MOTION PICTURES
TELEVISION
and
RADIO

a union catalogue

A
Reference
Publication
in
Film

Ronald Gottesman
Editor

MOTION PICTURES
TELEVISION
and
RADIO

*a union catalogue
of manuscript and special collections
in the western United States*

compiled and edited by
LINDA HARRIS MEHR

sponsored by
THE FILM AND TELEVISION STUDY CENTER, INC.

G.K.HALL *&*CO.
70 LINCOLN STREET, BOSTON, MASS.

Library of Congress Cataloging in Publication Data
Mehr, Linda Harris.
  Motion pictures, television and radio.

  (A Reference publication in film)
  Includes indexes.
  1. Moving-pictures — Archival resources — The West —
— Directories.   2. Television broadcasting — Archival
resources — The West — Directories.   3. Radio broadcasting
— Archival resources — The West — Directories.   I. Film
and Television Study Center.   II. Title.   III. Series.
PN1993.4.M37   016.791   77-13117
ISBN 0-8161-8089-X

This publication is printed on permanent/durable acid-free paper
MANUFACTURED IN THE UNITED STATES OF AMERICA

The Film and Television Study Center, Inc.

Catalogue Advisory Committee

*Project Director/*Anne G. Schlosser Librarian, Charles K. Feldman Library
Center for Advanced Film Studies
The American Film Institute

Elizabeth Armstrong Librarian, California Institute
of the Arts

Robert Knutson Head, Department of Special
Collections and Cinema Library
University of Southern California

Audree Malkin Head, Theater Arts Library
University of California, Los Angeles

Mildred Simpson Librarian, Margaret Herrick Library
Academy of Motion Picture Arts
and Sciences

Foreword

Film is the only new art form to emerge in the last 75 years. It is the literature of the 20th century. In 1969 there were 219 colleges and universities teaching film and television courses. Today there are 1075. We have all heard these familiar statements. They testify to the pervasiveness of film and television in our culture today.

Despite this widespread contemporary interest, film and television have yet to be recognized as subjects worthy of historical investigation. Most scholars have considered the movies to be merely mass entertainment, and have turned their energies to more weighty subjects. The entertainment industry has also ignored its own historical past. Scripts, stills, correspondence, and other production records are the primary source materials for studying the origins of film and television. Unfortunately the networks and studios have traditionally viewed these records as only a means to an end. Production records have been saved mainly for business and legal reasons, not for scholarly use. Filmmakers have been just as blind to the importance of their own personal memorabilia. One hates to think of the masses of archival records thrown away as producers, directors, writers, and others moved from place to place. Only through the efforts of a dedicated personal secretary or some other caring individual are many filmmaker's scripts, photographs, and scrapbooks still in existence. The following quote from a noted silent film director best captures Hollywood's attitude towards preservation of its archival materials:

> "During my productive years, I never dreamed that another
> generation would have the slightest interest in my work.
> It was my habit, at the end of each day's shooting to
> tear out the pages covered. When there were no more
> pages I knew the picture was finished. Ergo, no shoot-
> ing scripts among my meager memorabilia."

Even though this attitude has prevailed, many libraries, museums, and historical societies have over the years been collecting and preserving bits and pieces of movie and television memorabilia. Much of this work has been done without encouragement or support of administrations. Imagine any self-respecting institution acquiring movie stills, a run of PHOTOPLAY or even worse TV GUIDE, or perhaps

a set of television scripts to THE MANY LOVES OF DOBIE GILLIS! But
these librarians and curators, with foresight and vision, persisted;
and an amazing body of primary source material now exists. It awaits
the growing band of scholars, educators, and writers, and even some
filmmakers, who have at long last waked up to the importance of film
and television. These individuals have finally come to recognize that
this new art form has something to tell us today; that it contributes
to and reflects the social history of America in the past half
century.

It should not surprise anyone to hear that there is no one inclu-
sive listing of all these various film and television special collections. Unlike other disciplines, film and TV have until recently
lacked even the most basic reference guides to the primary and
secondary material. For many years Harold Leonard's THE FILM INDEX,
Vol. 1, The Film as Art (NY, H. W. Wilson and the Museum of Modern
Art Film Library, 1941) and André Veinstein's PERFORMING ARTS
LIBRARIES AND MUSEUMS OF THE WORLD (Paris, Centre National de la
Recherche Scientifique and UNESCO, 1967) were practically the only
entry points to the literature of film. Fortunately in the past
several years, a number of bibliographies, indexes, and directories
have been published for film literature. Television documentation is
still in a state of chaos, and lags some 8-10 years behind.

However, a comprehensive bibliography describing the vast array of
primary source materials in the United States was still wanting.
Because of the peculiarities of the material, the NATIONAL UNION CATA-
LOG OF MANUSCRIPT COLLECTIONS compiled by the Library of Congress
does not include many film and TV collections. Several individual
libraries such as those at the University of Southern California,
UCLA, and the University of Oregon have published catalogues of their
own holdings. As admirable and useful as these catalogues are, they
do not meet the demand for a comprehensive catalogue of holdings.
William C. Young's AMERICAN THEATRICAL ARTS: A GUIDE TO MANUSCRIPTS
AND SPECIAL COLLECTIONS IN THE UNITED STATES AND CANADA (Chicago:
American Library Association, 1971) attempted to fill the void.
Young's work was indeed a milestone. For the very first time film
and television special collections were identified and located. However, the institutional coverage was limited and the collection
descriptions were far too general and brief. The need still remained
for a comprehensive, authoritative, descriptive listing of all motion
picture, television and radio archival collections in the United
States. If the historical renaissance in the entertainment field was
to be fully supported, such a union catalogue was necessary.

With this in mind, and based on my experience in special libraries
devoted to the entertainment industry, I prepared a proposal for the
reference work you are about to consult: MOTION PICTURE, TELEVISION,
AND RADIO: A UNION CATALOGUE OF MANUSCRIPT AND SPECIAL COLLECTIONS
IN THE WESTERN UNITED STATES. Originally I envisioned the scope of
the catalogue to encompass the entire United States. I have not yet

lost that vision. However, when the Film and Television Study Center
voted to sponsor the project, the scope was limited to the western
United States. This was a more manageable size for a fledgling
organization to handle.

Founded in 1972, the Film and Television Study Center is a non-
profit cultural organization established to facilitate co-operative
projects in the areas of film/television archives, education, and
research. The member institutions of the Study Center are: The
Academy of Motion Picture Arts and Sciences, The American Film Institute, California Institute of the Arts, The Los Angeles County Museum
of Art, the Los Angeles International Film Exposition, Loyola Mary-
mount University, the National Academy of Television Arts and Sciences,
the University of California, Los Angeles, and the University of
Southern California.

The Union Catalogue was chosen as the first cooperative project
for the new organization. A one year grant was received from the
National Endowment for the Arts to support this bibliographical
undertaking. Because the NEA recognized the importance of such work,
the grant was renewed for a second year. Additional funding to support the work was graciously received from: Bing Crosby, E. E.
Fogelson, the Ford Motor Company Fund, Norman O. Houston, Hal B.
Wallis and Robert Wise. Mervyn LeRoy deserves special credit for his
generous assistance in helping us to raise these funds. Without the
Endowment's support and the help of these private donors, this undertaking would not have been possible.

The Board of Trustees of the Film and Television Study Center
appointed a Catalogue Advisory Committee to supervise the Union Catalogue. This Committee consisted of: Robert Knutson, Head of the USC
Department of Special Collections and Cinema Library; Audree Malkin,
Head of the UCLA Theater Arts Library; Mildred Simpson, Librarian of
the Margaret Herrick Library at The Academy of Motion Picture Arts
and Sciences; Elizabeth Armstrong, Head Librarian, California Institute of the Arts; and Anne G. Schlosser, Librarian of the Charles K.
Feldman Library at The American Film Institute. After considering a
number of applicants the Committee selected Linda Harris Mehr as the
Bibliographer. With a PhD in History and with research experience
in U.S. and foreign film archives, her credentials were outstanding.

The Catalogue itself was designed to locate, identify and describe
research collections currently available for use in established
institutions, libraries, museums, and historical societies in the
eleven western United States: Arizona, California, Colorado, Idaho
Montana, Nevada, New Mexico, Oregon, Utah, Washington, and Wyoming.
The original concept concentrated on film and television only. However, the discovery of extensive radio material led the Committee to
include these collections as well.

Foreword

The Committee insisted on two key elements in the compilation of the catalogue. First: on-sight investigation of each library collection by the Bibliographer was mandatory. Questionnaires and other secondary sources were to be used only in the preliminary stages of locating collections. Ms. Mehr visited nearly every institution listed here and personally inspected the collections. In addition, she wrote the bibliographic descriptions, which were then reviewed and approved by the librarian at each institution.

Second: a detailed index was of paramount importance. Listing and describing collections are valuable, but to be of complete service to scholars, an index is essential. Thus, two indexes were compiled; a general index by name, title, and subject, and an index by occupation. In this way one can find not only the Isobel Lennart Collection, but also the collections of other noted writers as well. In many ways, the Committee feels these indexes are the most outstanding contribution to this work.

After two and one-half years of work, starting Spring 1974 and ending Winter 1977, the Union Catalogue is finally completed. We hope it will provide the stimulus for further research and investigation into the history of the moving image in America. In addition we hope it will encourage studios and filmmakers alike to recognize the value of their material. Hopefully they will either establish their own company archives in the case of the major studios and networks, or in the case of filmmakers, they will deposit their personal papers in any of the institutions listed in this catalogue. Only in that way will the archival records of the entertainment industry be preserved and made available for use by present and future historians.

Many people deserve credit for their work on this catalogue: first, the members of the Catalogue Advisory Committee whose expertise and total support goes unsurpassed; second, Linda Mehr for her perseverance and dedication; and finally credit goes to the librarians and administrators who cooperated so generously. Without their interest and help it would have been impossible to produce such an authoritative and comprehensive union catalogue.

Anne G. Schlosser
Project Director

Contents

Contents

Contents

Contents

Preface

The first stage of this project involved locating institutions with appropriate resources. A list of possible sources in the eleven Western states was compiled, including public and private libraries, universities, archives, historical societies, museums and commercial institutions. Questionnaires were sent to these institutions to determine the location and availability of motion picture, television and radio manuscripts and special collections. All institutions that indicated possession of such material were then contacted and arrangements were made for inspection of these collections.

Over a two year period institutions throughout the West were visited and their collections examined. The entries that appear in this volume are based on personal inspection of the collections in conjunction with the institutions' inventories for their material, wherever available. All entries were first sent to the personnel in charge of the collections at the various institutions for their editing and approval. Of the 73 institutions whose collections were inspected and for which entries were compiled only the University of Wyoming Division of Rare Books and Special Collections failed to return the copy of their holdings for inclusion in this volume.

The collections described in this volume are listed by institution and contain the following type of material: production and/or personal papers of directors, writers, producers, actors, cinematographers, costume designers, art directors, composers, publicists, editors, inventors, etc.; screenplays, television scripts and radio scripts; advertising material such as posters, lobby cards, press books and programs; production and publicity stills, candid photos; clipping files; scrapbooks; oral histories; musical scores; art work; animation material; costume designs, costumes; props and equipment. Motion pictures, television films and tapes, and radio transcriptions and tapes have been mentioned only where they are part of a general collection. Because the primary focus of this work is on paper material, archives exclusively devoted to the collection of films, television tapes or radio transmissions have not been included: UCLA Film Archive, UCLA Radio Archive, UCLA National Academy of Television Arts and Sciences, University of Washington Milo Ryan Phono Archive.

Preface

To facilitate access to these institutional listings two types of
indexes have been provided. The General Index includes names, subjects and titles. The Index by Occupation is arranged by job category.

It should not be assumed that what is listed here is all that is
available. This catalogue lists only those collections identified
and described as of March 1977. Space prohibits complete itemization
of the contents of each collection. Although this volume attempts to
be as complete as possible, large bodies of materials may appear to
be omitted because they are not catalogued as separate collections.
This is due to the diverse manners in which material is organized
from one institution to another. The general description in the
entries should provide sufficient clues to aid the researcher in
locating specific items.

To the many individuals who aided in the preparation and comple-
tion of this catalogue, I would like to express my appreciation. I
am particularly indebted to Anne Schlosser, who first envisioned this
project, and who has been a constant source of encouragement and help.
She and the other Advisory Committee members: Mildred Simpson, Audree
Malkin, Robert Knutson and Betty Armstrong provided immeasurable
assistance and guidance on all aspects of this project, from its in-
ception to the final indexing. Tracey Thompson ably assisted with
research, typing and proofing. Those in charge of the various collections at the institutions included in this volume were most helpful
to me on my visits to their libraries, doing their utmost to expedite
my cataloging. They further gave of their time and effort to edit
all final entries. Since accessibility of their material depends on
knowing of its existence, their cooperation is most profoundly
appreciated.

Linda Harris Mehr
Compiler and Editor

Explanation of Entries

INSTITUTIONAL INFORMATION

Name and address of the institution are provided in the center of the page. The specific department housing the special collections is indicated at the left hand margin along with personnel in charge of special collections, hours of service, any restrictions on use of material, and special services provided.

Example:

ACADEMY OF MOTION PICTURE ARTS
AND SCIENCES (AMPAS)
8949 Wilshire Boulevard
Beverly Hills, California 90211

THE MARGARET HERRICK LIBRARY
Librarian: Mildred Simpson
Archivist: Sam Gill
(213) 278-4313
Hours: M, Tu, Th, F, 9-5
Open to the public.
Photograph duplication services available.

COLLECTION INFORMATION

Collection entries for each institution are listed alphabetically and numbered. The name under which an entry appears may be that of an individual, institution, organization, title of a production or a general subject category. Brief biographical information is given for the individuals, dates and releasing companies for the productions. The citation for each collection includes encompassing dates where known, size of the collection, a general description of the contents and mention of some of the more exceptional items. Unless otherwise indicated boxes are 5" document size. At the request of certain librarians some collections are listed in greater detail. The entry also indicates whether the library possesses a detailed listing of individual collection contents in the form of inventory, register or index.

Examples:

> AFI
> 6 Chandler, George, 1902-   . (actor)
>   Collection, 1935-1971. 20 boxes.
>   Motion picture and television scripts. The screenplay col-
>   lection is especially strong in films directed by William
>   Wellman. The television collection is strong in scripts from
>   various series of the 1950s and 1960s, with a long run of
>   scripts from LASSIE.
>   Unpublished register in library.

> UCLA(C)
> 5 CHARLEY VARRICK (U, 1973).
>   Collection of memos, scripts and treatments related to the
>   production of the film, 1972-1973. 18 items in 2 boxes.
>   Unpublished register in library.

> AMPAS
> 4 Biography Files. 360 ft.
>   Consist of information and photographs dealing with film-
>   makers of all crafts (actors, cinematographers, costume de-
>   signers, directors, writers, producers, etc.). Files contain
>   feature articles, newsclips, daily trade items, studio biog-
>   raphies and publicity releases, and portrait and publicity
>   stills. A card file of obituaries is also maintained.

INDEXES

Index entries are followed by institutional codes and collection
numbers.

The General Index includes names (individuals, organizations, institutions) production titles, and subjects. Production titles are
indexed only when they appear as a collection title, or where the
quantity of material relating to a specific television, radio or
motion picture series within a collection is so extensive as to war-
rant separate mention. Other titles cited in collection descriptions
are given to indicate the nature and extent of a collection but are
not indexed. The best approach for locating information on a title
not listed in the General Index is to check under the name of a major
person connected with the production such as the producer, director,
writer, etc.

The Index by Occupation is arranged by job category for the motion
picture, television or radio industry. This includes those involved
in all phases of production as well as those commenting on the industry such as critics, historians and columnists. The category writers
refers to script writers. There are separate listings for commen-
tators, columnists and critics/historians. Individuals who have
worked in more than one capacity, for example as both director and
producer, are listed under both director and producer categories.

Explanation of Entries

Examples:

GENERAL INDEX

equipment
    motion picture, AFI:8, 10, 27; AMPAS:34, 63, 84; ASC:1;
        CMSI:1; HCAA:10; LAMNH(A):1, 2, 8, 14, 15, 17; USC:75

GUNSMOKE (television), HuL:2; UO:15

Ince, Thomas H., 1882-1924 (producer, director, executive),
    AMPAS:54; HCAA:16; UCLA(A):46; UCLA(C):14a

INDEX BY OCCUPATION

COSTUME DESIGNERS
    Conley, Renie, USC:20
    Head, Edith, AMPAS:35; USC:62

DIRECTORS
    Cukor, George, AFI:1c; UCLA(A):69f, 70h; USC:24, 77
    Daves, Delmer, SU:1; USC:121

WRITERS
    Daves, Delmer, SU:1; USC:121
    Davis, Luther, USC:26

Abbreviations for Motion Picture Releasing Companies

Based on those used in Film Daily Year Book

AA	Allied Artists
AIP	American-International
AMI	American-International
ART	Artcraft Pictures
BRN	Brandon Films
BV	Buena Vista
CAI	Cari
CIN	Cinerama
CIO	Cinerama Releasing Corp.
CIV	Cinema V
CLU	W. H. Clune
COF	Continental Distributing
COL	Columbia
EDK	Edison-Kleine
EDU	Educational
EMB	Avco Embassy
F	Fox, Twentieth Century-Fox
FBO	Film Booking Offices
FN	First National
GB	Gaumont-British
GRI	D. W. Griffith Productions
GRV	Grove Press
IML	Imperial Dist.
INR	International Roadshows
LOP	Lopert
M	Metro
MAE	Maysles Film Distributors
MAG	Mage
MG	Metro-Goldwyn
MGM	Metro-Goldwyn-Mayer
MT	Mutual
MTC	Magna Pictures Corp.
NGP	National General Pictures
PAR	Paramount (Famous Lasky, etc.)
PAT	Pathe and RKO Pathe

Abbreviations for Motion Picture Releasing Companies

PCO   Pathe Contemporary
PEW   Peppercorn-Wormser, Inc.
PRI   Principal (1933)
RAT   Harry Rathner
REP   Republic
RGL   Regional Film Distributors, Inc.
RKO   RKO Radio
SCG   Screen Guild
SEZ   Selznick (1946)
SRO   Selznick Releasing Organization
SW   Stanley Warner Cinema Corp.
TRH   Trans-Lux Distributing
TRI   Triangle
U   Universal
UA   United Artists
US   U.S. Films
WA   Warner Brothers, Warner Brothers-Seven Arts, Ltd.
WW   Sono Art-World Wide

Geographical List of Institutions

ARIZONA
<u>ARIZONA</u>
    Arizona Historical Society (AHS)
    Arizona State University (ASU)

<u>CALIFORNIA</u>
    Academy of Motion Picture Arts and Sciences (AMPAS)
    Ackerman Archives (AA)
    American Film Institute Center For Advanced Film Studies (AFI)
    American Society of Cinematographers (ASC)
    Anaheim Public Library (AnPL)
    Burbank Public Library (BPL)
    California Institute of the Arts (CIA)
    California Lutheran College (CLC)
    California Museum of Science and Industry (CMSI)
    California State Library (CSL)
    California State University, Fullerton (CSUF)
    California State University, Long Beach (CSULB)
    California State University, Los Angeles (CSULA)
    California State University, Northridge (CSUN)
    Disney (Walt) Productions (DP)
    First Federal Savings and Loan Association of Hollywood
        (FFSL)
    Foothill College Electronics Museum (FC)
    Glendale Public Library (GPL)
    Hart (William S.) Park and Museum (HPM)
    Historical Society of Long Beach (HSLB)
    Hollywood Center for the Audio-Visual Arts (HCAA)
    Honnold Library, Claremont Colleges (HL)
    Huntington Library (HuL)
    Los Angeles County Museum of Natural History (LACMNH)
    Los Angeles Police Department (LAPD)
    Los Angeles Public Library (LAPL)
    Loyola Marymount University (LMU)
    McGeorge School of Law (MSL)
    Metro-Goldwyn-Mayer (MGM)
    Mount St. Mary's College (MSM)
    Occidental College (OC)

Pacific Film Archive (PFA)
Pacific Pioneer Broadcasters (PPB)
RKO General Pictures (RKO)
Riverside Municipal Museum (RMM)
San Diego Historical Society (SDHS)
San Diego Public Library (SDPL)
San Diego State University (SDSU)
San Francisco Museum of Modern Art (SFMMA)
San Francisco State University (SFSU)
San Jose State University (SJSU)
School of Theology at Claremont (STC)
Security Pacific National Bank (SPNB)
Southern California Edison Company (SCEC)
Stanford University Libraries (SU)
Stanford University Museum of Art (SUM)
Twentieth Century Fox (TCF)
Universal City Studios (US)
University of California, Berkeley (UCB)
University of California, Davis (UCD)
University of California, Los Angeles (UCLA)
University of California, San Diego (UCSD)
University of California, Santa Barbara (UCSB)
University of California, Santa Cruz (UCSC)
University of Redlands (UR)
University of Santa Clara (UStC)
University of Southern California (USC)

COLORADO
State Historical Society of Colorado (SHSC)
University of Colorado (UCo)

IDAHO
Idaho State University (ISU)
University of Idaho (UI)

NEW MEXICO
Albuquerque Public Library (APL)
Museum of New Mexico (MNM)
New Mexico State Records Center and Archives (NMSR)

OREGON
Northwest Film Study Center (NWFSC)
Oregon Historical Society (OHS)
University of Oregon (UO)

UTAH
Brigham Young University (BYU)
Utah State Historical Society (USHS)

WASHINGTON
University of Washington Libraries (UW)

Key to Institutional Codes

AA	Ackerman Archives
AFI	American Film Institute Center for Advanced Film Studies
AHS	Arizona Historical Society
AMPAS	Academy of Motion Picture Arts and Sciences
AnPL	Anaheim Public Library
APL	Albuquerque Public Library
ASC	American Society of Cinematographers
ASU	Arizona State University
BPL	Burbank Public Library
BYU	Brigham Young University
CIA	California Institute of the Arts
CLC	California Lutheran College
CMSI	California Museum of Science and Industry
CSL	California State Library
CSUF(A)	California State University, Fullerton (Archives of Popular Culture)
CSUF(B)	California State University, Fullerton (Department of Special Collections)
CSULA	California State University, Los Angeles
CSULB	California State University, Long Beach
CSUN(A)	California State University, Northridge (Department of Special Collections)
CSUN(B)	California State University, Northridge (Radio/TV/Film Department)
DP	Disney (Walt) Productions
FC(A)	Foothill College Electronics Museum (De Forest Memorial Archives)
FC(B)	Foothill College Electronics Museum (Electronics Collection)
FFSL	First Federal Savings and Loan Association of Hollywood
GPL	Glendale Public Library
HCAA	Hollywood Center for the Audio-Visual Arts
HL	Honnold Library, Claremont Colleges
HPM(A)	Hart (William S.) Park and Museum (House and Grounds)
HPM(B)	Hart (William S.) Park and Museum (Manuscripts and Special Collections)
HSLB	Historical Society of Long Beach
HuL	Huntington Library

ISU	Idaho State University
LAMNH(A)	Los Angeles County Museum of Natural History (Industrial Technology Department)
LAMNH(B)	Los Angeles County Museum of Natural History (Costume Department)
LAPD	Los Angeles Police Department
LAPL(A)	Los Angeles Public Library (Art and Music Department)
LAPL(B)	Los Angeles Public Library (Audio-Visual Department)
LAPL(C)	Los Angeles Public Library (History Department)
LAPL(D)	Los Angeles Public Library (Literature Department)
LMU(A)	Loyola-Marymount University (Charles Von Der Ahe Library)
LMU(B)	Loyola-Marymount University (Communication Arts Department)
MGM	Metro-Goldwyn-Mayer
MNM	Museum of New Mexico
MSL	McGeorge School of Law
MSM	Mount St. Mary's College
NMSR	New Mexico State Records Center and Archives
NWFSC	Northwest Film Study Center
OC	Occidental College
OHS(A)	Oregon Historical Society (Library)
OHS(B)	Oregon Historical Society (Film Department)
PFA	Pacific Film Archive
PPB	Pacific Pioneer Broadcasters
RKO	RKO General Pictures
RMM	Riverside Municipal Museum
SCEC	Southern California Edison Company
SDHS	San Diego Historical Society
SDPL	San Diego Public Library
SDSU	San Diego State University
SFMMA	San Francisco Museum of Modern Art
SFSU	San Francisco State University
SHSC	State Historical Society of Colorado
SJSU(A)	San Jose State University (Department of Special Collections)
SJSU(B)	San Jose State University (John Steinbeck Research Center)
SPNB	Security Pacific National Bank
STC	School of Theology at Claremont
SU	Stanford University Libraries
SUM	Stanford University Museum of Art
TCF	Twentieth Century Fox
UCB	University of California, Berkeley
UCD	University of California, Davis
UCLA(A)	University of California, Los Angeles (Department of Special Collections)
UCLA(B)	University of California, Los Angeles (Music Library)
UCLA(C)	University of California, Los Angeles (Theater Arts Library)
UCo	University of Colorado

Key to Institutional Codes

UCSB	University of California, Santa Barbara
UCSC	University of California, Santa Cruz
UCSD	University of California, San Diego
UI	University of Idaho
UO	University of Oregon
UR	University of Redlands
US	Universal City Studios
USC	University of Southern California
USHS	Utah State Historical Society
UStC	University of Santa Clara
UW	University of Washington Libraries

Institutional Listing of Collections

ACADEMY OF MOTION PICTURE
ARTS AND SCIENCES (AMPAS)
8949 Wilshire Boulevard
Beverly Hills, California 90211

THE MARGARET HERRICK LIBRARY
Librarian: Mildred Simpson
Archivist: Sam Gill
(213) 278-4313
Hours: M, T, Th, F, 9-5
Open to the public.
Photograph duplication services available.

The Library was founded in 1927 to serve as a central source of information on all facets of motion pictures. Its holdings consist of books, periodicals and pamphlets; files of clippings and still photographs; and special research and archival collections, all of which are related to the motion picture and its history. Listed below are the holdings in Special Files and Archival Collections.

SPECIAL FILES

1 Academy Files, 1927-   . 98 ft.
   Publicity, records books, scrapbooks and stills files documenting the Academy of Motion Picture Arts and Sciences; card files and publicity recording each year's Academy Awards Presentation.

2 Academy Publications.
   Extensive collection, including Academy Players Directory, Screen Achievement Records Bulletin, and Reminder List of Eligible Releases.

3 Awards Files. 8 ft.
     Clippings and programs on individual awards and award-
giving events, other than Academy Awards.

4 Biography Files. 360 ft.
     Consist of information and photographs dealing with film-
makers of all crafts (actors, cinematographers, costume
designers, directors, writers, producers, etc.). Files contain feature articles, newsclips, daily trade items, studio
biographies and publicity releases, and portrait and publicity
stills. A card file of obituaries is also maintained.

5 Directors Files, 1934-1975. 4 ft.
     Card files with over 4,000 entries give director's name,
and list film credits by title, release date and releasing
company.

6 Film Festivals Files. 12 ft.
     Clippings and programs on individual film festivals.

7 General Subject Files. 120 ft.
     Contains clippings, stills and pamphlets. These are
assigned subject headings and often form complete records of
an event, company, or special topic. Included are such subjects as censorship, women in motion pictures, three-
dimensional films and wide-screen processes, the motion picture industry and individual foreign countries, independent
producers and productions, film genres, individual companies,
guilds, unions, and associations.

8 Independent Producers and Distributors. 15 ft.
     Card files give names and addresses of independent produc-
tion companies and distributors.

9 Magazine Index, 1914-   . 15 ft.
     Card files provide reference access to library's almost
complete run of Photoplay. Magazine Index has been enlarged
to include more than 60 periodicals. Arranged alphabetically
by personality, film title, and subject.

10 Producers Files, 1968-1975. 4 ft.
     Card files give producer's name, and film credits by title,
release date and releasing company.

11 Production Files, 1894-   . 450 ft.
     These files contain information and photographs on more
than 40,000 American and foreign motion pictures. Still
photographs, programs, pressbooks, synopses, cast and credits
sheets and posters are usually included. Reviews, production
notes and other articles considered useful for reference or
research are systematically clipped and added to the files.

2

An important supplement to the production files is the Story Buys and Title Changes File (52 1/2 ft.). This card file contains announcements of purchase of literary properties as well as an extensive system of cross references to keep up with the many changes in title that a film may undergo before (or even after) it is released. Notes of proposed, but not produced, titles remain in the file indefinitely.

12 Television Files, 1950-____. 8 ft.
    Arranged by subject including television in foreign countries, television stations, subscription systems, surveys, quiz show investigations, children's programming, and many other topics.

13 Writers Files, 1934-1975. 9 1/2 ft.
    Card files give writer's name, tells if joint authorship, title of film, date of release and releasing company. Also tells source material if picture was based on a novel, play, etc.

ARCHIVAL COLLECTIONS

14 Balshofer, Fred J., 1878-1969. (cinematographer, producer)
    1 scrapbook, 1916-1917.
    Publicity on Metro-Yorke Film Corp. and its stars, Harold Lockwood and May Allison.

15 Barthelmess, Richard, 1895-1963. (actor)
    48 scrapbooks, 1916-1936.
    Scrapbooks contain clippings, reviews, programs concerning films of Barthelmess. Included in collection is material on the following films: WAR BRIDES (SEZ, 1916), BROKEN BLOSSOMS (GRI, 1919), WAY DOWN EAST (UA, 1920), TOL'ABLE DAVID (FN, 1921), and THE PATENT LEATHER KID (FN, 1927).
    Unpublished inventory in library.

16 Beal, Scott, 1890-1973. (actor, assistant director)
    2 scrapbooks, 1910-1965. 2 ft.
    Scrapbooks contain about 200 stills, clippings and correspondence relating to Beal's career as actor for American and Santa Barbara Motion Picture companies (1910-1914); and as assistant director, production manager and director for Universal (1914-1916; 1931-1936), Triangle (1917), National (1918-1920), Thomas Ince (1920-1921), Maurice Tourneur (1921-1924), First National (1925-1931), and Warner Brothers (1927-1931).
    Unpublished inventory in library.

17 Bischoff, Robert, ca. 1899-1945. (film editor)
    1 scrapbook, 1914-1945.
    Contains clippings and personal memorabilia primarily dealing with 1930s and early 1940s.

18 Blackton, J. Stuart, 1868-1941. (producer, director, executive, motion picture industry pioneer)
  Collection, ca. 1917-1938. 1 ft.
  Includes contracts, cast sheets, statements of accounts on
films, treatments for films, radio scripts, lecture notes,
manuscripts (including HOLLYWOOD WITH ITS HAIR DOWN or Hollywood Memories *** Forty Years of Movies, by J. Stuart
Blackton).
  Unpublished inventory in library.

19 Borzage, Frank, 1893-1962. (director)
  Collection, 1930s-1950s. 1 ft.
  Shooting scripts, production records, shooting schedules,
photos, clippings, souvenir film programs, correspondence,
receipts, golf pictures, and non-film material possibly relating to unrealized film projects. Scripts and/or production
materials on the following films: I'VE ALWAYS LOVED YOU (REP,
1946), MOONRISE (REP, 1948), CHINA DOLL (UA, 1958), and THE
BIG FISHERMAN (BV, 1959).
  Unpublished inventory in library.

20 Brabin, Charles, 1883-1957. (producer, director)
  Collection, pre-1920s. 1 ft.
  Synopses, scripts, diary (1913) on filmmaking in London.

21 Brando, Marlon, 1924-   . (actor)
  1 scrapbook, 1950-1955.
  Fan magazine clippings on Brando compiled by fan.

22 Brown, Joe E., 1892-1973. (actor)
  2 scrapbooks, 1932-1933, 1944.
  Contain clippings about Brown. 1944 scrapbook contains
publicity and reviews of book, Your Kids and Mine.

23 Browne, Frank L., 1880-   . (actor, theater manager)
  4 scrapbooks, 1897-1924.
  Clippings on productions Browne appeared in during early
part of century, as well as material on various theaters,
exhibition stunts and publicity campaigns he managed. Some
correspondence.

24 Bucquet, Harold S., 1892-1946. (director)
  Scripts and stills, 1937-1944.
  19 scrapbooks contain stills and clippings regarding the
films of this MGM director, with particular emphasis on the
DR. KILDARE series (1938-1941) and the CRIME DOES NOT PAY
series of shorts (1937-1939). Collection includes scripts
for these and other films but they are integrated with
Library's script collection.
  Unpublished inventory in library.

25 Carroll, Frank J., 1879-1944. (producer)
        1 scrapbook, 1910-1918, 1925.
        Contains stills, ads, reviews and photos from the period
    when Carroll was an executive with the Cheyenne Feature Film
    Co. and the Stellar Photo-Play Company. Large number of
    stills and related material on SCARLET WEST (FN, 1925). Bio-
    resume on Carroll.

26 Carroll, William A., 1876-1928. (actor)
        2 scrapbooks, 1903-1916, 1914-1916.
        Contain press clippings, reviews, programs, stills. One
    book of stills from various productions of American Film Co.,
    1914.

27 Chamberlin Scrapbooks, 1921-1932. 45 v.
        Clippings of articles and reviews of approximately 3,375
    films.
        Unpublished inventory in library.

28 Costello, Maurice, 1877-1950. (actor)
        Collection, ca. 1910-1940. 1/2 ft.
        Clippings, photographs, contracts, correspondence.
        Unpublished inventory in library.

29 Cramer, Duncan, 1901-   . (set designer)
        Collection, 1936-1959. 2 ft.
        Drawings, set designs, set stills, shooting schedules,
    budget estimates, production notes for following films:
    RAMONA (F, 1936), THE WOMAN IN THE WINDOW (RKO, 1944), THE
    FIGHTING SEABEES (REP, 1944), DELIGHTFULLY DANGEROUS (UA,
    1945), ABILENE TOWN (UA, 1946), THE DARK MIRROR (U, 1946), A
    NIGHT IN CASABLANCA (UA, 1946), COPACABANA (UA, 1947), THE
    FABULOUS DORSEYS (UA, 1947), LULU BELLE (COL, 1948), FOUR
    FACES WEST (UA, 1948), and D.O.A. (UA, 1949). Also material
    on television series TERRY AND THE PIRATES (1952) and YANCY
    DERRINGER (1958-1959).
        Unpublished inventory in library.

30 Harry Crocker Collection of Chaplin Material, pre-1920s-
    1950s. 4 ft.
        Material collected by Crocker (d. 1958), newspaper colum-
    nist and associate of Chaplin. Includes 11 books by and about
    Chaplin. Also manuscripts by Crocker, including chapters for
    Charlie Chaplin--Man and Mime. 3 scrapbooks of newspaper and
    magazine clippings about Chaplin and Marion Davies. Pro-
    grams from Chaplin films. 15 original pictures. 14 letters
    to and from Chaplin. Over 200 stills from various Chaplin
    films and others. Snapshots of Chaplin, Crocker and others.
        Unpublished inventory in library.

31 Dawley, J. Searle, 1877-1949. (director, motion picture industry pioneer)
    Collection, 1907-1948. 2 ft.
      Includes scenarios for 5 Edison films (1910-1911); weekly time books kept by Dawley for Edison Co. film productions (1907-1909); one notebook containing miscellaneous data by Dawley, including word sketches on Edwin S. Porter, D. W. Griffith and John Barrymore; 6 scrapbooks of stills from films directed by Dawley; 5 untranscribed tapes interviewing Dawley; 6 notebooks of Dawley's written memoirs (1948); lists of feature productions and stars personally directed by Dawley; business correspondence, contracts, clippings.
      Unpublished inventory in library.

32 Elinor, Carli D., 1890-1958. (music director)
      Motion picture programs (California Theatre, Los Angeles), 1919-1924. 5 v.
      Index to collection.

33 Eltinge, Julian, 1882-1941. (actor)
      1 scrapbook, 1919.
      Photographs of Eltinge's house.

34 Film History and Inventions.
      1 scrapbook, 1879-1948.
      Contains newspaper and magazine clippings, trade publica-tions, film advertisements, telegrams, correspondence, daily cast reports.

35 Fleischer, Stanley, ca. 1903-1973. (art director)
      Costume, set sketches and set stills, 1935-1965. 1/2 ft.
      12 original signed color costume sketches by Edith Head and 8 color sketches for THE GREAT RACE (WA, 1965). Set stills for: CAPTAIN BLOOD (FN, 1935), CHARGE OF THE LIGHT BRIGADE (WA, 1936), JEZEBEL (WA, 1938), CASABLANCA (WA, 1942), DESERT SONG (WA, 1943), LIFE WITH FATHER (WA, 1947), and MY FAIR LADY (WA, 1964).

36 Flippen, Jay C., 1898-1971. (actor)
      1 scrapbook, 1953.
      Photos, memorabilia, awards, certificates, press clippings.

37 Friedman, Harry B. (publicist)
      Publicity material, 1944-1968. 2 ft.
      Material covers publicity campaigns for 39 films from Universal (1944-1949) and Warner Brothers (1950-1968).

38 General Federation of Women's Clubs.
      2 scrapbooks, 1933-1934; 1934-1935.
      Clippings, articles, reprints, pamphlets and stills com-piled for the Committee on Motion Pictures.

39 Geraghty, Thomas, 1883-1945. (writer)
       2 scrapbooks, 1917-1919; 1920-1922.
       Clippings, publicity and reviews of films written by
    Geraghty.

40 Glass Slides, 1915-1935.
       Over 500 slides, many colored. Included are advertisements
    for films and admonitions to the audience (i.e. "Hats Off,"
    "No Smoking Please," etc.).
       Unpublished inventory in library.

41 Goldstein, Jack, 1906-   . (exhibitor)
       1 scrapbook, 1931-1935.
       Clippings and stills regarding exhibitor publicity cam-
    paigns, Boston, Massachusetts.

42 Goldstein, Leonard, 1903-1954. (producer)
       Collection, 1946-1954. 12 ft.
       Collection includes 58 bound scripts (1946-1953), 14 ring
    binders of scripts and production working papers (1952-1954),
    5 bound periodicals (1952-1953), and 5 scrapbooks of clippings,
    reviews, programs, letters and photographs (1946-1952) relat-
    ing to films produced by Leonard Goldstein primarily for
    Universal-International (1946-1952) and Twentieth Century-Fox
    (1952-1954). Production working papers include shooting
    schedules and script breakdowns, budget and weekly cost sum-
    maries, staff lists, cast selection lists, inter-office memos
    and letters from the Motion Picture Association of America
    regarding production code requirements.
       Unpublished inventory in library.

43 Gombell, Minna, ca. 1892-1973. (actress)
       Collection, 1931-1939. 3 scrapbooks, 1 autograph book.
       1 scrapbook of clippings (1933-1935) on Minna Gombell. 2
    scrapbooks of stills from 31 films featuring Minna Gombell
    (1931-1934). Autograph book (1932-1939) contains autographs
    from numerous entertainment people, some with lengthy messages
    and drawings.
       Unpublished inventory in library.

44 Grace, Henry, ca. 1908-   . (set decorator)
       4 scrapbooks, 1933-1954.
       Set stills from MGM films in which set decoration was
    done by Henry Grace.
       Unpublished inventory in library.

45 Graham, Sheilah, ca. 1908-   . (columnist)
       Collection, 1936-1937; 1946-1957. 1 ft.
       Clippings of columns by Sheilah Graham.

46 Grauman's Chinese Theatre.
        1 scrapbook, 1927.
        Contains photographs of the interior and exterior of the
    theater prior to dedication of theater May 18, 1927. Included
    are photographs of Sid Grauman with various stars putting im-
    pressions in the forecourt cement: Mary Pickford, Douglas
    Fairbanks, Norma Talmadge, Norma Shearer, Gloria Swanson.
    Also shots of the costumed staff and some original pen and
    ink illustrations of the theater.

47 Grieve, Harold, ca. 1900-   . (art director, interior
    designer)
        21 scrapbooks, 1920s and 1930s.
        Interior designs for homes, offices. Set designs for THE
    CONQUERING POWER (M, 1921) and TESS OF THE D'URBERVILLES
    (PAR, 1924).

48 Gwynn, Edith. (columnist)
        Collection, 1948-1954. 1 ft.
        Clippings of daily columns by Edith Gwynn.

49 Hart, William S., 1872?-1946. (actor)
        Collection, 1919-1921. 1 ft.
        Includes publicity releases by Paul Conlon, Director of
    Publicity for William S. Hart Co.; fictionalizations of Hart
    films by Conlon; synopses of Hart films; a few scripts and
    clippings.

50 Hayward, Susan, 1919-1975. (actress)
        1 scrapbook clippings, ca. 1955-1964.

51 Hersholt, Jean, 1886-1956. (actor)
        Collection, 1915-1954. 32 scrapbooks, 9 v.
        21 scrapbooks of clippings on Hersholt and films in which
    he appeared (1916-1948). 4 scrapbooks of photographs from
    films featuring Hersholt (1915-1934). 1 scrapbook of pub-
    licity pictures (1915-1934). 1 album of tribute to Hersholt.
    1 scrapbook of Christmas cards he received. 1 album of
    Academy of Motion Picture Arts and Sciences photographs (1929-
    1953). 3 scrapbooks relating to Motion Picture Relief Fund
    (1938-1942). Bound scripts for the following films: ALIAS
    THE DEACON (U, 1927), BATTLE OF THE SEXES (UA, 1928), EMMA
    (MGM, 1932), GRAND HOTEL (MGM, 1932), MEN IN WHITE (MGM,
    1934), THE COUNTRY DOCTOR (F, 1936), ONE IN A MILLION (F,
    1936), SINS OF MAN (F, 1936), and IN OLD CHICAGO (F, 1938).
        Unpublished inventory in library.

52 HOLLYWOOD CAVALCADE. (20th Century-Fox, 1939)
        2 research books for the film.

53 Hopper, Hedda, 1885-1966. (columnist)
       Collection, 1938-1966. 42 ft.
       29 scrapbooks of Hopper's articles which appeared in Sun-
    day and daily columns (1938-1966). Books, still photographs,
    trophies, plaques, clippings and manuscripts. Also Hopper's
    files which include unpublished articles, unedited tape
    transcripts of interviews, and personal correspondence. Use
    of these files is restricted.
       Unpublished inventory in library.

54 Ince, Thomas H., 1882-1924. (producer, director, executive,
    motion picture industry pioneer)
       Collection, 1912-1925. 12 ft.
       Synopses of films and 106 still books covering Ince's
    career in films.

55 Irene, 1901-1962. (costume designer)
       Collection, 1932-1949; 1960-1962. 7 scrapbooks, 2
    notebooks.
       7 scrapbooks of photographs, press clippings, and letters
    covering 1932-1949, 1960-1962. 2 ring binders of costume
    design photographs for over 30 films, including: GASLIGHT
    (1944), THE THIN MAN GOES HOME (1944), TWO GIRLS AND A SAILOR
    (1944), GOOD NEWS (1947), GREEN DOLPHIN STREET (1947), EASTER
    PARADE (1948), THE BARKLEYS OF BROADWAY (1949), NEPTUNE'S
    DAUGHTER (1949), all MGM features.
       Unpublished inventory in library.

56 Ivens, Joris, 1898-   . (producer, director, writer,
    cinematographer, editor)
       1 scrapbook, 1938-1943.
       Articles by and about documentary filmmaker Joris Ivens
    (1938-1943) and publicity, ads and reviews of OUR RUSSIAN
    FRONT (RAT, 1942).

57 James, Walter, 1886-1946. (actor)
       2 scrapbooks, 1900-1920; 1920-1925.
       Earlier scrapbook contains photo snapshots, latter con-
    tains publicity and reviews of film and stage appearances.

58 Johnson, Erskine. (columnist)
       Collection, 1939-1958. 1 1/2 ft.
       Clippings of daily columns by Erskine Johnson.

59 Lasky, Jesse L., 1880-1958. (producer, executive, motion
    picture industry pioneer)
       Collection, 1896-1959. 3 ft.
       Photographs, correspondence, plaques, awards, drawings,
    clippings, telegrams, sheet music, manuscripts and memora-
    bilia. Collection includes very early photographs of Lasky
    and his sister from vaudeville act, photos of Lasky during

various stages of his career, photos of several residences,
Lasky's hand-written letters and postcards (1917) concerning
cross-country trip in Stutz Bearcat, stock certificates for
Jesse L. Lasky Co. (1912), a bound selection of "special"
letters to Lasky, the television script for THIS IS YOUR LIFE
(1957) on Lasky, and a manuscript version of autobiography
I Blow My Own Horn which differs from published version.
Also 1 scrapbook of stills and work photos from THE MIRACLE
OF THE BELLS (RKO, 1948).
  Unpublished inventory in library.

60 Lennart, Isobel, 1915-1971. (writer)
      Scripts, 1942-1968. 23 v.
    Includes scripts for the following: LOST ANGEL (MGM, 1943),
A STRANGER IN TOWN (MGM, 1943), ANCHORS AWEIGH (MGM, 1945),
HOLIDAY IN MEXICO (MGM, 1946), IT HAPPENED IN BROOKLYN (MGM,
1947), SKIRTS AHOY (MGM, 1952), LATIN LOVERS (MGM, 1953),
THIS COULD BE THE NIGHT (MGM, 1957), THE INN OF THE SIXTH
HAPPINESS (F, 1958), MERRY ANDREW (MGM, 1958), THE SUNDOWNERS
(WA, 1960), PLEASE DON'T EAT THE DAISIES (MGM, 1960), TWO FOR
THE SEESAW (UA, 1962), and FUNNY GIRL (COL, 1968).
    Unpublished inventory in library.

61 Leonard, Robert Z., 1889-1968 and Gertrude Olmstead,
    1905-1975.
      Leonard-Olmstead Collection, 1900-1965. 29 scrapbooks, 1
    box, 2 framed water color sketches.
    Production stills, portraits, clippings, programs and
reviews relating to the careers of both Robert Z. Leonard and
Gertrude Olmstead. Material emphasizes Leonard's acting
career on the stage (1908-1911) and in motion pictures (1913-
1916) and directing career in motion pictures (1924-1950);
and Olmstead's acting career in motion pictures (1920-1930).
The collection includes material for such films as DANCING
LADY (MGM, 1933), THE GREAT ZIEGFELD (MGM, 1936), THE GIRL OF
THE GOLDEN WEST (MGM, 1938), PRIDE AND PREJUDICE (MGM, 1940),
IN THE GOOD OLD SUMMERTIME (MGM, 1949). Personal family
photos are also included.
    Unpublished inventory in library.

62 Lesser, Julian, 1915-   . (producer)
      Collection, 1952-1962. 2 transfer cases, 1 box, 1
    envelope.
    Advertising materials, correspondence, scripts relating to
2 television series, I SEARCH FOR ADVENTURE and BOLD JOURNEY.

63 Sol Lesser Collection of Historical Motion Picture Devices
    and Equipment, 1740-1922. ca. 90 items.
      Collection includes cameras, lanterns, slides, daguero-
    type plates and stereo photo apparatus. Among the items are
    the Praxinoscope Theatre of E. Reynaud (1877), Vitascope of

Thomas Edison (1894), Edison Projecting Kinetoscope, Type B (1910), Kinora Kesler Lumiere (1896), Phonoscope of Georges Demeny (1892), Muybridge Animal Locomotion Machine, Kodak Panoramic apparatus 6x9 roll film (1912).
Unpublished, illustrated catalogue in library.

64 Lester, Louise, 1867-1952. (actress)
    Collection, 1908-1925. 1 ft.
    Collection consists of 2 scrapbooks, one of photograph portraits and one of publicity clippings; and 200 stills, primarily from films produced by the American Film Company (1910-1916) in which Louise Lester appeared as a character actress and in her role of "Calamity Anne" (1912-1914).

65 Lobby Cards.
    Large collection filed with oversize stills alphabetically by film title.

66 Louise, Ruth Harriet, ca. 1906-   . (portrait photographer)
    2 scrapbooks, 1926-1927; 1927-1930.
    Fan magazine illustrations of MGM stars photographed by Ruth Harriet Louise.

67 LUX RADIO THEATRE, 1936-1953.
    Program scripts, 1936-1953. 85 v.
    Collection also includes clippings on Lux program from magazines and newspapers, press releases, publicity pictures, facts on programs, statistics, publicity promotion plans.
    Program and title index in library. Inventory of record discs held by Academy. Portion of records on tape in library.

68 Lyndon, Barre, 1896-1973. (writer)
    Collection, 1934-1970. 13 cartons.
    Screenplays, stage plays and television scripts, notebooks, drafts, working papers.
    Unpublished inventory in library.

69 MacDonald, Jeanette, 1906-1965 and Nelson Eddy, 1901-1967.
    4 scrapbooks, 1935-1947.
    Clippings from fan magazines on films and acting careers of MacDonald and Eddy.

70 Manson, Edward, ca. 1892-1969. (publicist, writer)
    Collection, ca. 1920s-1949. 1 ft.
    Material deals primarily with Warner Brothers and with industry activities during World War II, especially material related to the Goldwyn Girls Tour of 1942. 1 book of clippings and press material on the Hollywood Victory Caravan (1942). Portraits, memos, notes, photos. 1 typewritten manuscript of Charlie Chaplin Secrets written by Manson. Photos

of Chaplin and others and material on Chaplin-Lita Grey mar-
riage. Original stories and screenplays by Edward Sinclair
(Manson).
Unpublished inventory in library.

71 MGM Short Subjects.
Stills, 1928-1929.
Approximately 180 stills contained in this collection.

72 Moreno, Antonio, 1888-1967. (actor)
Collection, 1916-1938. 1 scrapbook, 1 folder.
Clippings, contracts, correspondence.

73 Morgan, Frank, 1890-1949. (actor)
2 scrapbooks, 1947.
1 book contains yachting clippings and photos; 1 book contains congratulatory telegrams on yachting race won by Morgan
in 1947.

74 Motion Picture Association of America, Inc.
MPAA Title Registration Reports, 1935-1972. 21 ft.
Record of registration of titles for films.

75 Motion Picture Patents Company and General Film Company.
Collection, 1909-1917. 1 ft.
Minutes of meetings, agreements, memos, etc. (1909-1917).
Also 6 volumes of United States of America, petitioners, vs.
The Motion Picture Patents Co., et al, defendants, 1912-1914.
Testimony at hearings includes that from the following:
J. Stuart Blackton, Albert E. Smith, Thomas Armat, William
Fox, Sigmund Lubin, George K. Spoor, Charles O. Baumann.

76 Motion Picture Society for the Americas.
Files of the organization, story ideas, scripts and correspondence. 15 ft.

77 Muir, Florabel, ca. 1890-1970. (columnist)
Collection, 1945-1947; 1949-1953. 1/2 ft.
Clippings of columns by Florabel Muir.

78 Office of War Information Bulletins, 1942-1943.
1 notebook.
Information sent to William Gordon at RKO with suggestions
on attitudes to be incorporated in films regarding war, defeat
of fascism, pushing for democracy after war, etc.

79 OLIVER TWIST. (First National, 1922)
1 still book.

80 Paramount Pictures.
Press Sheets, 1920, 1926-1965. 42 v.

81 Paramount Pictures.
    Production Facts File, 1914-1970.
    Card file organized alphabetically by film title (1914-
1970) and numerically by production number (1914-1931).
Examples of information given on card (though not all information on all films): director, assistant director, cast,
business manager, release and/or production dates, locale,
technical personnel, research personnel, other titles. Cross
references from plays, novels that were made into films.

82 Paramount Pictures.
    Stills and Scripts Collection, 1914-1970. ca. 700 ft.
    Consists of still books, stills and scripts from more than
2,200 Paramount productions.
    Unpublished inventory in library.

83 Parsons, Louella, 1881-1972. (columnist)
    Collection, 1915-1961.
    52 scrapbooks (1915-1961) containing clippings, reviews,
columns. 1 envelope of loose clippings, articles and programs (1926-1949). 1 album photos and clippings on party for
new magazine Ingenue (1959).
    Unpublished inventory in library.

84 Patent Material.
    352 original patent papers relating to motion pictures,
from pre-cinema to 1910.

85 Pathe Studio.
    Business Records, 1927-1931. 2 ft.
    Correspondence, budgets, balance sheets, etc.

86 Poster Collection, 1914-   .
    Over 2,000 posters, chiefly from American productions.
Some foreign titles. Filed by accession number--card key.
Collection is kept up to date.

87 Potel, Victor, 1889-1947. (comedian)
    1 scrapbook, 1910-1915; 1923-1924.
    Contains clippings, reviews, articles, ads on Potel who
played "Slippery Slim" in Essanay comedies, 1914-1915.

88 Quarberg, Lincoln, 1901-   . (publicity director)
    Collection, 1927-1955. 4 ft.
    Press releases, correspondence, pressbook material, busi-
ness letters for Caddo Co. Productions (Howard Hughes) (1927-
1933); press releases for Universal (1939-1942); correspondence, press releases, studio handbooks of publicity for RKO
(1943-1955). Manuscripts and articles by Quarberg including
original screen stories, outlines for stories. Memorabilia,
telegrams. Scripts, manuscripts and articles by others. 50
stills.
    Unpublished inventory in library.

89 Reid, Wallace, 1892-1923. (actor)
    Stills, 1914-1922. 1 ft.
    For Paramount films featuring Reid.

90 RKO Radio Pictures.
    980 still books and stills, 1929-1958.

91 Sais, Marin, ca. 1895-   . (actress)
    1 scrapbook, 1911.
    Scrapbook contains stills from Kalem films. Also loose
stills. Large number of stills for Marin Sais and Jack Hoxie
(a cowboy star).

92 Schallert, Edwin, 1890-1968. (columnist)
    Collection, 1946-1958. 3 ft.
    Clippings of daily columns by Edwin Schallert.

93 Script Collection.
    Approximately 1,200 motion picture scripts from ca. 1921
to date representing all the major studios. Also included
are a few television and radio scripts.

94 Selig, William, 1864-1948. (producer, executive, motion picture industry pioneer)
    Collection, 1905-1916. 10 ft.
    Collection includes copyright registrations, stills,
scripts, programs, campaign books, continuities for Selig
productions and correspondence. 1 album of clippings on the
Selig Zoo (1915-1916).

95 Sennett, Mack, 1880-1960. (producer, director, executive,
motion picture industry pioneer)
    Collection, 1913-1933. 101 ft.
    Collection consists of a Production File, Biography File,
Stories File, Subject File, Scrapbooks and Finance Records.
    The Production File contains stills, scripts, working
papers, title sheets, copyright information, continuity
sheets, synopses, preview notes on films in the following
series: Keystone Comedy Series (1913-1917), Triangle Series
(1915-1917), Triangle Komedy Series (1916-1917), Mack Sennett
Comedy Series (1917-1933). There are also lists of productions by number.
    The Biography File contains material on 262 persons asso-
ciated with Mack Sennett, including stills, publicity material, contracts, clippings and biographical information sheets.
6 series of approximately 400 photographs of Sennett covering
1912-1932 period in Sennett's career.
    The Stories File contains scripts, script ideas, stories,
treatments, suggestions that may or may not have been produced
on film. Listed by persons who may have appeared in them,
types of stories, and story titles.

The Subject File contains studio office records, correspondence relating to publicity matters, issues of <u>Mack
Sennett Weekly</u> (1917-1919), <u>Sennett News Bulletin</u> (1924, 1927),
publicity stills, pictures sent for casting purposes, refer-
ence stills (location and set), film rental billings, list of
Keystone releases (3/5/13 - 2/9/17) with director, working and
final title. Telegrams during crucial transition period from
Sennett's association with Triangle to his move to Paramount.
   Scrapbooks include 15 still books, ca. 1917-1926, and 4
books of clippings: one covering the year 1922; THE CROSSROADS
OF NEW YORK (FN, 1922); THE GOOD-BYE KISS (FN, 1928); HYPNO-
TIZED (WW, 1933).
   The Finance Records (1917-1933) include Sennett's declara-
tion of bankruptcy.
   Unpublished progress reports in library give greater details
on collection.

96 Seymour, James, 1895-1976. (writer)
       Collection, 1928-1974. 1 folder.
       Correspondence, papers, clippings, programs, pamphlets,
    poster and photograph. Collection includes correspondence
    from various industry personnel (1928-1971). 1 poster for
    GOLD DIGGERS OF 1933 (WA, 1933).
       Unpublished inventory in library.

97 Skolsky, Sidney, 1905-   . (columnist)
       Collection, 1936-1958. 3 ft.
       Clippings of daily columns by Sidney Skolsky.

98 Society of Independent Motion Picture Producers vs. United
    Detroit Theatres Corp., 1949. 1/2 ft.
       Documents include plaintiff authorizations, pre-answer
    pleadings, correspondence, outlines, working papers, proceed-
    ings, miscellaneous documents.
       Unpublished inventory in library.

99 Stone, George E., 1904-1976. (actor)
       6 scrapbooks, 1927-1933.
       1 album of clippings (1931-1933). 5 albums of portrait
    and production stills (1927-1932).

100 Thalberg, Irving, 1899-1936. (producer)
       2 scrapbooks, 1924-1929; 1929-1937.
       Production stills from MGM productions, including: THE BIG
    PARADE (1925), BEN HUR (1926), FLESH AND THE DEVIL (1927),
    HALLELUJAH (1929), MIN AND BILL (1930), CHINA SEAS (1935),
    MUTINY ON THE BOUNTY (1935), and THE GOOD EARTH (1937). Also
    some publicity shots.

101 TORA, TORA, TORA! (20th Century-Fox, 1970)
       Continuity sketches. 1/2 ft.

102   Tunberg, Karl, 1907-   . (writer, producer)
        6 scrapbooks, 1940s.
        1 still book of THE IMPERFECT LADY (PAR, 1947). 5 research
      notebooks containing background material on the period for
      various films--clothes, food, hairstyles, news of the day,
      music of the period, social customs, amusements, servants,
      etc.

103   Universal Pictures.
        Production still negatives of Universal pictures, 1945-
      1955. 260 boxes, 8x10x5.
        Collection contains close to 100,000 portraits, publicity
      pictures and stills.

104   USO Camp Shows, Inc., 1941-1957. 4 reels microfilm.
        Complete history of USO Camp Shows covering period of
      World War II and Korean War.

105   Van Riper, Kay, 1908-1948. (writer, actress)
        Collection, ca. mid-1930s-1940s. 5 ft.
        Includes scripts for radio and films, notes, correspondence,
      financial records.

106   Warner Bros. Catalogue of Classified Story Resumes.
        Compiled as of January 1, 1946.

107   West, Roland, 1877-1952. (producer, director)
        Collection, 1926-1933. 1 1/2 ft.
        Includes personal and business correspondence (1930-1933),
      check stubs (1926-1931), receipts and bills (1927-1932). Also
      screenplay for THE PURPLE MASK.
        Unpublished inventory in library.

108   Westmore, Perc, 1904-1970. (studio make-up artist, hair
      stylist)
        Collection, 1935-1950. 1 file drawer, 42 scrapbooks, 100
      records.
        Press clippings, pictures, articles, sketches covering
      Perc Westmore's years in motion picture business and as head
      of Westmore "family." 42 scrapbooks of press clippings
      (1935-1948). Approximately 100 records of Perc Westmore on
      radio programs. Master file on make-up, make-up charts, etc.
        Unpublished inventory in library.

109   Whalen, Michael, ca. 1902-1974. (actor)
        10 scrapbooks, 1927-1938.
        Press clippings, photos from stage shows, stills from
      films, reviews of stage and films. 1 scrapbook of clippings
      of Whalen as he appeared as model for newspaper and magazine
      ads (1927-1930), including many drawn by James Montgomery
      Flagg. Stills include those for the following films:

16

PROFESSIONAL SOLDIER (F, 1935), SONG AND DANCE MAN (F, 1936), COUNTRY DOCTOR (F, 1936), and POOR LITTLE RICH GIRL (F, 1936). Unpublished inventory in library.

110 White, Jules, 1900-   . (producer)
        Collection, 1933-1957. 10 1/2 ft.
     Stills and scripts for comedy shorts produced for Columbia by Jules White in the 1930s-1950s. These two-reeler shorts include those with The Three Stooges, Harry Langdon, Hugh Herbert, Vera Vague, Buster Keaton, and Andy Clyde.
     Unpublished inventory of scripts in library.

111 Winchell, Walter, 1897-1972. (columnist)
        Collection, 1930-1958. 3 ft.
     Clippings of columns by Walter Winchell.

112 Young, Clara Kimball, 1890-1960. (actress)
        1 scrapbook, 1890-1927.
     Contains photograph portraits, portraits in costume and stills from films starring Clara Kimball Young, emphasizing the period 1912 to 1922.

113 Young, Loretta, 1913-   . (actress)
        3 scrapbooks, 1932-1942.
     Clippings, magazine articles, photos. Both English and foreign language publications included.

ACKERMAN ARCHIVES (AA)
2495 Glendower Avenue
Hollywood, California 90027

Curator: Forrest J Ackerman
(213) 666-6326
Hours: By appointment.
Archives open to the public by special arrangement.

1 Science Fiction and Fantasy Collection.
     The material in this archive is the end product of 50 years of collecting by Forrest J Ackerman in the areas of science fiction, fantasy, the supernatural and horror/monster fiction and films. There are over 200,000 items in all, including books, periodicals, paintings, screenplays, television scripts, autographs, authors' photos, stills, posters, lobby cards, pressbooks and props. A clippings file containing production reviews and information, as well as information about science fiction writers and fantasy in general is maintained. A large section of the archive is devoted to the source material (i.e. books, magazine fiction) which provided the basis for many motion pictures.

   Motion picture stills (100,000) are arranged alphabetically
by title, as is the extremely large collection of 1, 2, and
3-sheets. There are a number of manuscripts by Ray Bradbury
and other science fiction writers. A large props collection
includes props from such films as KING KONG (RKO, 1933),
DRACULA (U, 1931), CREATURE FROM THE BLACK LAGOON (U, 1954),
ATLANTIS, THE LOST CONTINENT (MGM, 1961), and THE ILLUSTRATED
MAN (WA, 1969). Television material includes scripts for
STAR TREK and props for OUTER LIMITS. Other items include
various art work from films, studio life masks, phonograph
albums, Lon Chaney's make-up kit, Karloff and Lugosi film
rings, Fritz Lang's monocle and "Trixie" Award, and radio
tapes from various science fiction programs.

ALBUQUERQUE PUBLIC LIBRARY (APL)
501 Copper NW
Albuquerque, New Mexico 87102

FINE AND PERFORMING ARTS DEPARTMENT
Librarian: Mrs. Hester Miller
(505) 766-7722
Hours: M-Th, 9-9; F-Sat, 9-5:30
Open to the public.

1 Motion Picture and Television Material.
      The library has a small amount of material relating to
motion pictures and television. The clipping file includes
references to New Mexico motion picture activity. The information index contains complete indexing of TV Guide from
Vol. 9, April 1961 through the current issue. Photographic
material includes about 75 snapshots (ca. 1920s) of the Super
Chief Hollywood passengers such as Rudolf Valentino, Jackie
Coogan, Rin Tin Tin and C. B. DeMille as seen in the Albuquerque station. Also a few videotapes.

AMERICAN FILM INSTITUTE (AFI)
CENTER FOR ADVANCED FILM STUDIES
501 Doheny Road
Beverly Hills, California 90212

CHARLES K. FELDMAN LIBRARY
Librarian: Anne G. Schlosser
(213) 278-8777
Hours: M-F, 9-5:30

The primary function of the Charles K. Feldman Library is to serve the reading and research needs of the Fellows, Faculty and Staff of the Center for Advanced Film Studies. The Library's resources are also open to visiting film scholars and advanced graduate students, and members of the entertainment industry.

SPECIAL COLLECTIONS

1 <u>American Film Institute Film History Program--Oral History Transcripts.</u> Funded by the Louis B. Mayer Foundation.

    a. Berman, Pandro S., 1905- (producer). Oral history conducted and prepared by Mike Steen, 1972.

    b. Berndt, Eric M., 1903- (camera and sound equipment engineer). Interviewed by William C. Flaherty, 1972.

    c. Cukor, George, 1899- (director). Interviewed by Gavin Lambert, 1971.

    d. Dawn, Norman O., 1886- (cinematographer, special effects photographer). Oral history conducted by Stephen P. Cohen, 1974.

    e. Dwan, Allan, 1885- (director, producer, writer). Interviewed by Peter Bogdanovich, 1969.

    f. Friedhofer, Hugo, 1902- (composer). Interviewed by Irene Kahn Atkins, 1974.

    g. Gershenson, Joseph, 1904- (musical director, producer). Interviewed by Irene Kahn Atkins, 1976.

    h. Groves, George R., 1901-1976 (sound engineer). Oral history conducted by Irene Kahn Atkins, ca. 1975.

    i. Hoffman, George Jeremiah, 1900- (publicist, producer). Interviewed by Bob Nero, 1975.

    j. Kaper, Bronislaw, 1902- (composer). Interviewed by Irene Kahn Atkins, 1975.

    k. Koch, Howard, 1902- (screenwriter). Oral history conducted by Eric Sherman, 1974.

    l. Leisen, Mitchell, 1898-1972 (director, costume designer, art director). Interviewed by David Chierichetti, 1971.

    m. McCarey, Leo, 1898-1969 (producer, director). Interviewed by Peter Bogdanovich, 1969.

    n. MacDougall, Ranald, 1915-1973 (screenwriter). Oral history conducted by Joel Greenberg, 1973.

    o. Oral History with early sound and music editors: Milo Lory, s.e.; Walter Elliott, s.e.; Joseph Henrie, s.e.; Evelyn Rutledge, s.e.; Robert Tracy, m.e.; George Adams, m.e.; June Edgerton, m.e. Interviewed by Irene Kahn Atkins, 1975.

    p. Polonsky, Abraham Lincoln, 1910- (writer, director). Oral history conducted by Eric Sherman, 1974.

    q. Rennahan, Ray, 1898- (cinematographer). Interviewed by Charles Higham, 1970.

r. Rosson, Harold, 1895–   (cinematographer). Inter-
    viewed by Bill Gleason, 1971.
s. Ruttenberg, Joseph, 1889–   (cinematographer). Inter-
    viewed by Bill Gleason, 1972.
t. Seaton, George, 1911–   (writer, director). Oral
    history conducted by David Chierichetti, 1974.
u. Seitz, John F., 1893–   (cinematographer). Interviewed
    by James Ursini, 1972.
v. Sherman, Vincent, 1906–   (director). Oral History
    conducted by Eric Sherman, 1972.
w. Shurlock, Geoffrey, 1894–1976. (producer, director of
    MPAA code rating office). Interviewed by James M.
    Wall, 1970.
x. Stewart, Donald Ogden, 1894–   (writer). Interviewed
    by Max Wilk, 1971.
y. Swanson, Harold Norling, 1899–   (literary agent).
    Interviewed by Bob Nero, 1975.
z. Warren, Harry, 1893–   (song writer). Interviewed by
    Irene Kahn Atkins, 1972.
aa. The Western in the 1920s. An oral history with Irvin
    Willat (director), Virgil Miller (cinematographer),
    Hoot Gibson (actor), Ann Little (actress), Ted
    French (cowboy), Jim Rush (actor) and Edna Miller
    Rush (actress). Interviews conducted by Robert S.
    Birchard, 1961–1972.
bb. Wilbur, Crane, 1889–   (actor, writer, director).
    Interviewed by Bill Smith, 1971.

2 American Film Institute Film History Program--Research
   Associateships. Funded by the Louis B. Mayer Foundation.
   a. Knox, Donald E. AN AMERICAN IN PARIS: a documentary
       study of the MGM studio system. 1971. Contains
       interviews with Preston Ames (art director), Joe
       Cohn (Vice-President of MGM), Leslie Caron (actress),
       Adrienne Fazan (editor), Nina Foch (acresss), Arthur
       Freed (producer), George Gibson (head of scenic art
       department), Keogh Gleason (set decorator), Honore
       Janney (script timer), Gene Kelly (actor), Alan Jay
       Lerner (author & screenwriter), Lilly Messinger
       (agent), Vincente Minnelli (director), Mary Ann
       Nyberg (dress designer), Dore Schary (MGM head of
       production), Alan Antik (technical advisor), Irene
       Sharaff (ballet costume designer), Walter Strohm
       (head of production department), Ed Woehler (unit
       production manager); John Green and Saul Chaplin (co-
       music directors); Emily Torchia (publicist) and Rick
       Ingersoll (office boy).

   b. Koszarski, Richard. Erich von Stroheim Research Pro-
       ject. 1973. Contains interviews with Hal Mohr

(cinematographer), Grant Whytock (editor), James Wong
Howe (cinematographer), Fay Wray (actress), Ted Kent
(editor), J. J. Cohn (production manager), William
Margulies (first assistant camerman), Anita Loos
(author & screenwriter), Ray Rennahan (cinematographer), Lewis Milestone (director), Paul Ivano
(cinematographer).

c. Solomon, Aubrey. A Corporate and Financial History of
the 20th Century-Fox Studio. 1975.

3 American Film Institute Film History Program--Autobiographies.
Funded by the Louis B. Mayer Foundation.

a. Brook, Clive, 1887-1974 (actor). The eighty four ages
of Clive Brook, his life and times. London. ca. 1972.

b. Lee, Rowland V., 1891- (director). The adventures
of a movie director. Beverly Hills. ca. 1971.

c. Love, Bessie, 1898- (actress). Love from Hollywood.
London. 1973.

d. Perry, Harry F., ASC., 1889- (cinematographer).
Forty years behind a motion picture camera, with
Oscar G. Estes, Jr. Seal Beach, California. 1960.

4 American Film Institute/Seminar Transcripts.
Over 300 transcripts of seminars with professionals from
the motion picture/television industry held at the Center for
Advanced Film Studies. 1969.

Includes discussions with individuals from all areas of the
industry: producers/directors, screenwriters, cinematographers,
editors, actors/actresses, art directors/set designers, composers, costume designers, film critics, laboratory processes,
production managers, script clerks, special effects, story editors, stunt men. Among the individuals included are: Nina
Foch (actress), Henry Fonda (actor), Liv Ullmann (actress),
Lee Garmes (cinematographer), Elmer Bernstein (composer),
Andrew Sarris (film critic), Verna Fields (editor), Bernardo
Bertolucci (director), Howard Hawks (director), Paul Mazursky
(director), Vincente Minnelli (director), Fred Zinnemann
(producer), Eleanor Perry (screenwriter).

5 Blue, James.
A report on the Horizons and Today news films, by James
Blue. Unpublished manuscripts. New York, 1965.

6 Chandler, George, 1902- . (actor)
Collection, 1935-1971. 20 boxes.
Motion picture and television scripts. The screenplay col-
lection is especially strong in films directed by William
Wellman. The television collection is strong in scripts from
various series of the 1950s and 1960s, with a long run of
scripts from LASSIE.
Unpublished register in library.

7 Clipping Files.
   For motion pictures the files are organized by subject,
film title, countries, associations/organizations, production
companies and film festivals.
   For television the files are organized by subject, program
titles, associations/organizations.
   Also biography files for film and television personalities.

8 Columbia Pictures.
   Stills Collection, early 1930s–mid 1950s. ca. 100,000
stills.
   Collection includes portraits, general publicity stills,
studio and location stills, photographs of equipment, as well
as production stills.

9 Dubrey, Claire, 1894–   . (actress)
   Collection, 1915-1949, 1956. 3 boxes.
   Stills, portraits and clippings. Photos of other actors
and actresses as well as Dubrey.
   Unpublished register in library.

10 Fleischer, Max, 1883-1972. (animator)
   Patents and photographs, 1917-1942. 1 box.
   Contains original patents for moving picture apparatus,
techniques, and animation processes. Includes photographs of
Max Fleischer and his character, Betty Boop.
   Unpublished register in library.

11 Flicker, Theodore J., 1930–   . (writer, director)
   Collection, 1964-1968. 10 boxes.
   Screenplays by Theodore Flicker, including THE PRESIDENT'S
ANALYST (PAR, 1967). Final versions, first and second drafts,
treatments, continuities. Also production notes, memoranda,
production stills.

12 Hathaway, Henry, 1898–   . (director)
   Collection, 1932-1968. 83 v.
   Director's annotated shooting scripts. Scrapbooks contain
production stills, photographs, letters, telegrams, and
clippings about Hathaway's films.

13 Horner, Harry, 1910–   . (production designer)
   Collection, 1974-1975. 3 boxes and 4 oversize packages.
   Sketches, drawings, and other production records for set
and scenery design for the motion picture THE BLACK BIRD
(COL, 1976). Similar material for HARRY AND WALTER GO TO
NEW YORK (COL, 1976).
   Unpublished register in library.

14 Keaton, Buster, 1895-1966. (comedian)
   Scrapbook, ca. 1902-1909. 1 reel microfilm and hard copy
print out.

Clippings of the Keaton family in vaudeville. Microfilmed from Mrs. Keaton's personal scrapbook.

15 Leisen, Mitchell, 1898-1972. (costume designer, art director, director)
Collection, 1933-1967. 34 v., 9 boxes, 40 notebooks.
Motion picture and television scripts, production records, correspondence, stills and research notebooks. Annotated scripts and production records and correspondence from films directed by Mr. Leisen from 1933-1963; television programs from 1955-1967. Also included are stills and research notebooks from Mr. Leisen's motion pictures.
Unpublished register in library.

16 Levee, Michael C., 1889-1972. (producer, studio executive, talent agent)
Scrapbooks, 1926-1932. 4 v.
One volume contains clippings of M. C. Levee publicity regarding construction of new Burbank First National Studios, his work with United Artists and later Paramount, and the founding of the Academy of Motion Picture Arts and Sciences. Three volumes contain clippings regarding the origin, development, programs of the Screen Guild for the year 1932.
Unpublished register in library.

17 McCarey, Leo, 1898-1969. (director, producer)
Collection, ca. 1932-1969. 48 boxes.
Correspondence, production records, telegrams, scripts, story ideas, publicity, clippings and photographs relating to Mr. McCarey's career in motion pictures. Included among the screenplays are: MAKE WAY FOR TOMORROW (PAR, 1937), THE AWFUL TRUTH (COL, 1937), GOING MY WAY (PAR, 1944), THE BELLS OF ST. MARY'S (RKO, 1945), MY SON JOHN (PAR, 1952), and AN AFFAIR TO REMEMBER (F, 1957).

18 Manes, Stephen.
Sixty years of studio, a history by Stephen Manes. Unpublished manuscript. Los Angeles, 1971.

19 Mintz, Jack. (motion picture production)
Collection, 1922-1961. 3 boxes.
Assorted production materials from Mr. Mintz's career in the film industry. Includes motion picture scripts, production records, correspondence, and other materials; also stills. Contains material on Monty Banks, Paramount, California studios, Screen Writers Guild and Academy of Motion Picture Arts and Sciences.
Unpublished register in library.

20 Peckinpah, Sam, 1925-   . (writer, director)
Collection of Television Scripts and Films, ca. 1956-1966.

Television scripts include NOON WINE, GUNSMOKE, THE RIFLE-
MAN. Films of RIDE THE HIGH COUNTRY (MGM, 1962) and NOON
WINE. Also some commercials.
Unpublished register in library.

21 RADIO FLASH, 1933-1955. 20 v.
RKO house organ publication. Information on new productions, publicity, etc. Geared primarily for exhibitors,
distributors.

22 A REDBOOK Dialogue.
Taped interviews by Redbook Magazine, 1959-1968. 15 reels,
plus tearsheets.
Library has following interviews: Harry Belafonte, Anthony
Quinn, David Hemmings, Anna Kashfi, Danny Kaye, Dr. Tom
Dooley, Deborah Kerr, Peter Viertel, Miguel Dominguin, Debbie
Reynolds, Billy Graham.

23 Riskin, Ralph, 1931-   . (producer, executive)
Collection, 1969-1971. 7 boxes.
Scripts and production records from the television series,
THE COURTSHIP OF EDDIE'S FATHER, 1969-1971.
Unpublished register in library.

24 Sage, George Byron, ca. 1900-1974. (story analyst)
Collection, 1941-1973. 22 folders.
Story analyst files compiled at Twentieth Century-Fox,
1941-1973.
Unpublished register in library.

25 Script Collection.
About 2,000 motion picture scripts and continuities from
1918-   . Includes a large number of scripts from MGM,
Twentieth Century-Fox. About 500 television scripts from
1955 to date including series such as THE WALTONS, COLUMBO,
VISIONS, RICH MAN, POOR MAN, ALL IN THE FAMILY, MAUDE, and
GOOD TIMES, as well as movies for TV such as THE AUTOBIOGRAPHY
OF MISS JANE PITTMAN, JAMES MICHENER'S DYNASTY, THAT CERTAIN
SUMMER.

26 Seitz, George B., 1888-1944. (director, writer)
Collection, 1935-1944. 10 boxes.
Scripts, production records and correspondence. Scripts
(often annotated) and related materials from Mr. Seitz's MGM
films, especially the ANDY HARDY series. Stills from A FAMILY
AFFAIR (MGM, 1937). Script for THE VANISHING AMERICAN (PAR,
1925). Campaign books for exhibitors on serials.
Unpublished register in library.

27 <u>Sound Recording Manuals From Goldwyn Studios, 1929-1956.</u>
9 boxes.
 Western Electric Sound Recording Systems: operating in-
structions, methods and processes. Miscellaneous Western
Electric Publications. Technical information bulletins for
Westrex Corp. Equipment. Technical tracts.
 Unpublished register in library.

28 <u>TIME-LIFE Audio History of American Movies, 1971-1972.</u>
56 cassettes, 4 transcribed interviews.
 Library has the following interviews on tape: Judith
Anderson, Fred Astaire, Mary Astor (trs.), Gene Autry, Lew
Ayres (trs.), Lauren Bacall, Busby Berkeley, Pandro Berman,
Walter Brennan, Johnny Mack Brown, George Cukor, Bette Davis,
Andy Devine, Melvyn Douglas, Henry Hathaway, Howard Hawks,
Paul Henreid, James Wong Howe, Nunnally Johnson, Fritz Lang,
Arthur Laurents, Mervyn LeRoy, Anita Loos, Joel McCrea,
Reginald Owen, Joe Pasternak, Otto Preminger, Irving Rapper,
Vincent Sherman, Adela Rogers St. Johns, Max Steiner, James
Stewart (trs.), King Vidor, John Wayne, William Wyler (trs.).

29 <u>Twentieth Century-Fox Film Corporation.</u>
 Catalogue of unproduced literary properties, 1951-1971.
Unpublished manuscripts. Revised: December, 1971.

30 <u>von Stroheim, Erich, 1885-1957.</u> (actor, director)
 Collection, 1919-1923. 2 reels microfilm 16mm.
 Erich von Stroheim scenarios, continuities, treatments,
synopses revisions, subtitles, notes for: FOOLISH WIVES (U,
1922), MERRY-GO-ROUND (U, 1923), BLIND HUSBANDS (U, 1919),
and THE DEVIL'S PASSKEY (U, 1920).

AMERICAN SOCIETY OF
CINEMATOGRAPHERS (ASC)
1782 North Orange Drive
Hollywood, California 90028

<u>MUSEUM</u>
Curator: Charles G. Clarke
(213) 876-5080
Hours: M-F, 9-5
Museum open to the public.

 The prime purpose of the Museum is to preserve and display
material of real historic interest pertaining to the evolution of
the motion picture. The Museum was conceived by Charles G.
Clarke, ASC, and Arthur C. Miller, ASC, in 1958. The nucleus of

the collection of equipment was donated by Mr. Clarke. Most of the equipment on display was actually used by the film pioneers themselves.

1 Early Apparatus pertaining to the evolution of the motion picture, 1834-____. ca. 1,000 items.
   Collection of early historical equipment includes pre-cinema and cinema devices, such as the Phenakistoscope (1834), flip-books, Traumascope, magic lanterns, Edison Kinetoscope (1893), Lumiere projector head (ca. 1896), Edison Projection Kinetoscope (ca. 1900), Mutoscope with 1909 pictures of Motion Picture Patents Company founders, Eclair 35mm camera (1907), Edison Home Projector (1912), Pathe studio camera, Moy professional camera, Debrie camera, Akeley camera, Hausmann step printer 35mm, Technicolor "three-strip" camera and other exhibits of Technicolor system. Special exhibitions demonstrate the evolution of the anamorphic lens, the zoom lens, light meters, and wide-screen systems. There are also early finders, measuring devices, moviolas, and a series of tinted and toned frames from motion pictures.
   Descriptive inventory for most items on display is in Museum.

2 Photograph Collection.
   Museum has a number of historical pictures oriented around the camera, many of which show cameramen at work on various productions. There are also original photographs of a number of early film pioneers, including the founders of the Motion Picture Patents Company and Vitagraph, as well as an up to date series of photographs of Oscar and Emmy winning cinematographers.

3 Walt Disney Room.
   Collection of photographs, drawings, story sketches, celluloids, etc. documenting various aspects of Disney films. Material on loan from Walt Disney Productions. Displays to be changed periodically.

ANAHEIM PUBLIC LIBRARY (AnPL)
500 West Broadway
Anaheim, California 92805

MOTHER COLONY HISTORY ROOM
Curator: Mrs. Opal Kissinger
(714) 533-5221
Hours: M-F, 9-6
Material open to the public.

1 Disney collection, ca. 1930s-   .
   Books, press releases, maps, operating manuals, guidebooks, employee newsletters, newspaper clippings, pressbooks, posters, periodicals, photographs, Disney character merchandise, examples of tickets, handbills, advertising matter, comic books, big-little books, pop-out books, puzzles, games, biographical material, Disney music, 20th, 50th anniversary scripts (TV), Disneyland attractions.
   Disney collection is non-circulating.

ARIZONA HISTORICAL SOCIETY (AHS)
949 East Second Street
Tucson, Arizona   85719

RESEARCH LIBRARY
Archivist: Dr. Don De Witt
(602) 882-5774
Hours: M-F, 9-4; Sat, 9-12
Some of material open to public.

1 Motion Picture Photographs.
   100 still photographs, 1914-1972. Bulk of collection is from the period 1960-1972.

2 Motion Picture Posters.
   Included are posters for SO THIS IS ARIZONA, RIDERS OF THE CACTUS, and ARIZONA.

3 Old Tucson File, 1940-   . 4 inches.
   A collection of clippings, tear sheets and miscellaneous materials relating to Old Tucson and the movie industry in Arizona.

4 Oral History.
   Interviews by Kenneth Hufford conducted between 1969 and 1971 with actors, directors, and other persons connected with the motion picture industry including the following:
   a. Alderson, Floyd ("Wally Wales") (actor)
   b. Born, Dewey (projectionist)
   c. Cabot, Bruce, 1906-   (actor)
   d. Canutt, Yakima, 1895-   (stuntman)
   e. Clothier, William, 1903-   (cinematographer)
   f. Elam, Jack (actor)
   g. Gardner, Gail I. (cowboy-songwriter)
   h. Haley, Earl (stuntman)
   i. Hawks, Howard, 1896-   (director)
   j. Heisler, Stuart, 1894-   (director)
   k. Holden, William, 1918-   (actor)

1. Johnson, Ben, 1919–   (actor)
m. Little, Ann, 1894–   (actress)
n. Mullens, Johnny (cowboy-friend of Tom Mix)
o. Pratt, Jim (production manager)
p. Roberson, Chuck (stuntman)
q. Smith, Mrs. Albert E. (Jean Page), 1896–   (actress)
r. Taliaferro, Hal (actor)
s. Wayne, John, 1907–   (actor)
t. Williams, Jack (stuntman)

ARIZONA STATE UNIVERSITY (ASU)
Charles Trumbull Hayden Library
Tempe, Arizona 85281
(602) 965-3415

DEPARTMENT OF SPECIAL COLLECTIONS
Rare Books Librarian: Mrs. Marilyn Wurzburger
Hours: M-F, 8-5
Material open to the public.

1 Starr, Jimmy, 1904–___. (writer, columnist)
      Collection, 1920s–   . ca. 50 ft.
      Collection contains material relating to Jimmy Starr's
career as a screenwriter and newspaper columnist.
      Communications. Material consists of letters, notes and
memos collected by Starr during his newspaper career. Material is from varied sources: studios, such as Warner Brothers
and Paramount, individuals, and special interest groups requesting his help.
      Biographical File. Miscellaneous information pertaining
to individuals, primarily in the form of newspaper clippings.
In some cases there are also scrapbooks and other memorabilia
regarding that particular person. Individuals covered include
Tallulah Bankhead, Betty Grable, Audrey Hepburn, Marlon
Brando, Gene Autry, Richard Burton, and Howard Hughes.
      Motion Picture Productions. Press releases, preview
notices, handbills, cast sheets, synopses, indexes to films
by company and stills. Also production notes from such movies
as PRISONER OF ZENDA, BREAKFAST AT TIFFANY'S, and OUR TOWN.
      Scripts. Screenplays, stageplays, manuscripts, suggestions
for radio and television, story ideas by Starr and others.
Included among the nearly sixty scripts are screenplays for a
considerable number of late 1920s Warner Brothers features,
many of which are annotated by Darryl Zanuck. Screenplays
include: OH, WHAT A NURSE (WA, 1926), JAWS OF STEEL (WA,
1927), DON'T TELL THE WIFE (WA, 1927), A RENO DIVORCE (WA,
1927), THE CRIMSON CITY (WA, 1928), FROM HEAD QUARTERS (WA,
1929), KID GLOVES (WA, 1929), HAROLD TEEN (WA, 1934), KING OF

THE ROYAL MOUNTED (F, 1936), GONE WITH THE WIND (MGM, 1939), SPECTER OF THE ROSE (REP, 1946), FRIENDLY PERSUASION (AA, 1956), and BLESS THE BEASTS AND CHILDREN (COL, 1971). Included with the full scripts are a number of title sheets for silent movies.

Published material. Newspapers, chiefly motion picture sections, from California and several other states. Periodicals include trade and professional magazines as well as motion picture directories.

BRIGHAM YOUNG UNIVERSITY (BYU)
Harold B. Lee Library
Provo, Utah 84602

ARCHIVES AND MANUSCRIPTS
Curator: Dennis Rowley
(801) 374-1211, Ext. 2905
Hours: M-F, 8-5
Unrestricted material may be viewed by any qualified scholar, but scholars are requested to write or telephone prior to going to Provo.

1 Astor, Mary, 1906-   . (actress)
    1 scrapbook, 1940.
    The 150 page scrapbook contains press clippings from BRIGHAM YOUNG--FRONTIERSMAN (F, 1940).

2 Beck, Marilyn. (columnist-author)
    Copies of her columns, research files and interview notes. 2 ft.

3 Doty-Dayton Productions.
    Production files, scripts, books, publicity material, stills and financial records for SEVEN ALONE (1975), WHERE THE RED FERN GROWS (1974), AGAINST THE CROOKED SKY, PONY EXPRESS RIDER (1976). 8 ft.

4 Easton, Carol. (writer)
    Research files, drafts, manuscript and an annotated galley proof of her book. The Search for Samuel Goldwyn. 1 ft.

5 Jagger, Dean, 1903-   . (actor)
    Papers, 1903-1974. 3 boxes and 5 v. (2 ft.)
    Includes correspondence, photographs, scripts, tape recorded interviews with transcriptions, publicity material and production stills relating to Jagger's show business career. While material on most films is limited to a still or press clipping, the bulk of the collection covers the years

1934-1965 and comprehensively documents major theatre per-
formances and the motion pictures BRIGHAM YOUNG (F, 1940),
WESTERN UNION (F, 1941), and TWELVE O'CLOCK HIGH (F, 1949).
Register published in 1976 by Lee Library.

6 Karloff, Boris, 1887-1969. (actor)
    Correspondence, photographs and memorabilia. 1 ft.

7 Lindsay, Cynthia. (writer)
    Research files and manuscript for her book, Dear Boris.
    2 ft.

BURBANK PUBLIC LIBRARY (BPL)
110 North Glenoaks Boulevard
Burbank, California 91503

WARNER RESEARCH COLLECTION
Research Librarian: Mary Ann Grasso
(213) 847-9743
Hours: M-F, 9-6. By appointment only.

The Warner Research Collection was formerly the Warner Brothers
Research Library. Although the collection is a part of the Bur-
Bank Public Library, Warner Research is a closed access collection
operating on a fee schedule of $8.75 per one-half hour minimum,
$17.50 per one hour, or $15.00 per hour by advance purchase of
time. (The advance purchase is based upon a minimum purchase of
100 hours of research time paid for in advance of use.) Fees are
determined by the amount of time the research librarian must spend
preparing the request. Time is not charged for use of the material.

1   The collection consists of research material covering a vast
     range of topics, including architecture, costumes and person-
     alities. The majority of the material is found in clipping
     files organized by subject. There are about 500 Pictorial
     Research Compilations scrapbooks for Warner Brothers films,
     primarily of the 1930s and 1940s, and many include set stills.
     Miscellaneous items include a limited number of posters, set
     stills, screenplays.

CALIFORNIA INSTITUTE OF THE ARTS (CIA)
24700 McBean Parkway
Valencia, California 91355

LIBRARY
Director: Elizabeth Armstrong
Film Librarian: Margie Hanft

(805) 255-1050
Hours: M-F, 9-5
Material open to the public for reference use.

1 Screenplay Collection.
   Small number of screenplays, including BIRTH OF A NATION
   (UA, 1915), taken from 16mm print of original 12 reel version),
   THE GRAPES OF WRATH (F, 1940), THE OX-BOW INCIDENT (F, 1943),
   MY DARLING CLEMENTINE (F, 1946), 13 RUE MADELEINE (F, 1946),
   VIVA ZAPATA (F, 1952), THE LADYKILLERS (COL, 1956), SWEET
   SMELL OF SUCCESS (UA, 1957), THE HUSTLER (F, 1961), and A
   HIGH WIND IN JAMAICA (F, 1965).

CALIFORNIA LUTHERAN COLLEGE (CLC)
Thousand Oaks, California   91360

DRAMA DEPARTMENT
Contact: Don W. Haskell, Instructor
(805) 492-2411

1 Script Collection.
   Small number of scripts for motion pictures and television,
   including several for BONANZA, THOROUGHLY MODERN MILLIE (U,
   1967), THE RUSSIANS ARE COMING, THE RUSSIANS ARE COMING (UA,
   1966), THE GRADUATE (EMB, 1967), and THE CHAMPAGNE GENERAL.

CALIFORNIA MUSEUM OF SCIENCE
AND INDUSTRY (CMSI)
700 State Drive
Los Angeles, California   90037

Museum Director: William J. McCann
(213) 749-0101
Hours: 10-5 every day except Thanksgiving and Christmas.
Material open to the public.

1 Cinemagic Exhibit. ca. 100 items.
   Pre-cinema and cinema antique collection loaned by Universal Studios and Universal Studios Tour. Includes mechanical
   lantern slides, peep shows, panoramic fans, stereoscopes,
   Kaleidoscopes, Eastman camera (1885), Pocket Biographs, Praxinoscope, Viviscope, Edison 35mm Projectorscope (1898), Bio-
   scope 35mm camera (ca. 1900), Selig 35mm camera (ca. 1908),
   Pathe 35mm camera (ca. 1909), Pathe 35mm camera (ca. 1910)
   used by cameraman Billy Bitzer to film BIRTH OF A NATION

(UA, 1915), Universal 35mm camera (ca. 1917), DeForest "Phonofilm" adapter 1920 and 1925 models, DeForest "light valve" for optical sound recording, RCA Condenser Microphone (ca. 1929), Prizma Color Camera (ca. 1918) and Western Electric recording amplifier Model 13c--1922 model. Also a collection of home movie entertainment equipment, 1901-1930.

CALIFORNIA STATE LIBRARY (CSL)
Library and Courts Building
Ninth Street and Capital Mall
(mailing address: P. O. Box 2037,
Sacramento, California 95809)

CALIFORNIA SECTION
Head Librarian: Kenneth I. Pettitt
(916) 445-4149
Hours: 8-5 weekdays except State holidays
Material open to the public.
Photo services available.

1 Manuscripts.
    Small collection of early screenplays, 5 scene plots (1916) and 15 articles covering photoplay production from script to screen ("Movies in the Making").

2 Motion Picture Photographs. ca. 1911-1920s.
    Over 400 photographs including production stills and portraits. 66 stills for RAMONA (CLU, 1916), all identified by actors and by scene in film. 60 stills for 15 William S. Hart films (1917-1919) including BREED OF MEN, RIDDLE GAWNE, THE SILENT MAN, SQUARE DEAL SANDERSON, WAGON TRACKS, and WOLVES OF THE RAIL. 1 poster for the Hart film THE POPPY GIRL'S HUSBAND (ART, 1919) plus a few early handbills (ca. 1911).

3 Motion Picture Programs and Pressbooks.
    Approximately 100 programs (pre-1940s). Also 2 Lasky pressbooks for THE WINNING OF SALLY TEMPLE (PAR, 1917) and ALIEN SOULS (PAR, 1916).

4 Newspaper Index.
    This index to San Francisco newspapers, including the Chronicle and the Examiner, contains about 10,000 entries (7 card file drawers) of references to motion pictures, specifically motion picture reviews from 1904-1949.

CALIFORNIA STATE UNIVERSITY,
FULLERTON (CSUF)
Library
Post Office Box 4150
Fullerton, California 92634

A   ARCHIVES OF POPULAR CULTURE
Head: Dr. Robert Porfirio
(714) 870-2441
Material to be viewed by special arrangement.

1   Motion Picture Material.
Collection includes about 500 lobby cards (late 1920s-
1960s), about 100 1-sheets (1930s-1960s), clippings scrapbooks on silent films (1909-1916, 1918-1926) and screenplays,
among which are THE MALTESE FALCON (WA, 1941), DEAD RECKONING
(COL, 1947), D.O.A. (UA, 1949), and MR. ARKADIN (CAI, 1962).

2   Radio Programs.
60 hours of programs, 1932-1952.

3   Television Material.
Television scripts include about 80 for BATMAN (1965-1967)
and 15 for SUPERMAN. Also the original Superman costume.

B   DEPARTMENT OF SPECIAL COLLECTIONS
Librarian: Linda Herman
(714) 870-3444
Hours: M-T, 1-7; W-F, 9-12 noon
Open to the public.

1   Guiol, Fred, 1898-   . (director, writer)
Collection, ca. 1920s-1959.
Screenplays, treatments, and outlines for films of 1920s-
1949; screenplays, treatments, outlines and production material for films of 1950s. Scripts or treatments for 1920s films
include a number for Stan Laurel, Laurel and Hardy, Spat
Family, Glenn Tryon, Max Davidson and Charley Chase. Several
scripts from the 1930s are by Fred Guiol and George Stevens,
and Stevens was director for a number of the films from 1950s.
Among the screenplays of the 1940s and 1950s are 11 Hal Roach
scripts including TANKS A MILLION (UA, 1941), ABOUT FACE (UA,
1942), YANKS AHOY (1943), TAXI, MISTER (UA, 1943), and HERE
COMES TROUBLE (UA, 1948). Collection also includes scripts
for THIS THING CALLED LOVE (COL, 1941), PENNY SERENADE (COL,
1941), WOMAN OF THE YEAR (MGM, 1942), I REMEMBER MAMA (RKO,
1948), A PLACE IN THE SUN (PAR, 1951), THE HALF-BREED (RKO,
1952), SHANE (PAR, 1953), 20,000 LEAGUES UNDER THE SEA (BV,
1954), GIANT (WA, 1956), and DIARY OF ANNE FRANK (F, 1959).

Also in the collection are a few television scripts and miscellaneous periodicals and pamphlets.
Register with collection.

2 STAR TREK.
46 scripts from the television series, 1966-1969.

**CALIFORNIA STATE UNIVERSITY,
LONG BEACH (CSULB)**
Library
1250 Bellflower Boulevard
Long Beach, California 90840

FINE ARTS LIBRARY
Librarian: Henry DuBois
(213) 498-4023
Hours: M-Th, 8am-9:30pm; F, 8-5; Sat, 9:30-5:30; Sun, 1-5
Material open to public; however, material which is in manuscript
    form is restricted to use in library.

1 Music Scores from the MGM Music Library, ca. 1778, 1847-1964.
40 ft.
    Material includes popular songs, vocal and instrumental
scores for popular music, scores for films, scores for stage
musicals, operas and operettas. A number of the scores are
in manuscript form with annotations. Film scores include:
GOODBYE, MR. CHIPS (MGM, 1939), BATAAN (MGM, 1943), VACATION
FROM MARRIAGE (MGM, 1945), THE OTHER LOVE (UA, 1947), ARCH
OF TRIUMPH (UA, 1948), SO THIS IS NEW YORK (UA, 1948), THE
HAPPY ROAD (MGM, 1957), and THE LITTLE HUT (MGM, 1957).
There are works of a number of composers, including: Jerome
Kern, Noel Coward, Leonard Bernstein, Cole Porter, George
Gershwin, Irving Berlin, Victor Herbert, Richard Rogers,
Miklos Rozsa, and Adolph Deutsch.
    There is a complete inventory of the MGM materials but
they have not been kept together as a separate collection.
The material is integrated with the rest of the library's
music collection, catalogued by title and composer.

**CALIFORNIA STATE UNIVERSITY,
LOS ANGELES (CSULA)**
John F. Kennedy Memorial Library
5151 State College Drive
Los Angeles, California 90032

ARCHIVAL SPECIAL COLLECTIONS
Library Archivist: Ray Engelke

(213) 224-2212, 224-2201
Collection may be used only by special arrangement.

1 Anthony Quinn Collection, 1950s-1970s. 17 ft.
      Collection includes 276 screenplays, most of which were
   apparently unproduced, television scripts and miscellaneous
   proposals, pamphlets, books and correspondence. Among the
   produced screenplays are LA STRADA (TRH, 1956), THE SHOES OF
   THE FISHERMAN (MGM, 1968), THE MAGUS (F, 1968), A DREAM OF
   KINGS (NGP, 1969), R.P.M. (COL, 1970), VANISHING POINT (F,
   1970), THE HUNTING PARTY (UA, 1970), and JOHNNY GOT HIS GUN
   (CMT, 1971). There are 14 television scripts for MAN AND THE
   CITY (1971).
      Inventory to collection in Library Archivists Office,
   Library North B 540.

CALIFORNIA STATE UNIVERSITY, NORTHRIDGE (CSUN)
Oviatt Library
18111 Nordhoff Street
Northridge, California 91324

A   DEPARTMENT OF SPECIAL COLLECTIONS
    Curator: Dennis C. Bakewell
    (213) 885-2832
    Material may be viewed only through special arrangement.

    1 Martin, Ray. (composer, arranger)
          Collection, ca. 1950s-   .
          Collection includes 875 manuscript scores and arrangements
       for films and phonograph records. Includes musical scores
       for number of James Bond films such as GOLDFINGER (UA, 1964)
       and THUNDERBALL (UA, 1965).

    2 Television Scripts.
          Small collection of scripts for several different televi-
       sion series, including 26 volumes for BIG TOWN (1952-1955),
       and individual scripts for TWILIGHT ZONE (1963), ALFRED
       HITCHCOCK PRESENTS (1959), and CHEVY MYSTERY SHOW (1960).

B   RADIO/TV/FILM DEPARTMENT
    Contact: Dr. John Schultheiss
    (213) 885-2838
    Material may be viewed only through special arrangement.

    1 Script Collection.
          Collection includes television scripts for a variety of
       programs such as THE JOHNNY CARSON SHOW (1955-1956), RED

SKELTON (1953-1955), OUTER LIMITS (1964), and HAVE GUN, WILL TRAVEL (1959-1960). Also number of apparently unproduced screenplays.

DISNEY (WALT) PRODUCTIONS (DP)
500 South Buena Vista
Burbank, California 91521

WALT DISNEY ARCHIVES
Archivist: David R. Smith
(213) 845-3141
Hours: M-F, 8-5
Material available to serious researchers by prior arrangement.

The Archives contains or can provide access to material on most aspects of Disney enterprises--creative and business. There is material dealing with the history of the studio, its productions and enterprises such as Disneyland and Walt Disney World. Many recent legal and business files are restricted.

1 Algar, James, 1912-   . (producer, director)
Business correspondence and production files, 1940s-1950s. 15 ft.

2 Animation History.
Pre-Disney and elsewhere during Disney period. Small but growing collection. Correspondence with early animators.

3 Awards.
Awards that Walt Disney and the Disney company have won including Oscars.

4 Barks, Carl, 1901-   . (artist)
Business correspondence, fan mail with answers, 1950-1970. 1/2 ft.
Includes a few sketches and original art work of man responsible for many Donald Duck comic books.

5 Catalogues.
Catalogues of all of the domestic books from Disney, including names of illustrators. Catalogue of magazine articles on some aspect of Disney by subject and author. Bibliographies listing Disney films, books, sheet music, books and articles about Disney, Disney television shows and Disney comic books. Catalogues of Disney phonograph records, merchandise licenses, tape recordings.

6 <u>Disney, Roy O., 1893-1971.</u> (executive)
    Personal and business correspondence, 1930-1971. 15-20 ft.

7 <u>Disney, Walt, 1901-1966.</u> (animator, producer, executive)
    Personal and business correspondence, 1930-1966.
    80-100 ft. Gifts, office furnishings, miniature collection,
    memorabilia, press clippings.

8 <u>Disneyland, 1955- and Walt Disney World, 1971-   </u>.
    Press releases, employee magazines, press clippings, photo-
    graphs, training manuals, operating procedures, attendance
    reports, publication printed in print shops, tickets and
    ticket books, business records and correspondence files,
    scripts and programs for special events. File of information
    arranged by attraction, shop, or dining facility.

9 <u>Gillett, Burton, 1891-1971.</u> (animation director)
    Business papers, 1905-1935. 1 ft.
    Material going back to Mutt and Jeff and Koko the Klown.

10 <u>Hand, David, 1900-   </u>. (animation director)
    Company memos, 1935-1940. 1/2 ft.

11 <u>Sharpsteen, Ben, 1895-   </u>. (director, producer)
    Business correspondence, 1940s-1950s. 10 ft.

12 <u>Walt Disney Productions.</u>
    a. <u>Art Work, 1927-   </u>.
        Animation and various original art work. ca.
        50,000,000 drawings, 5,000 ft. Story sketches, pencil
        animation, painted backgrounds and cells. Organized
        by picture and sequence within the pictures. Also
        story meeting notes.
        Designs, blueprints and models for things at studio--
        sets, buildings, props, etc. Also for Disneyland and
        Walt Disney World.

    b. <u>Books, 1930-   </u>. 800 domestic titles.
        Children's books. Thousands of foreign Disney
        books, sometimes translations, sometimes produced in
        foreign country using Disney characters.

    c. <u>Business Records.</u>
        Correspondence and memos from various departments,
        1923-. Also complete collection of annual reports to
        stockholders, 1940-. Proxy statements, stock pro-
        spectuses, etc. Biographies of company employees.
        Production files. Film credits.

    d. <u>Character merchandise, 1928-   </u>.
        Toys, games, clothing, jewelry--anything using

Disney characters. Primarily since 1950. 500–600
large boxes of merchandise. Also photographs, catalogues, and contracts regarding this material.

e. Comic books, 1932–____.
      Complete collection of domestic; good collection of
      foreign comic books.

f. Comic strips, 1930–____.
      Proof sheets.

g. Disney insignia.
      Collection of photographs and correspondence re:
      insignia designed at Disney studio for military units,
      1940–.

h. Motion pictures, 1920–____. Over 1,000.
      This material not stored at archives, but archives
      has access to all.

i. Motion picture promotional material.
      Posters, press clippings, press releases and press-
      books. About 400 posters (1925–) for most features
      but missing many for shorts. About 200 pressbooks
      for all feature films (1937–) and some shorts (1928–).
      Press releases on all of productions and on company
      business. Press clippings by date and subject (1924–,
      ca. 200 ft.). Included are clippings on early years
      of Mickey Mouse Club. 300 scrapbooks (1923–) for in-
      dividual films.

j. Phonograph records.
      Records since 1950 produced by Disney. Prior to
      that a representative sampling of Disney records re-
      leased by other companies.

k. Photographs.
      500,000 negatives in Still Camera Department. 500–
      750 still books for all of productions. 8,000 pictures
      of Walt Disney.

l. Screenplays and Television scripts. ca. 1,000.
      For all productions. About 120 alone for feature
      films. Includes cutting continuities, drafts and in
      some cases annotated scripts. Also Walt Disney's own
      copies of scripts with his notes. All animators that
      worked on each sequence of each film listed.

m. Sheet music, 1930–____. 4 ft.

n. Tape recordings, 1930-   .
    Interviews of present and former Disney employees;
interview of Walt Disney done for book on Disney by
Pete Martin (1956); tapes of radio shows on which Walt
Disney appeared (1930-).
    Transcripts of most.

FIRST FEDERAL SAVINGS AND LOAN
ASSOCIATION OF HOLLYWOOD (FFSL)
Hollywood and Highland
Hollywood, California 90028

Contact: Bruce T. Torrence, Sr. Vice-President
(213) 463-4141
Material available to the general public by appointment.
Photograph copying services available.

1   Photographic Collection.
        Photographs of Hollywood, Santa Monica and motion picture
    studios, 1884-. ca. 10,000 photographs.
        Collection includes ground photos of Hollywood, 1884 to
    the present, catalogued by year and by number on each glacene
    envelope; aerial photos of Hollywood and the Santa Monica
    area; and ground and aerial photos of motion pictures studios,
    1909 to the present, catalogued by studio in chronological
    order. Photos of studios begin in 1909 with Selig and include
    a considerable number for Famous Players-Lasky, Ince Studios,
    Pickford Fairbanks-United Artists, Mack Sennett (Glendale and
    Studio City), Universal and Vitagraph. In all over 1,000
    photographs of about 80-85 studios.
        All photos are catalogued in a card index file by subject
    and category.

2   Reference Collection. ca. 45-50 ft.
        Books, periodicals, programs dealing with Hollywood, motion
    picture production companies and motion picture studios.

FOOTHILL COLLEGE (FC)
ELECTRONICS MUSEUM
12345 El Monte Road
Los Altos Hills, California 94022

A   DE FOREST MEMORIAL ARCHIVES
Archivist: Mrs. Estelle McLaughlin
(415) 948-8590

Hours: M-F, 8-5
Material may be viewed by special arrangement.

1 De Forest, Lee, 1873-1961. (radio inventor, pioneer)
      Papers, 1873-1961. 128,444 items + 3 1/2 file drawers.
      Correspondence, diaries, journals, notebooks detailing
   scientific work and inventions, documents relating to patents
   and other legal matters, awards, and scrapbooks. Also radio
   scripts.
      Access restricted.
      Library also has microfilm of the collection.
      Unpublished inventory and calendar in the repository.

B ELECTRONICS COLLECTION
   Curator: Jack Eddy
   Hours: M-Th, 9-5; F, 9-10pm; Sat-Sun, 1-5. Doors close one-half
      hour earlier.
   Material open to the public.

   1 Elektra.
         Electricity and magnetism experimental displays that have
      been designed to demonstrate the fundamental laws of elec-
      tricity and magnetism which form the basis of the world of
      radio and electronics.

   2 FN-San Jose Calling.
         Reconstruction of the first regularly scheduled radio
      broadcast station, FN, "San Jose Calling." The first wireless
      station to broadcast voice and music was built and operated
      by Dr. C. D. Herrold of San Jose in 1909. Original arc trans-
      mitter used by Dr. Herrold is on display in museum.

   3 Early Radio Broadcast Receivers.
         Receivers and loud speakers from early broadcast era. Ex-
      amples of magnetic, crystal and vacuum tube detectors are in
      the display. Atop exhibit are mural size photographs of some
      of country's popular radio performers and shows. Headphones
      connected to working old time radios permit museum visitor to
      hear radio signals just as first radio listeners did.

   4 Early Amateur Radio Station.
         Two amateur radio stations are a part of the Museum. One
      is a 1920 vintage amateur station complete with QSL cards,
      log books, the spark transmitter of Mr. L. A. Bartholomew
      (6LC) and a Navy type SE-143 receiver. The other is an up-
      to-date, licensed, operating station (WB6WSL).

   5 Radio Tube Display.
         Display unit housing representative radio tubes that date
      from the Fleming valve (1904) to representative tubes still
      in use today. The development of vacuum tubes from the

de Forest audion to the giant Varian 1,250,000 watt Klvstron is shown. The story of the Varian brothers occupies a central spot in the microwave display.

6 Spark and Arc Transmission.
   Display demonstrates the principles of early spark and arc transmitters.

GLENDALE PUBLIC LIBRARY (GPL)
222 East Harvard Street
Glendale, California 91205

DEPARTMENT OF SPECIAL COLLECTIONS
Special Collections Librarian: Barbara R. Boyd
(213) 956-2037
Hours: M-F, 9-12, 1-5
All material open to the public.

1 Documents.
   1. Letter from James W. Horne regarding Kalem Co. in Glendale from 1912 when he joined it. n.d.
   2. 1920 affadavit of C. M. Giffin (Production Manager for Pinnacle Productions) regarding Bachmann Studio (a part of Pinnacle Productions) and the advantages that would accrue to the city of Glendale by the location of this studio.
   3. 1915 petition with 243 signatures to the Glendale City Council to allow theaters to conduct their business on Sundays.

2 Moving picture editions of novels.
   Novels from early 1900-1930s which were filmed and contain stills from the production.

3 RKO Screenplay Collection, 1934-1941.
   About 50 scripts in various stages--treatments, outlines, first drafts, estimating scripts, continuities, final scripts. Collection includes scripts for FOLLOW THE FLEET (1936), MARY OF SCOTLAND (1936), OUTCASTS OF POKER FLAT (1937), CAREFREE (1938), LOVE AFFAIR (1939), GUNGA DIN (1939), ABE LINCOLN IN ILLINOIS (1940), TOM, DICK AND HARRY (1941), and CITIZEN KANE (1941). Collection also includes some stills for several films and programs.
   Inventory to scripts in library.

HART (WILLIAM S.) PARK
AND MUSEUM (HPM)
24151 Newhall Avenue
Newhall, California 91355

A GROUNDS AND HOUSE
Park Ranger: Mike Harrett
(805) 259-0855
Hours: Tu-Sun, 10 until one hour before sunset.
Grounds and house open to the public.

1 The Hart Ranch is now maintained by the Los Angeles County
Department of Parks and Recreation.

The original ranch house, built in 1910 and remodeled to
its present state in 1922, is furnished in the style of the
early 1900s and includes early motion picture props and materials. The tack room holds a collection of hand-tooled
saddles, lariats, spurs, and bridles. This ranch house was
also used as a movie set.

The retirement home, built in 1928, contains the original
furnishings, works of art, historical Indian artifacts and a
gun collection. Among the famous artists represented in the
art collection are Charles M. Russell, Frederic Remington and
James Montgomery Flagg.

The bunk house contains gambling equipment used in various
W. S. Hart productions.

Many of Harts' animals are buried on the property, including his Great Danes and the movie pony "Fritz."

Tours given every 15 minutes from 10-12:15 and from
1-4:45.

B MANUSCRIPTS AND SPECIAL COLLECTIONS.
Contact: Seymour Greben, Director, County of Los Angeles, Department of Parks and Recreation
(213) 749-6941, Ext. 501
Material may be viewed only by special arrangement.

1 Hart, William S., 1872?-1946. (actor)
Collection, ca. 1891-1930. ca. 20 ft. plus oversize scrapbooks and 3 trunks glass negatives.

Collection includes material on both Hart's stage career
(1891-1913) and his film career (1914-1926). There are photographs, clippings, theater programs, play scripts, screenplays,
original paintings for posters of his films, correspondence
original manuscripts for short stories, novels and films by
Hart, and financial papers. Considerable correspondence from
Hart's publicity director Paul Conlon and with Jesse Lasky and
Wyatt Earp. Among the screenplays are: THE TESTING BLOCK
(PAR, 1920), THREE WORD BRAND (PAR, 1921), THE WHISTLE (PAR,
1921), and WILD BILL HICKOK (PAR, 1923). Over twenty

scrapbooks, both large and small, contain clippings and photos covering various periods of Hart's career and private life. The glass negatives are from Hart's films. Financial papers include vouchers from the William S. Hart Company, general records, payroll book, records of film receipts and invoice records.

The Museum has prints of 13 Hart films, 1914-1925, many of which are screened each summer for the public.

HISTORICAL SOCIETY OF LONG BEACH (HSLB)
Rancho Los Alamitos
6400 Bixby Hill Road
Long Beach, California 90815

Contact: Mrs. Loretta Berner
(213) 422-6688
Hours: W, 1-5
Material open to the public.

1 Balboa Amusement Producing Company.
   1 scrapbook, July 1913-October 1914.
   Contains press clippings, advertisements, flyers on Long Beach motion picture company and its productions. Includes material on H. M. Horkheimer (president and general manager), E. D. Horkheimer (secretary and treasurer), various productions such as ST. ELMO, THE HUNCHBACK OF CEDAR LODGE, and WILL O' THE WISP, and particularly on the legal suit with Jack London over company's right to produce THE SEA WOLF.

HOLLYWOOD CENTER FOR THE
AUDIO-VISUAL ARTS (HCAA)
412 South Parkview
Los Angeles, California 90057

HOLLYWOOD MUSEUM
(Housed temporarily at Lincoln Heights Jail)
Contact: Dr. Walter J. Daugherty
(213) 383-7342
No set hours due to limitations of facilities and staff.
Material may be viewed only through special arrangement.

1 Balshofer, Fred J., 1878-1969. (cinematographer, producer)
   1 scrapbook, 1917-1918.
   Contains stills from various films including THE HAUNTED PAJAMAS (M, 1917) and THE AVENGING TRAIL (M, 1918).

2 Blue, Monte, 1890-1963. (actor)
    Scripts and clippings, 1926-1930. 1 carton.
    Collection includes 1 large album of clippings on Blue
    (1926-1928) and 15 scripts primarily from Warner Brothers
    (1927-1930). Included are scripts for: BITTER APPLES (1927),
    BRASS KNUCKLES (1927), TENDERLOIN (1928), FROM HEADQUARTERS
    (1929), ISLE OF ESCAPE (1930).

3 Borzage, Frank, 1893-1962. (director)
    Stills and publicity material, 1920-1961. 52 v., 12
    scrapbooks.
    Scrapbooks include personal memorabilia, correspondence,
    as well as clippings on Borzage and his films (1937-1940,
    1945-1961); 9 volumes of publicity (December 1931-October
    1937); 43 still books (1920-1946). Included are still books
    for: HUMORESQUE (PAR, 1920), CHILDREN OF DUST (FN, 1923),
    LAZYBONES (F, 1925), MARRIAGE LICENSE (F, 1926), SEVENTH
    HEAVEN (F, 1927), FAREWELL TO ARMS (PAR, 1932), STRANGE CARGO
    (MGM, 1940), and STAGE DOOR CANTEEN (UA, 1943).

4 Breil, Joseph Carl, 1870-1926. (composer)
    Collection, 1909-1932. 1 carton.
    Includes piano scores for BIRTH OF A NATION (UA, 1915) and
    AMERICA (UA, 1924), newspaper clippings, reviews, programs,
    correspondence, and original music manuscripts. Included is
    telegram from D. W. Griffith regarding the writing of music
    score for BIRTH OF A NATION, as well as an oversize auto-
    graphed photograph of Griffith.

5 Bylek, Rudolph, 1885-   . (technical director, art director)
    Collection, 1913-1939. 3 cartons.
    Included are set drawings for 11 films, most from Paramount
    (1921-1924) such as THE SHEIK (1921), BURNING SANDS (1922),
    MORAN OF THE LADY LETTY (1922), and BEYOND THE ROCKS (1922).
    Also stills, production notes, receipts, correspondence, per-
    sonal papers. Stills from early Biograph films (1914-1917)
    in which Bylek appeared as actor. 1 album of clippings and
    correspondence on JAVA HEAD (1923).

6 Coogan, Jackie, 1914-   . (actor)
    2 scrapbooks, ca. 1922.
    Includes personal and publicity photos of Jackie Coogan,
    many from OLIVER TWIST (FN, 1922).

7 Costumes.
    Collection includes about 150 costumes with accessories
    from films of various periods.

8 Crosby, Bing, 1904-   . (singer, actor)
    1 scrapbook, 1943-1944.
    Clippings, photos and correspondence relating to radio con-
    test for most popular singer.

9 Desmond, William, 1878-1949. (actor)
    1 scrapbook, 1901-1904.
    Contains clippings, theatre programs for productions in
which Desmond appeared, and some photos.

10 Equipment.
    Approximately 12-14 cameras, including 2/3 of the camera
used in filming BIRTH OF A NATION; 6 projectors, including
the first projector used in 1906 at Los Angeles' Tally Theatre; 1 mutoscope, 3 recorders, 2 Kinetoscopes, 2 Iconoscopes,
4 Balopticans, 2 TV sets, 3 stereopticans, 3 phonographs,
animatoscope, animatograph, graphophone, cinematograph, Koda-
scope, cameragraph, splicer, measuring machine, rewind, tape
splicer, step printer, densitometer, and silent picture
viewer.

11 Farnum, William, 1876-1953. (actor)
    Collection, 1891-1940. 4 cartons, 1 suitcase.
    Contains clippings, stills and costume shots from 1920s
films, publicity portraits of stars, scripts, and correspondence on Lambs Club.

12 Gebhart, Myrtle. (actress, columnist)
    Collection, 1924-1950s. 8 cartons.
    Press clippings, copies of stories printed in such maga-
zines as Screenland, Sunset and Picture-Play, press preview
invitations, personal correspondence, material on astrology,
unpublished manuscript.

13 Helfer, Bobby, d. 1970. (composer)
    OKLAHOMA (MTC, 1955). Music score and related material.
1 carton.
    Includes music cue sheets, recording data, interoffice
memos, shooting schedules, and complete musical score for
OKLAHOMA.

14 Hoyt, Vance Joseph, 1889-1967. (writer, physician, naturalist)
    1 scrapbook, ca. 1935.
    Material deals primarily with SEQUOIA (MGM, 1934) and in-
cludes clippings and final script. Also some assorted stills.

15 Imhoff, Roger, 1875-1958. (actor)
    1 scrapbook, ca. 1933-1936.
    Production stills for various films, including: PADDY, THE
NEXT BEST THING (F, 1933), HOOPLA (F, 1933), ONE MORE SPRING
(F, 1935), THE FARMER TAKES A WIFE (F, 1935), IN HIS STEPS
(GN, 1936).

16 Ince, Thomas H., 1882-1924. (producer, director, executive,
motion picture industry pioneer)
    Collection, 1912-1924. 1 carton.

Synopses and scripts for Ince productions (1912-1924).
2 volume manuscript, <u>Synopses: of Productions Made by Thomas
H. Ince During the Period April, 1912 to August, 1915</u>, 486 p.
with index. Also scripts, cutting continuities, synopses for
16 films (1918-1924), including BLUE BLAZES RAWDEN (1918),
RIDDLE GAWNE (1918), BRANDING BROADWAY (1918), and SELFISH
YATES (1918), all William S. Hart productions. 7 issues (1923-
1924) of <u>The Silver Sheet</u>.

17 <u>Laemmle, Carl, 1867-1939</u>. (producer, executive, motion picture industry pioneer)
Collection, 1906-1935. 3 cartons.
Includes original manuscript by Laemmle, <u>This Business of
Motion Pictures</u>, n.d., 227 p; newspaper clippings (1920s and
1930s); photos of Laemmle Film Service, Chicago (ca. 1900s);
photos of Laemmle and business associates, Laemmle and family
(ca. 1920s); financial data (1923-1924); scrapbook and clippings on 1931 Silver Jubilee Celebration. Also 6 Universal
film scripts: SPIRIT OF NOTRE DAME (1931), WATERLOO BRIDGE
(1931), BACK STREET (1932), COUNSELLOR-AT-LAW (1933), ONLY
YESTERDAY (1933), and IMITATION OF LIFE (1934).

18 <u>Lasky, Jesse, 1880-1958</u>. (producer, executive, motion picture
industry pioneer)
Collection, 1898-1951. 5 cartons, 7 oversize scrapbooks.
Includes early notebooks with ideas for vaudeville acts;
scrapbooks of clippings covering Lasky's career (1893-1951),
photographs, campaign literature, expense accounts, clippings,
programs; oversize scrapbooks containing interoffice memos,
telegrams, publicity work book, pre and post-production clippings on THE MIRACLE OF THE BELLS (RKO, 1948); 1 notebook of
editorial board notes (1932), including comments on prospective
films, actors, writers, story ideas; manuscript and galleys
for <u>I Blow My Own Horn</u> (1947), Lasky's autobiography, and 1
still book on THE POWER AND THE GLORY (F, 1933).

19 <u>Linkletter, Art, 1912-   </u>. (radio, television entertainer)
175 video tapes of the ART LINKLETTER SHOW, 1950s.

20 <u>Louis, Jean, 1907-   </u>. (costume designer)
10 costume sketches, n.d.

21 <u>Mayer, Louis B., 1885-1957</u>. (producer, executive)
Collection, ca. 1940s and 1950s. 1 carton.
Includes clippings, mostly 1950s; 1 notebook, "New York
Theater Figures," with details in film bookings and revenue;
copy of 1947 speech before House Un-American Activities Com-
mittee; and 3 screenplays.

22 <u>Menjou, Adolphe, 1890-1963</u>. (actor)
2 scrapbooks, 1921-1924.

Contains stills from various productions, including THE
KISS (PAR, 1921), THE THREE MUSKETEERS (UA, 1921), IS MATRI-
MONY A FAILURE (PAR, 1922), and THE WORLD'S APPLAUSE (PAR,
1923).

23 Motion Picture Memorabilia.
    A variety of items such as Ben Turpin's bronzed shoes,
Rudolph Valentino's automobile hood ornament, a propeller
from WINGS, Mabel Normand's personal clothes trunk, busts of
various actors, paintings of stars, makeup cases, awards, etc.

24 Motion Pictures.
    Approximately 433 films: governmental, documentaries,
shorts, features, television films and newsreels.
    Not stored with rest of collections.

25 Oral History.
    Interviews with entertainment personalities, ca. 1960s.
ca. 500 tapes, ca. 70 transcriptions.
    Included are interviews with: Edie Adams-Ernie Kovacs,
Fred Astaire, Lucille Ball, Jack Benny, Billie Burke, Maurice
Chevalier, Bing Crosby, Doris Day, Walt Disney, John Ford,
Jerry Giesler, Laurence Harvey, Alfred Hitchcock, Audrey
Hepburn, Gene Kelly, Burt Lancaster, Sol Lesser, Groucho Marx,
Marilyn Monroe, Paul Newman, Pat O'Brien, Mary Pickford,
Edward G. Robinson, Peter Sellers, Josef von Sternberg,
Spencer Tracy, Wally Westmore. A number of transcriptions
appear to be of interviews conducted by writer Pete Martin
for articles in early 1960s issues of Saturday Evening Post.

26 Photographs.
    Production and personality photographs, most prior to
1940. 45 file drawers. Collection of approximately 30-40,000
items includes photos of stars, producers, directors, film
executives, stuntmen, make-up, behind the scenes, etc.
Arranged both by production and personality.
    Dean Martin Collection, pre-1950. 4 file drawers. Col-
lection consists of negatives of photos of stars in candid
shots.

27 Radio Material.
    Transcription discs, sound tapes, scripts, publicity,
1937-1959.
    Scripts include: CBS YOU ARE THERE (ca. 150, 1948-1949);
ARMED FORCES RADIO (57 v., 1940s); THE WOMAN IN WHITE (10 v.,
1945-1946); CBS Columbia Shakespearean Cycle (1937).
    Vast collection of transcription discs or tapes include
those for the following shows: FIBBER MCGEE AND MOLLY (1937-
1953), THE GREAT GILDERSLEEVE (1941-1954), THE JUDY CANOVA
SHOW (1947, 1949, 1950-1952), NBC THEATRE (1949-1951), SCREEN
DIRECTORS PLAYHOUSE (1949-1951), THE BING CROSBY SHOW

(1946-1949), THE LIFE OF RILEY (1943-1948), DINAH SHORE SHOW (1953-1957), GROUCHO MARX'S "YOU BET YOUR LIFE" (1949-1959), ROSEMARY CLOONEY (1953-1954), EDDIE FISHER COKE TIME (1956-1967).

ARMED FORCES RADIO publicity, press clippings, photos, 1943-1947, 1950-1953. 10 oversize albums.

28 Ray, Charles, 1891-1943. (actor)
2 scrapbooks, 1912-1917; 1932-1942.

29 Roach (Hal) Studio Files, ca. mid-1930s-1950s. 28 file drawers.
Collection includes production papers, correspondence, story inquiries, title clearances, scripts, shooting schedules, cost sheets, wage scales, accounting department files.

30 Santschi, Tom, 1879-1931. (actor)
1 scrapbook.
Contains stills from early silent era.

31 Script Collection.
Motion picture and television scripts, ca. 1935-1958. ca. 100.
Includes number of scripts in various stages. Also some for films apparently never produced. Included are: HERE'S TO ROMANCE (F, 1935), MR. SMITH GOES TO WASHINGTON (COL, 1939), SERGEANT YORK (WA, 1941), THE MAN FROM DOWN UNDER (MGM, 1943), THE TWO MRS. CARROLLS (WA, 1947), MIRACLE OF THE BELLS (RKO, 1948), and HIT THE DECK (MGM, 1955). Television scripts include a number for various episodes of GALE STORM (1957-1958), ETHEL MERMAN SHOW, and PUBLIC DEFENDER.

32 Selbie, Evelyn, 1882-   . (actress)
Collection, 1898-1946. 2 cartons.
Number of stills of Evelyn Selbie, leading lady from Essanay, known as the original Bronco Billy Girl, ca. 1913, photos of friends of Selbie and other actors of period; clippings and memorabilia.

33 Sound Effects Material.
Large collection from former sound effects engineer includes recordings and equipment for making almost any sound such as waves, gunfire, fire, explosions, etc.
Card catalogue index to sounds.

34 Universal City Studios.
1 scrapbook, 1925.
Contains photos of the studio.

THE HONNOLD LIBRARY,
CLAREMONT COLLEGES (HL)
CLAREMONT COLLEGES (HL)
Claremont, California 91711

DEPARTMENT OF SPECIAL COLLECTIONS
Head: Ruth M. Hauser
(714) 626-8511, Ext. 3977
Hours: M-F, 9-12, 2-5
Material may be viewed only through special arrangement.

1 Oral History.
        Roach, Hal, 1892-   . (producer)
            Memories of a Film Career. 1965. 45 p.
        Mr. Roach sketches his life story. Then he discusses
    his view of the nature of acting and comedy, movie finan-
    ces, and the origins of his idea for the OUR GANG comedies.
    He presents vignettes of prominent film actors with whom
    he worked and had friendships: Charlie Chaplin, Harold
    Lloyd, Laurel and Hardy, Zasu Pitts and Will Rogers.
        Library has the edited transcript. Tape is in Oral
    History Office of Graduate School.

HUNTINGTON LIBRARY (HuL)
1151 Oxford Road
San Marino, California 91108

MANUSCRIPTS
Curator of Manuscripts: Jean Preston
(213) 681-6601
Hours: M-Sat, 8:30-5
Most material open to qualified readers and scholars.

1 Akins, Zoe, 1884-1958. (writer)
        Collection, 1878-1958. 34 ft.
    Manuscripts, correspondence, business papers, family papers,
photographs and miscellanea. Over 100 well-known authors,
critics, dramatists, editors, illustrators, and publishers are
represented among her correspondents. Letters from entertainment people include those from Ethel Barrymore, Billie
Burke, F. Scott Fitzgerald, Helen Hayes, and David O. Selznick.
Collection of business agreements, assignments, contracts, releases, etc., pertaining to Miss Akins' productions for the
legitimate stage, motion pictures, radio and television.
Articles, novels, plays, screenplays, radio broadcasts, critical essays and book reviews in various stages from treatments, outlines and synopses to final form. Inscribed
photographs of stage and screen stars. Among the screenplays

in the collection are those for the following films: ANYBODY'S
WOMAN (PAR, 1930), SARAH AND SON (PAR, 1930), GIRLS ABOUT TOWN
(PAR, 1931), WORKING GIRLS (PAR, 1931), OUTCAST LADY (MGM,
1934), CAMILLE (MGM, 1936), THE TOY WIFE (MGM, 1938), ZAZA
(PAR, 1939), and DESIRE ME (MGM, 1947). The stage play THE
GREEKS HAD A WORD FOR IT (1932) which was the basis for the
film HOW TO MARRY A MILLIONAIRE is also included.
　　Summary report in library.

2　GUNSMOKE.
　　　Radio and television scripts, 1952-1967.
　　　Collection contains 317 radio and 38 television scripts.

3　Lake, Stuart N., 1890-　　. (writer)
　　　Collection, ca. 1926-1961. 25 ft.
　　　Personal and business correspondence, original stories,
screenplays, outlines and treatments. Correspondents include
William S. Hart, Joel McCrea, George O'Brien, Max Hart Agency,
William Morris Agency, the various Fox studios, Universal
Pictures, Warner Brothers and Goldwyn Productions. Source
material for WELLS FARGO (PAR, 1937). Original story treat-
ment for WINCHESTER '73 (U, 1950) as well as material regard-
ing 1949 lawsuit over this film. Screenplay for WICHITA (AA,
1955) and 26 television scripts for the television series THE
LIFE AND LEGEND OF WYATT EARP (1960-1961).
　　Summary report in library.

4　Levien, Sonya, 1889-1960. (writer)
　　　Collection, 1908-1962. 17 ft.
　　　Biographical papers (1908-1956), publicity clippings, correspondence (1931-1958), diaries (1915-1917, 1921, 1924),
manuscript plays, musicals, screenplays with adaptations,
treatments and revisions; motion picture awards, photographs,
woman's suffrage papers, miscellany and ephemera. Included
are letters from Nunnally Johnson, Jesse L. Lasky, Oscar
Levant, John O'Hara, and Darryl Zanuck. Over 80 screenplays
in various stages, including 55 for produced films such as
THE EXCITERS (PAR, 1923), LUCKY STAR (F, 1929), MARIE GALANTE
(F, 1934), HERE'S TO ROMANCE (F, 1935), THE COUNTRY DOCTOR
(F, 1936), DRUMS ALONG THE MOHAWK (F, 1939), THE HUNCHBACK OF
NOTRE DAME (RKO, 1929), THE GREEN YEARS (MGM, 1945), THE
GREAT CARUSO (MGM, 1950), QUO VADIS (MGM, 1950), and HIT THE
DECK (MGM, 1954). Included in the collection is a 1937 dia-
logued treatment of DRUMS ALONG THE MOHAWK by William Faulkner.
　　Summary report in library.

5　London, Jack, 1876-1916. (writer)
　　　Papers, 1888-1932. 56 1/2 ft.
　　　Collection, which is highly restricted, contains correspondence, business papers, lawsuits, works, manuscripts,
notes, notebooks, photographs and ephemera. Within collection

are 5 folders containing agreements for motion picture rights
of Jack London's writings (1913, 1914, 1919). Lists of film
rights sold in Jack London's works.
Summary report in library.

6 Motion Picture Programs, 1914-1928, 1950s, 1960s. ca. 250
items.
One sheet programs and souvenir program books from Los
Angeles motion picture theaters. Theaters for which there
are programs include Clune's Auditorium, Kinema Theatre,
Majestic Theatre, Grauman's Metropolitan, Grauman's Million
Dollar Theatre, Grauman's Chinese, Grauman's Rialto, Loew's
State Theater, Egyptian Theater, Carthay Circle Theatre, Four
Star Theatre, and Mission Theatre.

7 Motion Picture Scripts, 1939- . 53 pieces.
Collection of motion picture production scripts and copies
of scripts. Included are publicity photographs and information, brochures, posters, etc. Among the screenplays are THE
GRAPES OF WRATH (F, 1940), THE OX-BOW INCIDENT (F, 1943), MY
DARLING CLEMENTINE (F, 1946), THE WOMAN ON THE BEACH (RKO,
1947), HIGH NOON (UA, 1952), FROM HERE TO ETERNITY (COL,
1953), MIDNIGHT COWBOY (UA, 1969), DIARY OF A MAD HOUSEWIFE
(U, 1970), and BLAZING SADDLES (WA, 1974).

8 Motion Picture Studio Photographs, 1918-1940. 19 items.
Photographs of various studios and studio sets, including
Ince Studio in Culver City (1918), Goldwyn Studios and sets
(1918), Pickford-Fairbanks Studio (1927), Jesse D. Hampton's
studios, and MGM and 20th Century-Fox studios and sets
(1939-1940).

IDAHO STATE UNIVERSITY (ISU)
Pocatello, Idaho 83209

SPEECH AND DRAMA DEPARTMENT
Contact: Professor Daniel W. Alkofer
(208) 236-3695
Material may be viewed by special arrangement.

1 Stevenson, Edward, 1906-1968. (costume designer)
Collection, 1920-1968.
Collection includes about 250-300 water color costume draw-
ings (14"x22") for film and television (1929-1968). Many of
the drawings are for 1930s First National films. Included in
the collection are drawings for such films as THE PAINTED
ANGEL (FN, 1930), SONG OF THE FLAME (FN, 1930), THE BITTER
TEA OF GENERAL YEN (COL, 1933), THE MAGNIFICENT AMBERSONS

(RKO, 1942), CHEAPER BY THE DOZEN (F, 1950), DAVID AND
BATHSHEBA (F, 1951), LADY GODIVA (U, 1955), and THE FIRST
TRAVELING SALESLADY (RKO, 1956). There are costume designs
for several actresses, including Joan Bennett, Marian Nixon,
Maureen O'Hara, and Barbara Stanwyck. Over 100 costume designs are for Lucille Ball for the various LUCY television
series. 5 scrapbooks contain clippings on Stevenson's career
from the mid 1930s-1940s, basically on his work at RKO. Also
some correspondence, contracts, photographs, and early
sketches (1920-1924) before he went to work in films.
Index for costume designs.

LOS ANGELES COUNTY MUSEUM OF
NATURAL HISTORY (LAMNH)
900 Exposition Boulevard
Los Angeles, California 90007

A   INDUSTRIAL TECHNOLOGY DEPARTMENT
Curator: Norwood Teague
(213) 746-0410
Material may be viewed only through special arrangement.

1   Amet, Edward H., 1860-1948.   (film equipment pioneer)
        Papers, ca. 1910. 1/2 ft.
        Copies of patents, drawings for inventions, correspondence.

2   Armat, Thomas, 1866-1948.   (camera pioneer)
        Papers, 1900-1935. 1/2 ft.
        Correspondence, drawings of inventions.

3   Animation Collection, 1930s. 6 1/2 ft.
        Animation cells (40), original frame sketches of Walt
    Disney, Walter Lantz, Max Fleischer. Original Disney camera
    and animation equipment. Original cells from STEAMBOAT
    WILLIE (1928) and THREE LITTLE PIGS (1933).

4   Biograph Mutoscope.
        Handbills, 1906-1910. ca. 50.
        Also catalogues, clippings, manuals, incorporation papers.

5   Blackton, J. Stuart, 1868-1941.   (director, producer, execu-
    tive, motion picture industry pioneer)
        Ephemera. ca. 1898-1910.
        Blackton's drawing of his New York first studio, 1898. His
    design for Vitagraph logo. Promotional biography, bronze
    bust.

6 Chaplin, Charlie, 1889-___. (actor, director)
    Scrapbook, 1931.
    Clippings on Chaplin. Also first Academy of Motion Pic-
ture Arts and Sciences Award for Distinctive Achievement,
1928.

7 Davies, Marion, 1898-1961. (actress)
    Scrapbooks, 1923-1928. 9 v.
    Contain clippings on the following motion pictures: LITTLE
OLD NEW YORK (G, 1923), YOLANDE (MG, 1924), LIGHTS OF OLD
BROADWAY (MG, 1925), ZANDER THE GREAT (MG, 1925), BEVERLY OF
GRAUSTARK (MGM, 1926), THE FAIR CO-ED (MGM, 1927), QUALITY
STREET (MGM, 1927), TILLIE THE TOILER (MGM, 1927), and THE
PATSY (MGM, 1928).

8 Dickson, W. Kennedy Laurie, 1860-1937. (camera inventor)
    Papers, late 1890s, 1932. 1/2 ft.
    Original drawings, letters of the man really responsible
for inventing camera--worked with Edison. 1932 recollection
of what he did in 1890s.

9 Farnum, William, 1876-1953. (actor)
    Papers, ca. 1940s and early 1950s. 1/2 ft. Stills, ca.
1907-1920s. 2 ft.
    Correspondence, clippings, original poems, production
stills and scrapbook of personal photographs.

10 Lawrence, Florence, 1888-1938. (actress)
    Papers, 1904-1925. 1 1/2 ft.
    Personal correspondence, clippings, programs, financial
papers. About fifteen manuscripts and scenarios from the
nickelodeon era of the motion picture industry.

11 Motion Picture Props.
    Various Charlie Chaplin material including his skates and
the back pack and shoe from THE GOLD RUSH (UA, 1925); a mini-
ature mock-up of KING KONG (RKO, 1933) and King Kong's hand;
the bat from DRACULA; and various items from Douglas
Fairbanks' MR. ROBINSON CRUSOE (UA, 1932).

12 Motion Picture Publicity Material, ca. 1920-1936.
    Lobby cards (ca. 150), programs (ca. 50), press books
(1 ft.), press releases (4 ft.).

13 O'Brien, Willis, 1886-1962. (special effects)
    Scrapbook, 1930s.
    Contains photographs of shots depicting special effects
for a number of films from the 1930s. O'Brien responsible
for special effects on KING KONG (RKO, 1933).

14 Patents Collection, 1860–1936.
     Jean A. LeRoy–United States Patent Collection for motion
pictures. Copies of all patents for motion picture equipment, 1860–1936.

15 Peters, Thomas Kimmwood, ca. 1884–1973. (camera inventor,
set designer)
     Papers, early 1900s–1950. 2 ft.
     Photographic and mechanical material. Business papers
pertain to camera he designed ca. 1909. Majority of material
unrelated to motion picture work.

16 Photograph Collection, 1920s–mid 1930s. 5 file drawers.
     Stills arranged by performers, directors, producers and
production. Large number of Wallace Reid and Jackie Coogan
in productions of 1920s.

17 Photographic Equipment.
     Ca. one dozen silent picture cameras, including those de-
signed by Lumiere, Eclair, Camera Graft, Pathe. Three strip
Technicolor cameras. Several early projectors, including
Edison Kinetoscope projector. Experimental projectors and
portable projectors.

18 Radio Material.
     Included are the following: one of the best collections of
vacuum tubes in the United States, dating from 1908–; incan-
descent lamps going back to 1880; a fair to good collection
of early AC receivers (1927–1940); a fair collection of early
wireless, both amateur experimental and radio telegraphy pre-
voice; some broadcast transmission material (1927–1928) from
a local radio station and other miscellaneous transmission
equipment from the early 1930s; good miscellaneous supportive
equipment, including test equipment, amplifiers, tuners, etc.,
from the mid-1930s on.

19 Screenplay Collection, 1906–1939. ca. 50.
     Includes final scripts, treatments, continuities, research
material. About 30 are scripts from 1906–1916. Later scripts
include WHEN A MAN'S A MAN (FN, 1924), THIS IS HEAVEN (UA,
1929), CIMARRON (RKO, 1931), LITTLE WOMEN (RKO, 1933), and ONE
IN A MILLION (F, 1936).

20 Selig, William, 1864–1948. (producer, executive, motion picture industry pioneer)
     Papers, ca. 1910, 1915.
     Ca. 50 press sheets, announcements, clippings.

21 Silent Film Music.
     Ca. 40 music cue sheets for silent films. Also piano music
for D. W. Griffith's ORPHANS OF THE STORM (UA, 1922).

22 Slides, 1914–1920s. ca. 1,000.
        Hand tinted slides for use in motion picture theaters.
    Many have messages ("Ladies, Kindly Remove Your Hats"). There
    are also portrait slides of the stars and song slides.

23 Turner, Florence, 1885–1946. (actress)
        Papers, 1914–1922. 1 1/2 ft.
        Collection includes 4 still books for LOST AND WON (1914),
    MY OLD DUTCH (U, 1915), FAR FROM THE MADDING CROWD (MT, 1916),
    and GRIM JUSTICE (1916). Also 2 scrapbooks of clippings.
    Deals with work done in England when Turner was producing and
    starring in her own films.

24 Van Guysling, George, 1865–1946. (executive, motion picture
    industry pioneer)
        Scrapbook, 1898–1900.
        Clippings on Van Guysling, early general manager for
    Biograph.

B   COSTUME DEPARTMENT
    Director: Margaret Switzer
    (213) 746-0410
    Motion picture material may be viewed only through special
        arrangement.

    1 Costumes and accessories–motion picture.
           Costumes and accessories from motion pictures, primarily
       of the silent era. Includes costumes worn by Lon Chaney,
       Charlie Chaplin, Mary Pickford, Douglas Fairbanks, and Mae
       Murray. Also Fred Astaire's dancing shoes from TOP HAT (RKO,
       1935).
           Costumes at present are not on display but may be viewed
       for research purposes by special arrangement.

LOS ANGELES POLICE DEPARTMENT (LAPD)
150 North Los Angeles Street
Los Angeles, California 90012

PUBLIC AFFAIRS SECTION, OFFICE OF SPECIAL SERVICES
Historian: Judy Kosbau
(213) 485-3281
Material may be used by appointment only.

1 DRAGNET Radio Program.
       Tapes of programs, February 1940–May 1953. ca. 100.

LOS ANGELES PUBLIC LIBRARY (LAPL)
630 West Fifth Street
Los Angeles, California 90071

A ART AND MUSIC DEPARTMENT
Department Head: Katharine Grant
(213) 626-7461
Hours: M-Th, 10-9; F-Sat, 10-5:30
All material open to the public.

1 Film Reviews.
     Clippings from Los Angeles *Times*, 1972-   . Organized
     alphabetically by year.

2 Shefter, Bert, 1904-   . (composer, conductor)
     Collection, 1959-1965. 36 reels of tape.
     Tape recordings of 11 movie soundtracks, 1959-1965. In-
   cluded are those for the following films: THE SAD HORSE (F,
   1959), YOUNG GUNS OF TEXAS (F, 1962), CATTLE KING (MGM, 1963),
   THE LAST MAN ON EARTH (AMI, 1964), and CURSE OF THE FLY (F,
   1965).

3 Hal Weiner Collection.
     Portrait collection, 1920-1960s.
     Represents almost 400 names in the fields of opera, con-
   cert stage, motion pictures, musical comedy, and dance. Performing groups as well as individuals are represented.
     The collection is arranged in vertical files. Each folder
   in these files contains anywhere from one to several dozen
   black and white 8x10 glossy publicity stills. Included are
   photographs for such individuals as Frank Albertson, Pearl
   Baily, Eddie Bracken, Sid Caesar, Leo Carrillo, Judy Garland,
   Louis Hayward, Henry Mancini, Louis B. Mayer, Basil Rathbone,
   Hazel Scott, and Walter Slezak.
     Portrait Index at reference desk.

B AUDIO-VISUAL DEPARTMENT
Department Head: Bill Speed
(213) 626-7461
Hours: M-Th, 10-9; F-Sat, 10-5:30
All material open to the public.

1 Picture Collection.
     Included in this vast collection covering a wide range of
   subjects are approximately 5 file drawers of photographs for
   motion pictures, television and radio. There are production
   stills, Xerox reproductions, publicity stills and clippings
   of photographs from magazines. Some are listed under actors
   and actresses, others under motion pictures and still others
   are filed by individual personality.

C HISTORY DEPARTMENT
   Department Head: Mary Pratt
   (213) 626-7461
   Hours: M-Th, 10-9; F-Sat, 10-5:30
   All material open to the public.

   1 Motion Picture Studios, 1937-1939.
      About 50 photographs of studio exteriors, interiors and
      sets from WPA project.

   2 Motion Picture Theaters, 1894-____.
      About 600-700 photographs of California motion picture
      theaters. Collection includes photographs of Grand Theater
      when it was Orpheum (1894), Tally's (ca. 1908), Clune's and
      Million Dollar Theatre (1918).
      Listed in card file index by city and then by name of
      theater.

   3 Story, Ralph.
      RALPH STORY'S LOS ANGELES, 1964-1969. 12 v.
      Type-script of programs no. 1-248 aired over KNXT-Channel
      2, January 14, 1964-November 29, 1969.
      Table of contents for each volume indicating segment topics.
      No composite index.

D LITERATURE DEPARTMENT
   Department Head: Helene Mochedlover
   (213) 626-7461
   Hours: M-Th, 10-9; F-Sat, 10-5:30
   All material open to the public.

   1 Radio Scripts.
      18 NBC GREAT PLAYS series scripts (1938-1939), 1 SHERLOCK
      HOLMES script ("The Strange Case of the Girl with the
      Gazelle," 1946).

   2 Screenplays.
      Small collection includes first drafts and final scripts,
      an original story and a synopsis. Screenplays include: THE
      PRISONER OF ZENDA (UA, 1937), THIS THING CALLED LOVE (COL,
      1941), THE APACHE TRAIL (MGM, 1942), THE MOON IS BLUE (UA,
      1953), RAGE AT DAWN (RKO, 1955), STAGE STRUCK (BV, 1958), and
      THE BROTHERS KARAMAZOV (MGM, 1958).

   3 Stengler, Mack. (cinematographer)
      Screenplay and television script collection, 1927-1952.
      ca. 187 items.
      Collection of scripts for motion pictures and television
      for which Stengler was chief cameraman. Many annotated with
      comments regarding shots, film and processing. Most scripts
      contain lists of all people involved in making film and many

contain shooting schedules. Heaviest concentration for 1930s and 1940s. Special items include 16 Mack Sennett scripts (1930s), 12 for Hopalong Cassidy Productions (1946-1948), 2 for all black casts: DOUBLE DEAL (INR, 1939) and MYSTERY IN SWING (INR, 1940), 42 for Monogram (1941-1949) and 25 short subjects. 58 television scripts (1951-1952) including 23 episodes for MYSTERY THEATER.
Collection is housed in Library Annex.

4 <u>Television Scripts</u>.
16 television scripts from a number of different shows, 1958-1970.

LOYOLA MARYMOUNT UNIVERSITY (LMU)
7101 West 80th Street
Los Angeles, California 90045

A CHARLES VON DER AHE LIBRARY
Librarian: Mrs. Dorothy O'Malley
(213) 642-2788
Hours: M-Th, 8am-11pm; F, 8am-10pm; Sat, 9-5; Sun, 1-11pm
Material open to the public.

1 <u>Television Script Collection, 1956-1968</u>.
Approximately 350 television scripts for a wide variety of series, including DANIEL BOONE (1966-1968), GET SMART (1966-1967), I DREAM OF JEANNIE (1966-1967), PLEASE DON'T EAT THE DAISIES (1966-1967), THE VIRGINIAN (1966-1967), and VOYAGE TO THE BOTTOM OF THE SEA (1966-1967).

B COMMUNICATION ARTS DEPARTMENT
Contact: Professor Ben Abbene
(213) 642-3030
Material may be viewed only through special arrangement.

1 <u>O'Connell, Arthur, 1908-   </u>. (actor)
Collection, 1934-1972. ca. 30 ft.
Screenplays, television scripts, stage play scripts, clippings, contracts, correspondence, financial papers, photographs, personal papers and plaques. Large amount of American National Theater and Academy material, including tapes of various A.N.T.A. conferences (1966). Television scripts are from a wide variety of series (ca. 1958-1972) and include 26 episodes for THE SECOND HUNDRED YEARS (1966-1967). 40 screenplays (1955-1972) include PICNIC (COL, 1955), THE SOLID GOLD CADILLAC (COL, 1956), THE MAN IN THE GRAY FLANNEL SUIT (F, 1956), BUS STOP (F, 1956), ANATOMY OF A MURDER (COL, 1959),

CIMARRON (MGM, 1960), THE SILENCERS (COL, 1966), FANTASTIC
VOYAGE (F, 1966), and BEN (CIN, 1972).
Unpublished register with collection.

2 Script Collection.
Small number of screenplays and television scripts.
Screenplays include FOXFIRE (U, 1955) and LOVER COME BACK (U,
1961). Various television scripts (1958-1961, 1972) including
10 episodes for BANYON (1972).

McGEORGE SCHOOL OF LAW (MSL)
3282 Fifth Avenue
Sacramento, California 95817

LAW LIBRARY
Librarian: Mrs. Alice J. Murray
(916) 452-6167
Hours: Telephone for information.
Material may be viewed only through special arrangement.

1 PERRY MASON Television Scripts, 1956-1963. 29 v.
Collection of approximately 174 scripts donated by Raymond
Burr also includes diagrams of sets.
Scripts may not be photocopied or loaned.

METRO-GOLDWYN-MAYER (MGM)
10202 West Washington Boulevard
Culver City, California 90230

RESEARCH DEPARTMENT LIBRARY
Librarian: James J. Earie
(213) 836-3000
Hours: M-F, 9-5
Material may be viewed only through special arrangement.

This library functions as a picture collection and book research center for the studio and the various companies connected
with it. Research on a wide range of topics is provided for the
making of films and television programs.

1 Art Direction.
Set blueprints for Metro and MGM films, 1919-.

2 Catalogues on MGM Films.
Compilations of information on various aspects of MGM
films, including:

Costume Design Credits, 1923–.
Synopses of MGM films, 1968–.
Thematic Catalogue of MGM films, 1930–1972.
List of all MGM films by production number.

3 Motion Picture Promotional Material.
Miscellaneous posters, pressbooks, 1930s–.

4 Photographs.
Set stills (8x10 glossies) from Metro and MGM films, 1919 to date. ca. 100 ft.
Catalogue of matte shots used in MGM films, 1934 to date. ca. 24 v.

5 Production Research Notebooks for MGM Films, 1935–1950. ca. 300.
Notebooks contain photographs and research notes.

MOUNT ST. MARY'S COLLEGE (MSM)
12001 Chalon Road
Los Angeles, California 90049

LIBRARY
Librarian: Deirdre D. Ford
(213) 476-2237
Hours: M-F, 8-5
Material open to the public.

1 KPFK Radio Tapes, 1961–1967. ca. 900.
Tapes from various KPFK programs, including discussions on art and politics, contemporary music, sociological studies and plays.

2 Screenplays.
Small collection of screenplays including THE LAST OUTLAW (PAR, 1927), THE TAMING OF THE SHREW (UA, 1929), SARATOGA TRUNK (WA, 1945), and THE YEARLING (MGM, 1946).

3 SONG OF BERNADETTE (F, 1943).
2 production research notebooks.

MUSEUM OF NEW MEXICO (MNM)
Box 2087
Santa Fe, New Mexico 87503

PHOTO-ARCHIVES
Photographic Archivist: Arthur L. Olivas
(505) 827-2559
Hours: T-F, 9-5; M & Sat by appointment only.
Photograph reproduction services available.

1 Photograph Collection.
   In this extremely large collection of photographs dealing
with various aspects of New Mexico are a small number of on-
location photographs for several motion pictures made in New
Mexico. Included are those for THE SANTA FE TRAIL (WA, 1940),
A DISTANT TRUMPET (WA, 1964), and THE HALLELUJAH TRAIL (UA,
1965).

NEW MEXICO STATE RECORDS CENTER
AND ARCHIVES (NMSR)
404 Montezuma
Santa Fe, New Mexico 87503

HISTORICAL SERVICES DIVISION
Contact: James Purdy
(505) 827-2321
Hours: M-F, 8-5
Material open to the public.

   The State Records Center and Archives collects material about
New Mexico, New Mexicans and things made in New Mexico. Over the
past decade a special effort has been made to compile information
on the history of filmmaking in New Mexico since 1897. Besides
the collections listed below, the Archives maintain civil and
criminal court records which involve film companies in New Mexico
during the Territorial Period.

1 Governors' Papers: John E. Miles, 1939-1942; Thomas J. Mabry,
   1947-1950; and David F. Cargo, 1967-1970.
   Included in the official papers of these three New Mexico
Governors is information concerning the state's efforts to
attract the movie-making industry.

2 Historical Film Collection - Archives. 1 file drawer.
   Clippings, correspondence, interviews, research material,
and photographs. Files include information on various individuals involved in New Mexico filmmaking such as Romaine

Fielding, Tom Mix, Mary Pickford, Mae Marsh, Paul Brinegar, and Don Alvarado. Information also on Governor Miles' attempts to bring more filmmaking to New Mexico (1940s), on filming in Carlsbad Caverns National Park (1924-1969) and in Gallup (1928-1965). About 300 photographs include production stills and location shots for a number of films made in New Mexico. Other items include lists of films made in New Mexico in the early period and more recent times, and an index to Tom Mix films. Several unpublished manuscripts on early filmmaking in New Mexico and the Southwest based on newspaper stories, recollections and research include:

    "Romaine Fielding and the Lubin Moving Picture Company. Silver City and Las Vegas, New Mexico. 1913." 85 p.

    "Tom Mix and the Selig Polyscope Company. Las Vegas, New Mexico. 1915." 7 p.

    "Mary Pickford, 'The Biograph Girl,' D. W. Griffith and Mack Sennett in Albuquerque, New Mexico. 1912." 9 p.

    "Another White Hope Bites the Dust: The Jack Johnson-Jim Flynn Heavyweight Championship Fight in Las Vegas, New Mexico. 1912."

    "Pioneer Movie Making in Arizona. The Lubin Company on Location. 1912." 22 p.

3 <u>Historical Film Collection, 1897-   </u>. ca. 100 films.
    Collection of films depicting the landscape, artistic heritage, historical events, people, and life of the State of New Mexico. Earliest film is INDIAN DAY SCHOOL (1897). Others include JACK JOHNSON VS. JOE FLYNN (1912), LOCAL COLOR (1916) with Tom Mix, A PUEBLO LEGEND (1912) with Mary Pickford, Romaine Fielding's THE RATTLESNAKE (Lubin, 1914), THE TOURIST (Biograph, 1912) with Mabel Normand, and AS WE REMEMBER HIM, a film on the life of John E. Miles (1917).

4 <u>Jones, Andrieus A., 1862-1927</u>. (attorney, U.S. Senator)
    Papers, 1884-1927. 10 1/2 ft.
    Material is limited to period of Jones' career as Las Vegas, New Mexico attorney. Collection includes 58 motion picture scripts for, and stock certificates of the Bible Film Company, ca. 1917.

NORTHWEST FILM STUDY CENTER (NWFSC)
Portland Art Museum
Southwest Park and Madison Streets
Portland, Oregon 97205

Director: Robert Sitton
(503) 226-2811
Hours: M-F, 9-5
Material open to the public.

1 Clippings File. 2 file drawers.
   Newspaper, magazine clippings organized by film personality.

2 Motion Picture Promotional Material.
   50 posters (1965-) and 4 cartons pressbooks (1965-).

3 Northwest Film Study Center Material.
   Index of feature films shown at NWFSC (1973-); index of
   festivals and shorts by independent filmmakers, students, etc.
   shown at NWFSC; program notes on feature films shown at NWFSC
   (1973-); scrapbook on NWFSC (1973-). Back issues of The
   Animator, NWFSC newsletter on regional film activities. Film
   library of classics and independent films for circulation and
   in-house use (150 titles).

4 Oral History Interviews--"The Movies," a series on films and
   filmmaking.
   Tapes of interviews by Robert Sitton for Pacifica Radio
   Network (New York and San Francisco), 1965-1972. Study Center
   has the following:
   a. Bertolucci, Bernardo, 1940- (director) and Pierre
       Clementi (actor), 9/24/68.
   b. Brennan, Paul (actor). Topic: SALESMAN (MAE, 1969),
       4/29/69.
   c. Brook, Peter, 1925- (director). Topic: TELL ME LIES
       (COF, 1968), 1968.
   d. Brown, Bruce (director, writer, producer). Topic: THE
       ENDLESS SUMMER (CIV, 1966), Winter 1967.
   e. Bute, Mary Ellen (director, writer, producer). Topic:
       PASSAGES FROM "FINNEGAN'S WAKE" (GRV, 1970), 10/16/67.
   f. Clarke, Shirley, 1925- (director, producer, writer)
       and Louis Brigante (film editor). Topic: Formation
       of Filmmakers Cooperative in New York, 1/66.
   g. Corwin, Sherrill C. (president, National Association
       of Theater Owners). Topic: The theater owners,
       5/25/67.
   h. Crawford, Joan, 1908-1977 (actress), 8/17/66.
   i. Evans, Edith, 1888-1976 (actress). Topic: THE
       WHISPERERS (LOP, 1967), 7/14/67.
   j. Gilliatt, Penelope (film critic), 8/14/67.
   k. Grieco, Marie (program director, Flaherty seminar),
       8/13/68.
   l. Hitchens, Gordon (film critic). Topic: Asian films,
       1968.
   m. Korty, John, 1936- (director, producer, animator,
       writer) and Peter Bonerz (actor, director). Topic:
       FUNNYMAN (Korty Films, Inc., 1968), 12/14/67.
   n. Lelouch, Claude, 1937- (director). Topic: LIVE FOR
       LIFE (UA, 1967), 1967.
   o. Lerner, Murray (cinematographer, director, producer,
       writer) FESTIVAL (PEW, 1967) (Newport Folk Festival),
       3/11/68.

p. Mancia, Adrienne (film critic). Topic: Revolt at
    Pesaro (Pesaro film festival), 7/1/68.
q. Matko, Zelimir and Boris Kolar, 1933- (animator).
    Topic: Animation in Zagreb, 3/12/68.
r. Maysles, Al, 1933- and David (documentary film-
    makers). Topic: SALESMAN (MAE, 1969), 4/14/69.
s. Medak, Peter (director). Topic: NEGATIVES (COF,
    1968), 10/16/68.
t. Mekas, Jonas, 1922- (director, writer, producer,
    film critic). Topic: Filmmakers Cooperative, 1/66.
u. Polanski, Roman, 1933- (director), 12/65.
v. Preminger, Otto, 1906- (producer, director), 6/26/67.
w. Ribovska, Malkah (actress). Topic: THE OTHER (F,
    1971), 9/29/67.
x. Rooks, Conrad (producer, director, writer). Topic:
    CHAPPAQUA (RGL, 1967), 10/25/67.
y. Rossellini, Roberto, 1906-1977 (director). Topic:
    THE RISE OF LOUIS XIV (BRN, 1970), 9/27/67.
z. Shaye, Bob (film distributor). Topic: Founding of New
    Line Cinema, 12/3/68.
aa. Skobtseva, Irina (actress). Topic: WAR AND PEACE (COF,
    1968), 4/20/68.
bb. Skolimowski, Jerzy, 1938- (director, writer). Topic:
    BARRIER (Arcturus Films, 1967), 9/22/67.
cc. Starr, William (film critic). Topic: National Federa-
    tion of Film Societies, 1967.
dd. Stevens, George Jr., Richard Kahlenberg and other
    officers of AFI. Topic: American Film Institute,
    Summer 1967.
ee. Szabo, Istvan, 1938- (director). Topic: FATHER (COF,
    1967), 9/29/67.
ff. Turrell, Saul J. and Bill Becker (executives of Janus
    Films), 6/13/68.
gg. Vogel, Amos (film critic). Topic: Film in Czecho-
    slovakia, 8/27/68.
hh. Voiss, Dr. Daniel (psychiatrist). Topic: IMPRESSIONS
    of Cassavetes' A WOMAN UNDER THE INFLUENCE (Faces
    International Films, 1974), 3/21/75.
ii. Watkins, Peter, 1935- (producer, director). Topic:
    THE WAR GAME (PCO, 1967), 4/1/67.
jj. Whitehead, Peter (director, producer). Topic: TONIGHT
    LET'S ALL MAKE LOVE IN LONDON (Universal Education
    and Visual Arts, 1968), 9/29/67.
kk. Wiseman, Frederick, 1930- (producer, documentary
    filmmaker). Topic: American documentary filmmakers,
    9/67.

5 Oral History Interviews--"Minorities of One." NWFSC film
   series, 1974.
       Tapes from series' sessions dealing with topic of individ-
   uality within sub-cultures. Study Center has the following:

"The Outsider": THE BOY WITH GREEN HAIR (RKO, 1948)
Speaker: Dr. Wilson Record (Professor of Sociology,
PSU), 6/13/74.
"The Lawbreaker": IN COLD BLOOD (COL, 1967)
Speaker: Dr. Tom Gaddis (psychologist, writer),
6/20/74.
"Racism": NOTHING BUT A MAN (CIV, 1964)
Speaker: William McClendon (Professor of Black
Studies, Reed College), 6/27/74.
"The Alternatives": BLACKJACK'S FAMILY (1973) and
LIVING TOGETHER (1972)
Speaker: Dr. Shirley Kennedy (Assoc. Prof. of
Anthropology, PSU), 7/18/74.

6   Other Interviews on Tape.
a.   Gish, Lillian, 1899– (actress). Interviewed by Tom
Shales (film critic) KBPS, 4/24/74.
b.   Godard, Jean Luc, 1930–   (director), 1968.
c.   Renoir, Jean, 1894–   (director). Interviewed by
Arthur Knight (film critic), 1970.

7   Photographs.
Personality and production stills, 1965– . 4 file
drawers.

OCCIDENTAL COLLEGE (OC)
Mary Norton Clapp Library
1600 Campus Road
Los Angeles, California   90041

DEPARTMENT OF SPECIAL COLLECTIONS
Librarian: Michael C. Sutherland
(213) 259-2852
Hours: M-F, 1-5
Material may be viewed only through special arrangement.

1   E. T. Guyman Collection of Mystery and Detective Fiction,
1770-1960. ca. 15,000 v.
All first or special editions. Also manuscripts, including Dashiell Hammett's original story idea for The Thin Man,
written in 1930, three years prior to his writing of final
and quite different version adapted for the screen. Many
books in collection have been adapted for the screen--works
of Hammett, Dorothy Sayers, Stuart Palmer. Also 21 PERRY
MASON television scripts (1957-1959) and Drexel Drake's radio
scripts for THE FALCON (1945-1947).

2 Henry, Bill, 1890-1970. (journalist)
      Collection, ca. 1920-1970. ca. 60 boxes.
      Includes 5 boxes of letters, a number of which are from
   entertainment personalities, including Judy Canova, Frank
   Capra, Cecil B. DeMille, Alice Joyce, Art Linkletter, Mae
   Marsh, Zasu Pitts, and Mack Sennett.
      Name and subject index to letters in library.

3 Kiesling, Barret C., 1894-   and Lillian W.
      Collection, ca. 1920- .
      Collection remains in possession of Kiesling. Arrange-
   ments for viewing it must be made through library.
      Includes autographed books, screenplays, photographs, cor-
   respondence, clippings, memorabilia, diaries and paintings
   collected by Kiesling who was a publicist for Sam Goldwyn and
   MGM. Autographed books and pictures are from many film personalities including Greer Garson, Sam Goldwyn, Jimmy Durante,
   Janet Gaynor, William S. Hart, Bob Hope, Jean Hersholt, Elsa
   Lanchester, Joan Crawford, and Marie Dressler. Autographed
   screenplays include DAVID COPPERFIELD (MGM, 1935), OKLAHOMA
   (MTC, 1955), TEAHOUSE OF THE AUGUST MOON (MGM, 1955), and THE
   TEN COMMANDMENTS (PAR, 1956).
      Register of collection in library.

OREGON HISTORICAL SOCIETY (OHS)
1230 West Park Avenue
Portland, Oregon 97205

A   LIBRARY
   Chief Librarian: Louis Flannery
   (503) 222-1741
   Hours: M-Sat, 9-5
   Material available to public by appointment.

   1 Cook, Lewis Clark, 1909-   . (cinematographer)
         Papers, 1926-1931. 1 folder.
         Collection includes original political cartoons (1931),
      movie handbills (1926-1931), and contract forms.

   2 Kirkham, Arthur P.
         Correspondence, scrapbooks, miscellany concerning career
      in Portland radio and involvement in various activities such
      as conservation of natural resources, tourism, the Oregon
      Centennial (1959), sports, and various civic affairs. 1 box,
      2 scrapbooks.

   3 Pascal, Ernest, 1896-   . (writer)
         CANYON PASSAGE (U, 1946). Final shooting script.

Screenplay by Pascal from the novel by Ernest Haycox, August 1, 1945. Cover includes autographs by members of the cast.

4   Platt, Helen.
Unpublished manuscripts on radio broadcasting, Portland, Oregon.
History of radio station KGW, Portland, Oregon, including chapters on the "Hoot Owls," radio music and drama, sports broadcasting, educational programs, news and special events coverage, religious and farm news, public service, and station engineering.

5   Radio Scripts.
Collection of scripts from radio plays based on data from case files of Portland Police Department, presented by radio station KGW, 1939. 1 v.

B   FILM DEPARTMENT
Contact: Lewis Cook
(503) 222-1741
Hours: M-Sat, 9-5
Material may be viewed only through special arrangement.

1   The Film Department collects and preserves film of Oregonian historical value. Included are 1,200-1,500 reels of historical footage (1905-1940, primarily 1920s). Many of the films are early newsreels shot by a number of cameramen, including Jesse G. Sills (International Newsreel and Webfoot Weekly), Lewis Cook (Universal, Paramount), Parris Emery (Pathe), Eric Mayo (Fox) and Charlie Piper (Oregonian Screen News). There are a few entertainment films photographed in Oregon from the 1920s and 1930s, 1914 lantern slides of Oregon-Columbia River, World War II training films and various production stills. The Film Department also produces films relating to Oregon and Pacific Northwest history.

PACIFIC FILM ARCHIVE (PFA)
University Art Museum
Berkeley, California 94720

Director: Tom Luddy
(415) 642-3035
Hours: M-F, 9-5
Some of material may be viewed only through special arrangement.

The prime purpose of this regional center of film information is the gathering and preservation of films. Over 3000 films from

countries around the world are presently under Pacific Film
Archive custodianship.

1 Clippings Files. 6 file drawers.
       Includes material on films, people, festivals and various
   subjects.

2 Photographs. 5 file drawers.
       Motion picture production stills.

3 Posters.
       Over 3,000 one-sheets, 1950s.

PACIFIC PIONEER BROADCASTERS (PPB)
6255 Sunset Boulevard
Suite 609
Hollywood, California 90028

ARCHIVES
Director of Acquisitions: Martin Halperin
Archivist: Ron Wolf
(213) 461-2121
Hours: By appointment.
Material may be used only through special arrangement.

   Pacific Pioneer Broadcasters is a non-profit organization
dedicated to preserving irreplaceable broadcasting material of
historical interest. Eligibility for membership requires at least
20 years in radio or television or in some phase of the broadcasting industry.

1 Anthony, John J., 1898-1970. (radio commentator)
       Collection, 1938-1946, 1957, 1960s. 42 items.
       Plaques, correspondence, photographs, telegrams, all
   mounted and framed. Also tapes of broadcasts from late 1960s.

2 Bixby, Carl L. (writer)
       Radio script collection, 1937-1954. 148 v.
       Collection of writer's scripts for 5 programs, including a
   complete set for LIFE CAN BE BEAUTIFUL (99 v., 1938-1954).
   Scripts also for BIG SISTER (1937-1938), SECOND HUSBAND
   (1937-1938), THIS DAY IS OURS (1938-1940), and THE MAN I
   MARRIED (1939-1942).

3 CBS-KNX Radio Script Collection, 1939-1958. 106 ft.
       Collection includes scripts for over 100 different radio
   series, often with property purchase records included. The
   large collection of scripts for LIFE WITH LUIGI (1948-1953)

includes the first episode broadcast under the title "The Little Immigrant." Other series include LEAVE IT TO JOAN (1948-1950), JOHNNY MERCER SHOW (1953-1954), BING CROSBY (1955-1958), BROADWAY'S MY BEAT (1949-1954), ADVENTURES OF PHILIP MARLOWE (1948-1950), SWEENEY AND MARCH SHOW (1946-1948), DOORWAY TO LIFE (1947-1948), and TENNESSEE ERNIE FORD SHOW (1954-1958).

4 CBS Radio Master Tape Collection, ca. 1953-1961. ca. 1,500 tapes.
    Collection includes tapes for a large number of programs, among which are: THE BEST OF BENNY (1953-1958), OUR MISS BROOKS (1955-1957), GUNSMOKE (1955-1956), SUSPENSE (1955-1956), JOHNNY DOLLAR (1955-1956), AMOS 'N' ANDY SUNDAY SHOW (1954-1955), CBS RADIO WORKSHOP (1956-1957), HAVE GUN WILL TRAVEL (1958-1960), and CBS news broadcasts (1957-1961).

5 DRAGNET Radio Program.
    Original transcriptions, February 1950-May 1953. Approximately 100 programs.

6 Equipment.
    Broadcasting equipment of historical interest from both radio and television, including amplifiers, receivers, microphones, radio consoles (Fada, Everready, Scott), projection type television sets (RCA, Philco), NBC remote unit, early iconoscope television tube, CBS machine for playing sound effects, and an Ampex magnetic tape recorder (200A #1, ca. 1948).

7 Johnstone, Jack. (writer, producer, director)
    Collection, 1934-1950. 2 ft.
    Includes scripts adapted, produced and directed by Jack Johnstone for such programs as THRILL OF THE WEEK, FLASH GORDON, YOU SAID IT, FRONT PAGE NEWS, THE PSYCHIC DETECTIVE, and SOMEBODY KNOWS. Also research material.

8 LUX VIDEO THEATRE.
    Scripts and set stills, 1952-1957. 16 ft.
    Television scripts (80 v.) for approximately 260 episodes and about 600 set stills.

9 Mills, Billy, d. 1971. (composer, arranger)
    Music Library, ca. mid-1930s-1955. 79 ft.
    Contains scores and orchestrations, original music for FIBBER MCGEE AND MOLLY (King's Men and orchestra numbers) radio program and for THE GREAT GILDERSLEEVE radio program. Also Chicago CBS music collection, 1 scrapbook of clippings, programs and correspondence (1911-1918, 1930-1941), and 1 photo album (ca. 1940s). Reference recordings of most music used on FIBBER MCGEE AND MOLLY.

10 Morse, Carlton E., 1901-___. (writer)
  ONE MAN'S FAMILY script collection, 1948-1957. 14 ft.
  Collection includes scripts for radio (1948-1957) and
television (1950-1952) programs of ONE MAN'S FAMILY. Also
recordings of ONE MAN'S FAMILY (1949-1953).

11 Mullen, Frank, 1896-___. (NBC executive)
  Collection, 1920s-1940s. 17 ft.
  Business papers, correspondence, paid vouchers. Much of
material from Mullen when he was NBC executive vice-president
and concerns attempts to break up NBC network. Included on
this topic are national hearings and commission reports.
Also material related to NATIONAL FARM AND HOME HOUR radio
program including production reports.

12 NBC-KFI Radio Scrapbooks, 1923-1953. 84 v.
  Oversize scrapbooks contain newspaper clippings and
publicity.

13 Oral History--Audio History Library.
  Tapes of interviews with radio personalities. Unless otherwise indicated individuals were interviewed by Les Tremayne.
PPB has tapes of the following:
  a. Allen, George W. (director, producer), 5/16/73.
  b. Allman, Elvia (actress), 1/29/75.
  c. Arquette, Cliff (actor) and Grace Lenard (actress),
    1/30/73.
  d. Backus, Alice (actress). Interviewed by Alice
    Reinheart, 3/19/75.
  e. Ballin, Bob (musician), 9/2/72.
  f. Barton, Fred (announcer), 8/30/72.
  g. Brown, Jeanne DeVivier (talent coordinator). Inter-
    viewed by Alice Reinheart, 3/2/75.
  h. Butler, Frank (actor), 1/2/74.
  i. Carroll, Carroll (writer), 2/14/73.
  j. Fisher, George (Hollywood commentator), 10/18/76.
  k. Fuller, Barbara (actress). Interviewed by Alice
    Reinheart, 3/19/75.
  l. _____ (Pacesetters KTLA), 3/22/75.
  m. Gerson, Betty Lou (actress), Bret Morrison (actor),
    and Vincent Pelletier (announcer), 2/5/75.
  n. Gregg, Virginia (actress). Interviewed by Alice
    Reinheart, 3/26/75.
  o. Jordan, Jim (actor), 2/5/73, 2/7/73.
  p. Krugman, Lou (actor), 8/30/72.
  q. Lauria, Lew (actor), 8/23/72.
  r. Lewis, Forrest (actor), 9/13/72.
  s. Olmsted, Nelson (actor), 9/21/73.
  t. Prentiss, Ed (actor), 1/8/72, 1/16/72.

u. Reinheart, Alice (actress), 2/19/75.
v. Rickles, Donald (announcer).
w. Selinger, Donald (news commentator), 1/29/73.
x. Summers, Hope (actress), 8/16/72.
y. Tedrow, Irene (actress), 3/9/75.
z. Tobias, Harry (musician), 8/16/72.
aa. Tremayne, Les (actor). On "Acting"-Ivar Seminar,
       10/27/73.
bb. Von Zell, Harry (announcer, actor), 1/22/75.
cc. Waring, Fred (music director), 3/15/73.
dd. Worth, Frank (music director), 1/15/75.

14 Photographs.
    Portraits, publicity photos, on-the-air photographs of various radio personalities, 1930-1950, ca. 1,000.
    Special items include:
    Raymond R. Morgan Advertising Agency. 7 notebooks (1940s) for various radio programs and personalities, including Tom Breneman and BREAKFAST IN HOLLYWOOD, HEART'S DESIRE, LUCKY U RANCH, and REX ALLEN SHOW. Also 3 v. scripts for commercials (1947-1948) for Planters Nut and Chocolate Co., White King Soap and Scotch Triple Action Cleanser.
    DR. CHRISTIAN. Stills (1946-1952) including pictures from 13th, 15th and 19th anniversary parties.
    THE GREAT OLD DAYS OF RADIO. ca. 300 mounted photographs used for this KCET 1976 broadcast.
    Small number of posters for films featuring radio personalities including THANKS FOR THE MEMORY (PAR, 1938), ARKANSAS TRAVELER (PAR, 1938), and HIT PARADE OF 1941 (REP, 1940).

15 Radio and Television Script Collection, ca. 1932-1967. 76 ft.
    Scripts for a wide variety of radio programs including A DATE WITH JUDY (1946-1950), DUFFY'S TAVERN (1944-1947), JERRY LESTER SHOW (1943-1944), RAILROAD HOUR (1948-1954), THE MAD HATTERFIELDS (1937-1939), LIFE WITH FATHER (1953-1954), MIDSTREAM (1938-1940), and WILD BILL HICKOK (1952-1954). Particularly extensive radio collections include:
    FIBBER MCGEE AND MOLLY, 1937-1950. 35 v.
    BUCK ROGERS, 1932-1936. 4 file drawers.
    THE CAMEL PROGRAM (Jimmy Durante and Garry Moore), 1943-1947. 24 v.
    Scripts for television programs include DECEMBER BRIDE (1953-1956), OUR MISS BROOKS (1950-1955), BETTY HUTTON (1959-1960), SPACE PATROL (1951-1952), LORETTA YOUNG SHOW (1955-1958), and DEAN MARTIN SHOW (1966-1967).
    Index to most scripts in library.

16 Radio Tapes Collection, ca. 1912-1960.
    Collection includes tapes for entertainment programs, news broadcasts, film promotions, commercials, etc. The earliest item is a recorded speech of Theodore Roosevelt, ca. 1912.

Entertainment programs on tape include: FRED ALLEN (1935–1949), JACK BENNY (1932–1954), BURNS AND ALLEN (1934–1952), Orson Welles programs including CAMPBELL PLAYHOUSE (1938–1940), MERCURY THEATER and ORSON WELLES ALMANAC (1941–1944); LUX RADIO THEATER (1936–1955), SUSPENSE (1942–1959), ART LINKLETTER HOUSE PARTY (1953–1957), and ROSEMARY CLOONEY SINGS (1950s).

Index to tapes in library.

17 Radio Transcription Discs.
Records from a wide variety of programs including ARMED FORCES RADIO (1940s and 1950s), KFI news and entertainment programs (1937–1948), THE WHISTLER (1942–1953), SUSPENSE (1943–1955), LIFE WITH LUIGI (1949–1953), GUNSMOKE (1952–1955), MY FRIEND IRMA (1947–1954), ESCAPE (1947–1954), OUR MISS BROOKS (1948–1955), CURT MASSEY SHOW (1949–1953), BROADWAY IS MY BEAT (1949–1954), JACK BENNY PROGRAM (1949–1955), and AMOS 'N' ANDY PROGRAM (1949–1955).

18 Rosenberg, E. J. (producer)
Radio and television script collection, 1946–1953. 34 v.
Producer's scripts for a variety of shows including CHARLIE WILD (1950–1952), THE CLOCK (1946–1949), WILLIE PIPER (1946–1948), and TOP GUY (1951–1953).

RKO GENERAL PICTURES
A Division of RKO General, Inc.
129 North Vermont Avenue
Los Angeles, California 90004

RKO RADIO PICTURES CORPORATE ARCHIVES
West Coast Manager/Archivist: John Hall
(213) 387-4238
Hours: M–F, 9–5
Material open to qualified researchers who have made advance
    appointments or requests in writing.

1   This is the complete working archives of 35 years of RKO Radio Pictures, 1923–1958. Most of material relates to the sound era but there is some silent material as well. Included in the collection are the following: alphabetical files containing production, personnel, legal, literary and general matters; story submission files; scripts, cutting continuities and synopses; screen advertising credit files; author/story/title index; scriptwriting teams index; literary property cards; western stories synopses; story continuity index and records; title registration matters; stage play reviews; daily production files; short features production files; short

features index; dance files; musical scores; music cue cards; contracts index; actors starts and closes; other payroll starts and closes; miscellaneous accounting records.

Other items include: Hughes era scrapbooks of press clippings; unproduced properties synopses; press books; press kits; copyright data; produced property surveys; and RKO Flash files.

Current files are maintained on: correspondence; remakes; copyright renewals; suppliers; scholars; lists of clearances; new synopses; day-to-day records; clips clearances rolodex.

The Archives also contains the Story Department Library consisting of plays, novels, some scripts, and a small number of reference works.

Index and floor plan to collections.

RIVERSIDE MUNICIPAL MUSEUM (RMM)
3720 Orange Street
Riverside, California 92501

Curator of History: Warren H. Schweitzer
(714) 787-7273
Hours: Tu-Sat, 9-5
Open to the public, however, an appointment with the Curator of
    History is required for access to the collection.

1 Rin Tin Tin--Lee Duncan Collection, 1918-1965. 899 items.
    Collection contains material on Rin Tin Tin and his
    trainer, Lee Duncan. There are approximately 268 photographs,
    252 television scripts, 8 radio scripts and 17 miscellaneous
    scripts, some of which are for motion pictures. Included also
    are pedigree certificates, news releases, books, magazines,
    booklets, comics, artifacts, and personal, fan and business
    correspondence.
    Inventory to collection in museum.

SAN DIEGO HISTORICAL SOCIETY (SDHS)
Serra Museum
Presidio Park, P. O. Box 81825
San Diego, California 92138

LIBRARY AND MANUSCRIPTS COLLECTION
Librarian: Sylvia Arden
(714) 297-3258
Hours: Tu-F, 10-5; Sat, 12-5.

Use of the library is restricted to adult researchers. No charge to members of the San Diego Historical Society. Fee for non-member researchers.

1 Grossmont Studios, Inc. Box File, 1922-1928.
   Box file materials are a small part of The Fletcher Collection.
   Collection deals with a company taken over by Col. Ed Fletcher to satisfy claims. Studios were located at La Mesa in 1925 and were taken over by the Grossmont Studios early in 1926. Productions listed in these records are BATTLING BOOK-WORM and ONE MINUTE TO GO. The Grossmont Studios were liqui-dated shortly after 1928. The collection includes minutes of meetings of Board of Directors (1925, 1926), Journal (cash book, 1925, 1928), Day Book (S-L-Studios, 1922, 1923), and list of stockholders (1924), miscellaneous bills and receipts, by-laws, correspondence, stockholders report, and stock certificates.

2 Elizabeth MacPhail Scrapbook, 1929.
   Includes material on movie shorts shot in San Diego.

3 Motion picture studios in San Diego area.
   Information on the following studios: Allan Dwan and the American Film Co., Lubin Studio in Coronado (1915), Essanay Co.--La Mesa, and Pollard Pictures Co. of San Diego headed 1916 by Harry Pollard. Information contained in interviews, scrapbooks, newspaper articles, biography and vertical files.
   Subject entries under "motion pictures" and "moving pic-tures" provide information on location of this material.

4 Vertical Files.
   Files which contain material on motion pictures, television and radio include: Antiques and Collectibles, Motion Picture Industry San Diego, Radio, Television, and Theatres, General (articles listing early movie theaters, programs, etc.).

SAN DIEGO PUBLIC LIBRARY (SDPL)
820 E Street
San Diego, California 92101

CALIFORNIA ROOM
Head Librarian: Rhoda Kruse
(714) 236-5834
Hours: M-Th, 10-9pm; F-Sat, 9:30-5:30
Material open to the public for reference use.

1 Film companies using San Diego Park grounds, 1915-1930.
   Portfolio of letters from film companies requesting permission to film on park grounds, 1915-1930.

2 San Diego Union Card Index, 1858-____.
   Newspaper index has over 735,000 entries. About 700
entries under "moving pictures" and related headings deal
with studios and filming in the San Diego area from 1930 to
date. Many cards have abstracts of the articles.

SAN DIEGO STATE UNIVERSITY (SDSU)
Malcolm A. Love Library
San Diego, California 92182

MICROFORMS AND LISTENING CENTER
Supervisor: Ms. Judith Vartanian
(714) 286-6792
Hours: Library hours vary according to school calendar.
Material open to the public.

1 THE INCREDIBLE MR. LIMPET. Production material, 1960-1964.
   ca. 9 ft.
   Pre- and post-production material for the film THE INCRED-
IBLE MR. LIMPET (WA, 1964), including treatments, outlines,
synopsis, screenplay, business correspondence, agreements,
contracts, research material, Navy material, publicity, and
sneak previews information.
   Inventory of scripts in library.

2 THE MOTHERS IN-LAW.
   Script and Video-tape Collection, 1966-1969.
   Collection includes scripts for 74 episodes of the tele-
vision series as well as video tapes of the programs.
   Inventory of scripts in library.

SAN FRANCISCO MUSEUM OF MODERN ART (SFMMA)
McAllister and Van Ness Avenue
San Francisco, California 94102

FILM DEPARTMENT
Film Curator: Kenneth DeRoux
(415) 863-8800
Hours: 10-5
Material may be viewed only through special arrangement.

1 "Art in Cinema" Film Series, 1946-1953.
      Collection of program notes, publicity, clippings, corres-
   pondence and audience ratings on experimental films shown in
   "Art in Cinema" series. 4 file drawers.
      Collection includes notes on filmmakers and films, bro-
   chures, press releases, newspaper clippings, catalogues, paid
   bills, comments from the audience, Frank Stauffacher's scenario
   for CHARLES SHEELER and correspondence from a number of filmmakers (1946-1947): Hans Richter, Eli Willis and Lewis Jacobs,
   John and James Whitney, Maya Deren, Douglass Crockwell,
   Herman G. Weinberg, and Oskar Fischinger.

2 Photographs.
      Motion picture production stills, 1920s- . 1 file drawer.
   Many of photographs are from experimental films shown in
   "Art in Cinema" series.

SAN FRANCISCO STATE UNIVERSITY (SFSU)
Library
1630 Holloway
San Francisco, California 94132

DEPARTMENT OF SPECIAL COLLECTIONS
Head: Robert Berg
(415) 469-1617
Hours: M-F, 1-5
Material open to the public.

1 Radio Collection, ca. 1928-1935.
      Radio scripts, correspondence, notes on music for radio
   programs. Most of material for programs originating in San
   Francisco. Over 1,000 scripts for various programs, includ-
   ing FRIENDLY NEIGHBORS (1934-1935), HOME FOLKS (1935), MEMORY
   LANE (1928-1933), UNCLE HARRY'S CHILDREN'S HOUR (1934), SHIP-
   WRECKED (1932), VIGNETTES OF LIFE (1934), and CHRISTOPHER AND
   HIS FRIENDS (1934).

2 Screenplay Collection, 1926-1969.
      About 200 screenplays, including ROSE OF THE TENEMENTS
   (FBO, 1926), STOLEN KISSES (WA, 1929), GONE WITH THE WIND
   (MGM, 1939), DUEL IN THE SUN (SRO, 1946), SWEET ROSIE O'GRADY
   (F, 1943), PORTRAIT OF JENNY (SRO, 1948), HALLS OF MONTEZUMA
   (F, 1950), THE SLENDER THREAD (PAR, 1965), THE CHASE (COL,
   1965), and JIGSAW (U, 1968).
      Catalogued by title and writer.

3   Television Script Collection, 1951-1970.
      About 1,000 television scripts for a wide number of pro-
    grams, including ARMSTRONG CIRCLE THEATRE (1951-1952), CBS
    NEWS SPECIAL REPORT (1964-1967), CBS NEWS (1960-1967), HAVE
    GUN, WILL TRAVEL (1958-1962), HONG KONG (1960-1961), MAVERICK
    (1960-1961), MYSTERY THEATER (1951-1952), RAWHIDE (1962-1964),
    SCIENCE IN ACTION (1954-1961), THAT GIRL (1966-1970), and
    YANCY DERRINGER (1958-1959).
      Catalogued by series title and writer.

SAN JOSE STATE UNIVERSITY (SJSU)
250 South Fourth Street
San Jose, California   95115

A   DEPARTMENT OF SPECIAL COLLECTIONS
    Collections Coordinator: Robert L. Lauritzen
    (408) 277-3399
    Hours: M-F, 9-4
    Material may be viewed only through special arrangement.

    1   Television Script Collection, 1950-1962.
          Collection contains about 57 television scripts in various
        stages from first to final draft along with revisions. Many
        scripts are annotated. Among the series for which there are
        scripts are RAWHIDE (1962), THE LLOYD BRIDGES SHOW (1962),
        THE DICK POWELL SHOW (1962), and ROBERT MONTGOMERY PRESENTS--
        YOUR LUCKY STRIKE THEATRE (1950-1953).

B   JOHN STEINBECK RESEARCH CENTER
    Contact: Dr. Martha Cox
    (408) 277-2745
    Hours: M-F, 1-4

    1   Screenplay Collection.
          Screenplays written by or based on works by John Steinbeck.
        Collection includes THE GRAPES OF WRATH (F, 1940), TORTILLA
        FLAT (MGM, 1942), THE MOON IS DOWN (F, 1943), LIFEBOAT (F,
        1944), VIVA ZAPATA (F, 1952), and THE WAYWARD BUS (F, 1957).

SCHOOL OF THEOLOGY AT CLAREMONT (STC)
1325 College Avenue
Claremont, California   91711

ROBERT AND FRANCES FLAHERTY STUDY CENTER
Director: W. J. Coogan
(714) 626-3521

Hours: By appointment.
Material may be viewed only through special arrangement.

1   Flaherty, Robert J., 1884-1951. (producer, director, pioneer
    in documentary film)
        Collection, ca. 1920-1972.
        Collection consists of still photographs, films, tapes and
    audio disc recordings. There are approximately 5,000 photo-
    graphs and these include production stills, exhibition prints,
    publicity photos, photo lithographs, lantern slides, and
    candid shots. There are negatives for many but not all photo-
    graphs, and the Study Center plans eventually to have prints
    or slides for all. A visual index to the still photographs
    contains a small reproduction of each photograph in the col-
    lection and is arranged by film title and within that category
    by subject matter. Films for which there are a considerable
    number of stills include NANOOK OF THE NORTH (PAT, 1922),
    MOANA (PAR, 1925), MAN OF ARAN (GB, 1934), ELEPHANT BOY (UA,
    1937), and LOUISIANA STORY (LOP, 1948). There are also 238
    audio tapes of Robert Flaherty, Frances Flaherty and others
    as well as music tracks related to films. About 30 audio
    disc recordings feature Robert Flaherty or others talking
    about Flaherty on various radio programs primarily in the
    1940s.
        The Flaherty Study Center has a considerable number of
    Flaherty films as well as films about Flaherty and can make
    arrangements for viewing these and others held at the Flaherty
    Farm in Vermont. A large collection of documents, including
    correspondence, diaries, financial records, scripts, publicity
    materials, books, short stories and articles are on deposit
    at the Butler Library at Columbia University, NYC.
        Unpublished guide to Flaherty Collections held by School
    of Theology at Claremont, Flaherty Farm in Vermont and Columbia
    University is in Study Center.

SECURITY PACIFIC NATIONAL BANK (SPNB)
333 South Hope Street
Los Angeles, California   90071

HISTORICAL COLLECTION
Bank Historian: Victor R. Plukas
(213) 613-6843
Hours: 9-4 by appointment.
Material may be viewed only through special arrangement.

1   Motion Picture File.
        Photographs of personalities, motion picture studios and
    sets, production stills, equipment and motion picture theaters.

SOUTHERN CALIFORNIA
EDISON COMPANY (SCEC)
2244 Walnut Grove Avenue
(mailing address: P.O. Box 800)
Rosemead, California 91770

HISTORICAL COLLECTION
Company Historian: William A. Myers
(213) 572-2084
Hours: By appointment.
Material may be viewed only through special arrangement.

1 Historical Photographs, 1880-___. ca. 70,000 (12,000 glass
   plates; 58,000 nitrate)
       Collection deals primarily with electrical related subjects
   in Los Angeles and Southern California such as street lighting
   and street railways (Pacific Electric and Los Angeles Railways). About 12 photos deal with methods of motion picture
   studio lighting pre-1920s. Collection not completely catalogued, perhaps includes more photos dealing with early
   filmmaking.

2 Motion Pictures.
       A few prints of early films, some commercial, some on
   Edison Company and Pacific Electric Railway.

STANFORD UNIVERSITY LIBRARIES (SU)
Department of Special Collections
Stanford, California 94305

MANUSCRIPTS DIVISION
Chief of Special Collections: Florian Shasky
(415) 497-4054
Hours: M-F, 8-5; Sat (during session), 9-12
Material may be viewed only through special arrangement.

1 Daves, Delmer Lawrence, 1904-1977. (writer, director,
   producer)
       Papers, 1930-1965. 83 boxes.
       Screenplays, stage plays, correspondence, treatments of
   novels, adaptations, drafts, lists, photographs, diagrams and
   working papers of Mr. Daves' career in the motion picture
   industry in Hollywood from 1930-1965. The collection contains
   correspondence with many of the industry's leading figures,
   particularly those at 20th Century-Fox such as executives
   Darryl F. Zanuck, Al Lichtman, Charles Einfeld and Fred L.
   Metzler; producers Julian Blaustein, Philip Dunne, Robert L.
   Jacks, Fred Kohlmar, Jules Buck, Louis D. Lighton, Frank

McCarthy and Frank Ross; production personnel Jason S. Joy,
Ray A. Klune, Lew Schreiber and Charles LeMaire; publicity
director Harry Brand, special effects director Fred Serson,
story editor Julian Johnson, music director Alfred Newman,
casting directors William Gordon and William Mayberry, director Harmon Jones and writers Michael Abel and Michael
Blankfort. Nearly 70 screenplays, the majority of which were
produced, include: CLEAR ALL WIRES (MGM, 1933), DAMES (WA,
1934), STAGE DOOR CANTEEN (UA, 1943), DESTINATION TOKYO (WA,
1943), BROKEN ARROW (F, 1950), BIRD OF PARADISE (F, 1951),
RETURN OF THE TEXAN (F, 1952), THE TREASURE OF THE GOLDEN
CONDOR (F, 1953), THE ROBE (F, 1953), A SUMMER PLACE (WA,
1959), SUSAN SLADE (WA, 1961), and YOUNGBLOOD HAWKE (WA,
1964). Considerable production material is filed with each
screenplay.
    Unpublished register in library.

2 Motion Picture Promotional Material.
    Collection includes about 200 souvenir motion picture play-
bills, 550 programs, 250 posters, and 200 lobby cards.

3 Photographs.
    Collection includes approximately 7,500 loose photographs
of actors, actresses, directors, writers, other film personnel
and production stills from the silent era on. There are also
photograph albums, many with biographical insert and clippings,
for the following: Barrymore Family, Jack Benny, Sarah
Bernhardt, Billie Burke, James Cagney, Charles Chaplin, Ronald
Colman, Bette Davis, Marie Dressler, Douglas Fairbanks Sr.,
Geraldine Farrar, Pauline Frederick, Clark Gable, Dorothy and
Lillian Gish, Gilda Gray, Victor Moore, Alla Nazimova, Mary
Pickford, Tyrone Power, Anita Stewart, Gloria Swanson, Norma
and Constance Talmadge, Rudolph Valentino, and Mae West.
    There is also a group of collotype prints from Eadweard
Muybridge's Animal Locomotion which demonstrate pre-cinema
motion.

4 Radio Scripts.
    DRAGNET, 1955. 3 v.

5 Screenplay Collection, 1930-____.
    About 100 screenplays for films from all the major studios
including GRAND HOTEL (MGM, 1932), PETER IBBETSON (PAR, 1935),
CAMILLE (MGM, 1936), YOU CAN'T TAKE IT WITH YOU (COL, 1938),
THE MALTESE FALCON (WA, 1941), LIFEBOAT (F, 1944), THE GUN-
FIGHTER (F, 1950), BELL, BOOK AND CANDLE (COL, 1958), SONS
AND LOVERS (F, 1960), PATTON (F, 1969), ZABRISKIE POINT (MGM,
1970), THE STING (U, 1973), and DOG DAY AFTERNOON (WA, 1975).

6 Steinbeck, John, 1902-1968. (writer)
    Collection, 1926-1968. 25 ft.

Includes correspondence, manuscripts, books, ephemera and photographs. 57 letters from Steinbeck to Max Wagner (writer) and Jack Wagner (actor) during the years just before and just after World War II. These letters focus on the Hollywood world, Steinbeck's success in adapting his writings to the screen, and range over a wide variety of subjects touching both his private and professional life. Screenplays in the collection include THE GRAPES OF WRATH (F, 1940), TORTILLA FLAT (MGM, 1942), THE MOON IS DOWN (F, 1943), THE WAYWARD BUS (F, 1957), and THE RED PONY (Omnibus Productions, ca. 1972) [N.B. this must be the television film broadcast in 1973].
Catalogue for collection in library.

7 Television Scripts, ca. 1950s-___.
   Over 600 scripts for various television programs, including ABC-TV MOVIE OF THE WEEK (1970-), DRAGNET (1955-1958), EMERGENCY (1972-), IRONSIDE (1970-1974), MANNIX (1971-), MEDICAL CENTER (1971-), MISSION IMPOSSIBLE (1971-1972), KOJAK (1973-), OWEN MARSHALL (1971-1973), TOMA (1973-1974), and THE SIX MILLION DOLLAR MAN (1973-).

STANFORD UNIVERSITY MUSEUM OF ART (SUM)
Museum Way and Lomita Drive
Stanford, California 94305

Curator of Photography: Anita Ventura Mozley
(415) 497-4177
Hours: Tu-F, 10-4:45; Sat, Sun, 1-4:45
Open to the public.

1 Muybridge, Eadweard J., 1830-1904. (pioneer photographer of the American West; made the first analytical photographs of fast motion, 1878, and the first synthesis of photographed motion, 1879)
   Collection, 1867-1886.
   Collection includes a working Zoopraxiscope, a replica made with some of Muybridge's equipment; glass slides banded together with tape to form a circle, possibly to be used with the Zoopraxiscope; 5 sets of lantern slides made of the motion experiments at Leland Stanford's Palo Alto Stock Farm (1878-1879); 4 of the 6 "Horse in Motion" cards (1878); a copy of Attitudes of Animals in Motion (1881) with the original photographs made during the experiments of 1878-1879; 250 collotype prints from Animal Locomotion (1884-1886); photographs and stereographs of Yosemite, San Francisco, Mills College, the California coast, and Central America (1867-1875); glass negatives of the Stanford homes in San Francisco and Sacramento (1872 and 1877/78); a pictorial index to Muybridge's

"view" work, prepared by Robert Haas for his biography of
Muybridge; also other supportive and supplementary material.

2 Pre-Cinema Devices Showing Motion. ca. 25 items.
    Various optical toys, including lantern slides with move-
able parts, a dissolving view lantern and slide sets, chromo-
tropes and Carlo Ponti's Megalethoscope of 1866.

STATE HISTORICAL SOCIETY
OF COLORADO (SHSC)
Colorado State Museum
200 - 14th Avenue
Denver, Colorado 80203

DOCUMENTARY RESOURCES
Curator: Maxine Benson
(303) 892-2305
Hours: M-F, 9-5
Most material open to the public.

1 Filmmaking in Colorado.
    Small collection of clippings and stills relating to film-
making in Colorado. Includes some location shots of Tom Mix.
Also some from more recent period.

2 Oral History.
    Library has the following tapes:
    Kohn, Max. "Early motion picture industry in Colorado."
      1960
    Rice, Harold E. "Early theatres in Denver." 1963
    Reproductions of these tapes, on either reel to reel or
cassette, may be purchased for $7.50.

3 Radio Broadcasts, ca. 1945-1958.
    Programs primarily local, but some national also. 145
tapes.

4 Television Broadcasts, 1960-1973.
    KOATV news programs from local stations. Approximately
500 reels a year. Though the scripts are not housed here,
Historical Society can provide access to them.
    Index to programs.

TWENTIETH CENTURY-FOX (TCF)
10201 West Pico Boulevard
Los Angeles, California
(mailing address: Box 900
Beverly Hills, California 90213)

RESEARCH LIBRARY
Head Librarian: Kenneth Kenyon
(213) 277-2211
Hours: M-F, 9-12, 1-5
Material may be viewed only through special arrangement.

This library functions as a research center for the studio
and the various companies connected with it. Research on a wide
range of topics is provided for the making of films and television
programs. Only through special arrangement is this resource
available to outside, independent filmmakers and historians at a
charge of $12.50 per hour.

1 Clippings Files.
    Newspaper and magazine clippings, photographs, pamphlets,
etc. on a wide range of topics. 5 folders contain material
on Fox history (1916-present). There are also folders for
such topics as cartoons, Disney, censorship, ratings, Keystone Cops, continuity sketches, and producers and directors.

2 Pre-Production Research Photos and Notebooks for Fox/
Twentieth Century-Fox films, late 1920s-1970. ca. 400.
    Card file and 4 notebooks of indexes to contents of re-
search books.

UNIVERSAL CITY STUDIOS (US)
100 Universal City Plaza
Universal City, California 91608

RESEARCH DEPARTMENT
Librarian: Robert Andrew Lee
(213) 985-4321
Hours: M-F, 8:30-6
Material may be viewed only through special arrangement.

This library functions as a research center for the studio
and the various companies connected with it. Research on a wide
range of topics is provided for the making of films and television
programs. Only through special arrangement is this resource
available to outside, independent filmmakers and historians at a
charge of $15 per hour.

1 Clippings Files. ca. 5,000 folders.
      In this vast collection which covers a wide range of topics
   only a small portion is related to film or television. Some
   material on MCA-Universal.

2 Motion Picture Promotional Material.
      Small collection of posters, pressbooks and campaign lit-
   erature for Universal films of the last few years.

3 Screenplays.
      Small collection of screenplays for Universal films of
   the last decade.

UNIVERSITY OF CALIFORNIA, BERKELEY (UCB)
Bancroft Library
Berkeley, California 94720

MANUSCRIPTS DIVISION
Head of Manuscripts: Estelle Rebec
(415) 642-3781
Hours: M-F, 9-5; Sat, 1-5
Material open to the public.

1 Coolidge, Dane, 1873-1940. (writer)
      Papers, 1889-1942. 9 ft.
      Correspondence, including letters from his wife, friends,
   publishers, agents, university officials, writers, scientists,
   etc.; manuscripts of stories, articles and movie scenarios;
   notebooks; personal accounts; clippings. Many of movie
   scenarios which may be from pre-1920 period are in outline
   and synopsis form.
      Unpublished report in library.

2 Goldberg, Rube, 1883-1970. (cartoonist)
      Papers, ca. 1907-1960. 129 ft.
      Correspondence, over 5,000 original drawings for comic
   strips and editorial cartoons (1907-1960); clippings, scrapbooks, manuscripts of articles, stories and songs; books
   written by him, photographs, records and film; manuscripts of
   plays. 1 still book of photographs from SOUP TO NUTS (F,
   1930), the scenario of which was written by Goldberg. Also
   includes photographs of Goldberg's sketches of some of the
   members of the cast. Still book is in Portrait Collection in
   library.
      Unpublished report in library.

3 GREED (MG, 1924).
      1 album of stills and cast photo from GREED.

4 Howard, Sidney Coe, 1891-1939. (writer)
    Papers, 1903-1939. 33 ft.
    Correspondence to and by Howard (1903-1939); typed tran-
scripts of diary entries (1927-1933, 1935-1939); 30 play
manuscripts and notes for plays not written; 11 screenplay
manuscripts both produced and unproduced including notes,
drafts and interoffice communications; manuscripts of stories
and articles, notebooks; playbills and programs for Howard's
plays; contracts, financial records, awards, clippings;
papers of Mrs. Sidney Coe Howard, Howard family papers and
memorabilia. Much of Howard's correspondence relates to his
life as a Hollywood screenwriter. Included in the collection
are letters from Michael Blankfort, Samuel Goldwyn, Max
Gordon, Lillian Hellman, Arthur Hornblow, Jr. (1932-1939 re:
THE LIGHT THAT FAILED); MGM correspondence from Sam Marx,
Lucien Hubbard and Hunt Stromberg (1935-1939 re: NORTHWEST
PASSAGE); Margaret Mitchell and David O. Selznick (1936-
1939 re: GONE WITH THE WIND). Screenplays in the collection
include Howard's version of GONE WITH THE WIND, DODSWORTH
(UA, 1936), THE LIGHT THAT FAILED (PAR, 1939), THE REAL
GLORY (UA, 1939), and NORTHWEST PASSAGE (MGM, 1940).
    Unpublished report in library.

5 Parker, Robert Allerton, 1888-1970. (writer)
    Papers, 1940-1963. 7 ft.
    Correspondence (1940-1961), unpublished novels, book re-
views, synopses of screen stories, fragments of plays,
articles on art, notes in daybooks (1947-1963), clippings.
    Unpublished report in library.

6 Wilson, Harry Leon, 1867-1939. (writer)
    Papers, 1879-1938. 6 1/2 ft.
    Correspondence, manuscripts of plays, screenplays, notes,
synopses, clippings, typescripts of articles, photographs
and scrapbook for MERTON OF THE MOVIES (PAR, 1924).
    Unpublished report in library.

UNIVERSITY OF CALIFORNIA, DAVIS (UCD)
Shields Library
Davis, California 95616

DEPARTMENT OF SPECIAL COLLECTIONS
Head: Don Kunitz
(916) 752-1621
Hours: M-F, 8-5
Material open to the public.

1 <u>Loney, Glenn, 1928-   </u>. (theater critic, professor)
   Papers, ca. 1950s-1972. 13 boxes.
   Collection includes clippings files primarily for theater
but contains some material on films. There are clippings of
Loney's articles for <u>Christian Science Monitor</u>, New York
<u>Times</u>, New York <u>Herald Tribune</u>, and other significant jour-
nals; his <u>Cue</u> interviews, published and unpublished reviews,
stories, drafts, correspondence, personal papers, GERMANY
TODAY radio series scripts, and radio tapes for SWEDISH
SPECTRUM (1968-1972) and CURTAIN TIME IN EUROPE.

2 <u>Motion Picture Programs, 1917-1974</u>. ca. 135.

3 <u>Personalities Section</u>.
   Items pertaining to theatrical personalities--actors, play-
wrights, theater managers, etc.--including photographs, clippings, engravings, programs and correspondence. While this
collection is primarily for theater there is material on a
number of film personalities who also did theater including
Ethel Barrymore, Mary Pickford, Fred Astaire and Brian Aherne.

4 <u>Photographs</u>.
   Motion picture production stills, 1964-1972. ca. 600.

UNIVERSITY OF CALIFORNIA,
LOS ANGELES (UCLA)
405 Hilgard Avenue
Los Angeles, California 90024

A   <u>DEPARTMENT OF SPECIAL COLLECTIONS</u>, University Research Library
    Department Head: James V. Mink
    (213) 825-4879; 825-4988
    Hours: M-Sat, 9-5
    Open to all who have occasion to consult its holdings.
    Materials to be used only in department's reading room.

   1 <u>Abdullah, Achmed, 1881-1945</u>. (writer)
      Collection of 166 typescripts of plays, novels, screen-
   plays, short stories, n.d. 8 boxes.

   2 <u>Akins, Zoe, 1884-1958</u>. (writer)
      Collection of literary manuscripts, including plays,
   screenplays and stories. ca. 1915-1958. 4 boxes.
      Included are screenplays for: THE TOY WIFE (MGM, 1938),
   PRIDE AND PREJUDICE (MGM, 1940), and HATTER'S CASTLE (PAR,
   1948).
      Unpublished register in library.

3　Animated Pictures.　Collection of animated pictures on long
　　paper strips for zootropes (wheel of life) and praxinoscope
　　theatre.　ca. 1870-1880.　5 items.
　　　　Zootrope was invented in 1834 by W. G. Horner under the
　　name Daedaleum.　It was introduced commercially by William E.
　　Lincoln, Providence, patent no. 64117, in 1867.　Praxinoscope
　　theatre was invented in 1879 by Emile Reynaud, Paris.　The
　　strips have black background.

4　Animated Pictures.　Collection of animated pictures, variously
　　called phantascopes, fantascopes, phenakistoscopes, optical
　　illusions, moving panoramas, and magic panoramas.　London and
　　Paris, ca. 1830.　89 items.
　　　　These items consist of cardboard wheels with drawings on
　　them showing minute variations.　When spun, they give the
　　effect of a moving picture.

5　Andrews, Robert Douglas, 1903-1976 (Robert Hardy Andrews).
　　(writer)
　　　　Papers, ca. 1945-　.　4 boxes.
　　　　This collection comprises literary manuscripts, movie and
　　television scripts, and ephemera.
　　　　Unpublished register in library.

6　Ardrey, Robert, 1908-　　.　(writer)
　　　　Papers, ca. 1935-1960.　4 boxes.
　　　　Includes letters from Ardrey to his wife and children; 14
　　motion picture scripts, and ephemera.
　　　　Unpublished register in library.

7　Aroeste, Jean Lisette (Buck), 1932-　　.　(writer)
　　　　Literary manuscripts.　ca. 1968-　.　1 box.
　　　　Mrs. Aroeste wrote two scripts for television serial STAR
　　TREK.
　　　　Unpublished register in library.

8　Bacher, William, 1900-　　.　(producer, director, writer)
　　　　Collection of miscellaneous screenplays by various persons
　　and related materials submitted to Mr. Bacher.　ca. 1930-
　　1960.　23 boxes and 8 oversize packages.
　　　　Included in collection are radio scripts 1932-1942 and
　　phonograph recordings of various musical scores connected
　　with Bacher's productions.　Among the screenplays are the
　　following: SEVENTH HEAVEN (F, 1927), WILSON (F, 1944), and
　　BATTLE CRY (WA, 1955).
　　　　Unpublished register in library.

9　Ballin, Hugo, 1879-1956.　(producer, director)
　　　　Papers, ca. 1890-1956.　25 boxes and 9 oversize packages.
　　　　Correspondence; literary manuscripts; book; photographs of
　　Hugo and Mabel Ballin, family, friends, residence, paintings

by Ballin; ephemera; scrapbooks relating to the Ballins; and
original sketches and water colors by Ballin. Letters from
Joan Crawford, Gloria Swanson, Louis B. Mayer, Edward G.
Robinson, Lionel Barrymore, Walter Damrosch, Samuel Goldwyn,
Jean Hersholt, David Selznick, Darryl Zanuck, Walt Disney,
Louis Untermeyer, Louis Bromfield, Howard Pyle, Millard
Sheets, Reginald Marsh.
Unpublished register in library.

10 Barrymore, Lionel, 1878-1954. (actor)
Collection of music by Lionel Barrymore. Los Angeles,
v.d. 13 boxes and 1 oversize package.
Most of this music is manuscript. Some of it is printed.
Collection also includes some correspondence, pictures and
ephemera.
Unpublished register in library.

11 Bellem, Robert Leslie, d. 1968. (writer)
Collection of short stories, novels, movie scenarios,
radio scripts, and television plays, all by Bellem.
1931-1968.
Collection includes several scripts for television series
77 SUNSET STRIP, DEATH VALLEY DAYS, THE F.B.I., and PERRY
MASON.
Unpublished register in library.

12 Benny, Jack, 1894-1975. (comedian)
Papers, ca. 1930-1967.
Collection representing fifty years of show business memo-
rabilia includes 900 radio scripts and electrical transcriptions from 1932-1955; 296 television scripts from time of
Benny's TV debut in 1950. There are also scrapbooks, entire
business correspondence, and hundreds of still photographs.
Among the radio shows are THE JACK BENNY PROGRAM (Lucky
Strike), 1944-1955; GRAPE NUTS PROGRAM, 1942-1944; SPECIAL
RADIO SHOWS, 1932-1934, 1940-1941; THE JELLO PROGRAM, 1934-
1940. Included in television scripts are THE JACK BENNY HOUR,
1959-1966 and SHOWER OF STARS, 1955-1958. Production stills
from motion pictures are for the years 1929-1940.
Use of correspondence and business records restricted.

13 Beyer, Walter, 1913-1969. (engineer)
Papers, ca. 1935-1968. 47 boxes, 2 oversize packages.
Collection contains letters, files, ephemera, slides, and
artifacts relating to motion picture engineer Walter Beyer's
work with Paramount Pictures, the development of Vista Vision,
Wide Screen and 3-D process, the Motion Picture Research
Council, and Universal Pictures.
Unpublished register in library.

14   Bibo, Irving, 1889-1962. (composer)
     Papers, ca. 1920-1962. 1 box (ca. 100 pieces) and 1 v.
(oversize) manuscripts, photographs, and printed material.
     Letters, photographs, clippings, sheet music, and song
books of Irving Bibo, song-writer and composer. Bibo wrote
tunes for the Ziegfeld Follies and other theatricals in 1920;
in 1930, as a Los Angeles resident, he composed motion picture
scores and college songs. Includes one phonograph record
shelved in records collection.

15   Birdwell, Russell, 1903-   . (publicist)
     Papers. 67 boxes.

16   Blue, Ben, collector. 1900-   . (comedian)
     Collection of radio scripts for comedy shows. ca. 1935-
1955. 45 boxes.
     Includes scripts for Jack Benny, Burns and Allen, Milton
Berle, Eddie Cantor, and others.

17   Boyer, Charles, 1899-   . (actor)
     A collection of photographs, scrapbooks, screenplays,
clippings and ephemera. ca. 1935- . 2 boxes, 4 oversize
packages.
     Collection relating to Charles Boyer contains two scrap-
books, approximately 200 photographs, and miscellaneous
ephemera. Screenplays included are THE GARDEN OF ALLAH (UA,
1938) and ARCH OF TRIUMPH (UA, 1948).
     Unpublished register in library.

18   Brandt, George, 1916-1963. (writer)
     Papers, ca. 1925-1950. 16 boxes and 1 oversize package.
     George Brandt wrote for radio, movies and television. He
also worked in public relations for various companies including the Douglas Aircraft Corporation. Included in collection
are scrapbooks compiled by Mr. Brandt on various subjects.

19   Brennan, Frederick Hazlitt, 1901-   . (writer)
     Collection of 184 scripts by Mr. Brennan for the WYATT
EARP television show. ca. 1955-1959. 7 boxes.
     Includes four shooting schedules.

20   Cantor, Eddie, 1892-1964. (comedian)
     Papers, ca. 1915-1964. 49 boxes and 33 oversize packages.
     The collection contains radio and television scripts,
awards, tributes, scrapbooks, correspondence, oil portraits
and photographs, sheet music, orchestrations, and recordings.
     Unpublished register in library.

21   Chandler, Raymond, 1888-1959. (writer)
     Collection of manuscripts, books, periodicals, ephemera
and correspondence, by or relating to Raymond Chandler, ca.
1930-

Included in collection is screenplay for DOUBLE INDEMNITY (PAR, 1944) written by Raymond Chandler and Billy Wilder, from the story by James M. Cain, 1943. Annotations by Billy Wilder.

22 Chase, Stanley, 1928-   . (producer)
    Papers, ca. 1950- . 59 boxes.
    Collection consists of scripts and related materials for Broadway, motion picture and television productions. Largely unorganized.
    List of box contents in library.

23 Churchill, Sir Winston Leonard Spencer, 1874-1965.
    SAVROLA, adapted for television by Frank and Doris Hursley from a novel by Winston Churchill... NBC [1956]
    "Devised and directed by Albert McCleery." Presented November 15, 1956, starring Sarah Churchill. With this: "Savrola" by Winston S. Churchill, adapted by Michael Dyne. This version unacceptable to Churchill, and was not produced. Also: comments by Churchill on Dyne's script; comments by Sarah Churchill on the meeting with her father about Dyne's script.

24 Curtis, Tony, 1925-   . (actor)
    Papers. v.p., ca. 1948- . 20 boxes and 7 oversize packages.
    Collection consists of motion picture scripts (56) and related materials--shooting schedules, press clippings, background materials, correspondence, and production and publicity stills. Included are scripts for: WINCHESTER 73 (U, 1950), HOUDINI (PAR, 1953), TRAPEZE (UA, 1956), SWEET SMELL OF SUCCESS (UA, 1957), THE DEFIANT ONES (UA, 1958), SOME LIKE IT HOT (UA, 1959), SPARTACUS (U, 1960), SEX AND THE SINGLE GIRL (WA, 1964), and THE BOSTON STRANGLER (F, 1968).
    Unpublished register in library.

25 Daly, Carroll John, 1889-1958. (writer)
    A collection of 163 typescripts of short stories, novella, radio scripts and television scripts. 7 boxes.
    Some of this material was published. Included is a copy of Mr. Daly's record book.
    Unpublished register in library.

26 Dick, Oliver Lawson, 1920-   . (writer)
    PORTRAIT OF ROBERT FLAHERTY...produced by W. R. Rodgers. Third Programme, Tuesday, September 2, 1952...[London, British Broadcasting Company] 1952.
    A radio script in which Orson Welles, John Huston, Lillian Gish, Jean Renoir, Alexander Korda, Henri Matisse, Oliver St. John Gogarty, Sabu, Denis Johnston, Pat Miller, and others reminisce about Flaherty.

27 Edwards, Anne, 1927-____. (writer)
      Papers. ca. 1965-____. 5 boxes.
      This collection consists of literary manuscripts, galleys,
   and screenplays.
      Unpublished register in library.

28 Englund, Ken, 1914-____. (writer)
      A collection of screenplays, play scripts, press clippings,
   research material, published works and personal papers.
   1940-____. 89 boxes and 1 package. (Roughly arranged)
      Collection contains over 50 boxes of scripts.

29 Federal Theatre Project.
      Collection of materials issued by the Federal Theatre
   Project of the Works Progress Administration, 1936-1939.
   9 boxes.
      Included are plays, synopses of plays, lists of plays,
   radio scripts, and three volumes of folk songs and ballads.
      Unpublished register in library.

30 Fine, Mort. (writer, producer)
      Papers of Mort Fine and David Friedkin, ca. 1950-
   18 boxes.
      Radio, motion picture, and television scripts, and related
   materials. Business records of Friedkin and Fine--contracts,
   production reports and story ideas. Included is screenplay
   THE FOOL KILLER (AMI, 1965).
      Unpublished register in library.

31 Fitzsimmons, Cortland. (writer)
      Papers. 1930s and 1940s. ca. 100 pieces. 4 boxes.
      Papers include screenplays, treatments, story ideas, and
   short stories. Screenplay for THE ARKANSAS TRAVELLER (PAR,
   1938).

32 Freedman, David.
      Radio scripts, ca. 1930-1940. 286 items in 10 boxes.
      The collection comprises scripts for radio programs in
   which Al Jolson, Bert Lahr, Fanny Brice, Eddie Cantor, Red
   Skelton, Tommy Dorsey, and others starred. Some were presented over a period of years as weekly shows. Also: 1 box
   scripts, jokes by Ben, Noel, and Nancy Freedman.

33 Gamet, Kenneth Seaton, 1907-1971. (writer)
      Papers, ca. 1910-1970. 33 boxes.
      Collection contains screenplays (over 80), story outlines,
   treatments, production notes, radio and television scripts
   by western screenwriter Kenneth Gamet. Also memoranda and
   correspondence. Included are screenplays for: SMART BLONDE
   (WA, 1936), FLYING TIGERS (REP, 1942), CANADIAN PACIFIC (F,
   1949), LAST OF THE COMANCHES (COL, 1952), and THE LAST POSSE

(COL, 1953). Television scripts include 16 episodes of the
CASEY JONES series (1957-58).
List of screenplays in Collection File.

34 George P. Johnson Negro Film Collection.
    On microfilm.
    Contains correspondence, playbills, advertising materials,
still photographs, posters, display cards, and magazine and
newspaper clippings concerning the Negro in motion pictures,
a collection assembled by George P. Johnson, the brother of
the actor Noble Johnson, ca. 1916- .
    Unpublished register in library.

35 Glass, Maude Emily, 1899-   . (writer)
    Papers, ca. 1912-1970. 5 boxes.
    Collection of correspondence, manuscripts, screen treat-
ments, and research materials of freelance writer, Maude Emily
Glass, and materials relating to her friendship with the
Wilshire Family, Julian Hawthorne, and Ruth St. Denis.
    Unpublished register in library.

36 Glazer, Benjamin, 1887-   . (producer, writer)
    Papers, ca. 1930-1950. 18 boxes.
    The collection is made up of screenplays (over 50) by or
produced by Glazer, and related material--correspondence,
synopses, music scores, business materials, notes, ephemera.
Screenplays include: A FAREWELL TO ARMS (PAR, 1932), MATA
HARI (MGM, 1932), DOUBLE OR NOTHING (PAR, 1937), and TORTILLA
FLAT (MGM, 1942).
    Unpublished register in library.

37 Grot, Anton F., 1884-   . (set designer)
    Collection of 869 sketches for moving pictures. L.A.
ca. 1930-1955. 26 packages.

38 Haase, John, 1924?. (writer)
    Collection of literary manuscripts. L.A. 1958- . 5
boxes.
    Included is screenplay of NOON BALLOON, 1968.

39 Hall, Norman Shannon, 1896-   . (writer)
    Collection of 111 screenplays and 19 television plays by
Norman Shannon Hall. Los Angeles, ca. 1925-1960. 11 boxes.
    Included are 17 items (plays, screenplays, and television
plays) by friends of Hall.

40 Heisler, Stuart, 1894-   . (director)
    Papers, ca. 1913-1967. 14 boxes, 1 oversize package.
    Collection contains motion picture and television scripts,
film story ideas, photographs, correspondence, clippings,
contracts, musical scores and legal documents. Oral history

of Heisler's career (4 tapes). Television scripts include
number from series LAWMAN (1958-1960) and THE DAKOTAS (1962-
1963). Among the screenplays are THE HURRICANE (UA, 1937),
THE BISCUIT EATER (PAR, 1940), ALONG CAME JONES (RKO, 1945),
TOKYO JOE (COL, 1949), THE STAR (F, 1953), and BEACHHEAD (UA,
1954). Also included is Lillian Hellman's story for the
documentary THE NEGRO SOLDIER (1944).
Unpublished register in library.

41 Hollywood literature.
A collection of books about Hollywood [v.d.] 247 books,
13 boxes.
The collection is chiefly fiction but includes some nonfiction exposes and biographies.

42 Hollywood Studio Strike.
Papers, 1945-1948. 3 boxes (approx. 600 pieces).
A collection of materials dealing with the Hollywood
Studio Strike, consisting of newspaper clippings (mainly from
the Hollywood Sun and the LSU News, both union publications),
mimeographed statements to the union membership, ephemera,
correspondence.
Unpublished register in library.

43 Horsley, William, 1870-1958. (producer, motion picture
industry pioneer)
Papers, 1903-1947. 1 box.
Photographs, correspondence, ephemera, memorabilia, peri-
odicals containing articles by and about Horsley, founder of
Universal Studios.
Unpublished register in library.

44 Houseman, John, 1902-   . (producer, director, writer)
Papers, ca. 1930- . 24 boxes and 7 oversize packages.
Included are correspondence, director's scripts for stage,
movies (14), radio, and television; newspaper clippings and
ephemera. Screenplays include: THE BLUE DAHLIA (PAR, 1946),
THE BAD AND THE BEAUTIFUL (MGM, 1952), JULIUS CAESAR (MGM,
1953), EXECUTIVE SUITE (MGM, 1954), and LUST FOR LIFE (MGM,
1956).
Unpublished register in library.

45 Hunter, Todd. (writer)
Papers, ca. 1940- . 2 boxes. (Unarranged)
This collection primarily of radio and television scripts
by Mr. Hunter.

46 Ince, Thomas H., 1882-1924. (producer, director, executive,
motion picture industry pioneer)
Synopses of productions made by Thomas H. Ince during the
period April, 1912 to August, 1915. Inceville Studios.

Includes an alphabetical index and numerical index to
scenarios.

47 Karlson, Phil, 1908-___. (director)
    Collection of screenplays and related materials, directed
by Phil Karlson. L.A., 1954- . 3 boxes.
    Screenplays (8) annotated. Included are scripts for:
TIGHT SPOT (COL, 1955), KEY WITNESS (MGM, 1960), THE YOUNG
DOCTORS (UA, 1961), and THE SILENCERS (COL, 1966). Also
story board for THE SILENCERS.
    Unpublished register in library.

48 Kovacs, Ernie, 1919-1962. (writer, comedian)
    Papers, ca. 1951-1961. 35 boxes, 53 oversize packages.
    The collection contains scripts, skits, character sketches
and recordings of Kovacs television shows. Also Illustrated
Profuselies, original ink drawings. Screenplays include:
OPERATION MADBALL (COL, 1957), BELL, BOOK AND CANDLE (COL,
1958), and OUR MAN IN HAVANA (COL, 1960).

49 Kramer, Stanley, 1913-___. (producer, director)
    Papers, 1949-1968. Approx. 150 boxes.
    Scripts in various stages. Production notes, stills, re-
visions, treatments, final drafts, cutting, continuity
scripts, music que sheets, music scores, publicity, corres-
pondence files, box office figures, budgets, actors' con-
tracts for nearly all films made by Kramer up to 1968.
Included among scripts are the following: CHAMPION (UA, 1949),
HOME OF THE BRAVE (UA, 1949), THE MEN (UA, 1950), CYRANO
DE BERGERAC (UA, 1950), DEATH OF A SALESMAN (COL, 1951),
MEMBER OF THE WEDDING (COL, 1952), HIGH NOON (UA, 1952), THE
JUGGLER (COL, 1953), THE CAINE MUTINY (COL, 1954), NOT AS A
STRANGER (UA, 1955), PRIDE AND THE PASSION (UA, 1957), THE
DEFIANT ONES (UA, 1958), ON THE BEACH (UA, 1959), INHERIT
THE WIND (UA, 1960), JUDGMENT AT NUREMBERG (UA, 1961), PRES-
SURE POINT (UA, 1962), IT'S A MAD, MAD, MAD, MAD WORLD (UA,
1963), INVITATION TO A GUNFIGHTER (UA, 1964), SHIP OF FOOLS
(COL, 1965), and GUESS WHO'S COMING TO DINNER (COL, 1967).

50 Laughton, Charles, 1899-1962. (actor)
    Papers, ca. 1930-1962. 23 boxes.
    This collection consists of correspondence, screen and
stage plays in which Laughton starred or collaborated, radio
and TV materials relating to Laughton, manuscripts of works
by Laughton, ephemera, and pictures. Screenplays include:
THE MAN FROM DOWN UNDER (MGM, 1943), THE CAINE MUTINY (COL,
1954), THE NAKED AND THE DEAD (WA, 1958), and IRMA LA DOUCE
(UA, 1963).
    Unpublished register in library.

51 LeMay, Alan, 1899-   . (writer)
        Papers, ca. 1940- . 23 boxes.
        The collection includes manuscripts of novels, story out-
    lines, screenplays for television and motion pictures, corres-
    pondence and ephemera.
        Unpublished register in library.

52 LOS ANGELES DAILY NEWS Morgue File, ca. 1923-1954.
        39 boxes in morgue files on films, alphabetized by title.
    Information also on film personalities and various aspects of
    motion pictures. Stills, research material, clippings.

53 McCoy, Horace, 1897-1955. (writer)
        Papers, ca. 1925- . 6 boxes.
        This collection comprises literary manuscripts, screenplays,
    books, correspondence and business contracts (ca. 30 pieces),
    ephemera, and pictures, all by or relating to Horace McCoy.

54 MacDonald, Jeanette, 1906-1965. (actress)
        Scrapbooks, 1931-1951. 5 volumes.
        Mounted newspaper clippings, press reviews, photographs,
    and programs documenting Jeanette MacDonald's stage, movie
    and opera career.

55 Macgowan, Kenneth, 1888-1963.
        Papers, ca. 1915-1970. 68 boxes.
        Consists of correspondence, manuscripts, books, clippings,
    scrapbooks, drawings, pamphlets, programs, and related ephemera
    mainly concerning the American theater, but also relating to
    Mr. Macgowan's activities in motion pictures, university
    teaching, anthropology, and archaeology.

56 Meehan, Elizabeth, 1905-   . (writer)
        Collection of television scripts, screenplays, and treat-
    ments, by Elizabeth Meehan and various collaborators. ca.
    1930-1955. 23 items in 1 box.
        Part of a gift of Mrs. Meehan's daughter. The majority of
    the scripts from this gift are catalogued in the Theater Arts
    Library, UCLA.

57 Mills, Hugh Mortimer Travers, 1906-1971. (writer)
        Papers. 13 boxes, 8 oversize packages.
        Manuscripts, including drafts, story notes and construc-
    tions for novels, plays and film; correspondence and ephemera.
    Collection includes the novel, screenplays and clippings for
    PRUDENCE AND THE PILL (F, 1968).
        Unpublished register in library.

58 Mirisch Productions, Inc.
        Production files, ca. 1955-1974. ca. 34 ft.

95

Collection contains correspondence, contracts, production data, and scripts of the motion pictures produced by Mirisch Corp. for United Artists. Over 60 scripts in various stages, including cutting and dialogue continuities, music cues and shooting schedules. Among the scripts included are SOME LIKE IT HOT (1959), THE APARTMENT (1960), ONE, TWO, THREE (1961), A SHOT IN THE DARK (1964), THE RUSSIANS ARE COMING, THE RUSSIANS ARE COMING (1966), IN THE HEAT OF THE NIGHT (1967), THE LANDLORD (1971), FIDDLER ON THE ROOF (1971), and MR. MAJESTYK (1973).

Unpublished register in library.

Papers restricted to permission of donor Walter Mirisch [consult Brooke Whiting, Assistant Head, Special Collections].

59 Moll, Elick, 1907-   . (writer)
Papers, ca. 1957- . 4 boxes.
This collection chiefly contains literary manuscripts of Elick Moll; among them are television plays.
Unpublished register in library.

60 Motion Picture Patents Co., et al., defendants.
Papers, 1911-1915. 4 boxes.
Briefs and other records, newspaper clippings, ephemera, in connection with the trial of the U.S. vs. Motion Picture Patents Co., from the files of the law firm of Caldwell, Masslich and Reed who represented the major defendants in this case.

61 Moving picture and theatre editions of novels.
ca. 1895- . 4 boxes.
A collection of reprints or novelizations of motion pictures and plays containing photographs of players and scenes from the productions.

62 National Broadcasting Company, Inc.
NBC. MATINEE THEATER. Scripts and production material. Los Angeles, 1955-1958. 20 boxes.
Scripts for 125 television shows.

63 National Broadcasting Company, Inc.
THE FURTHER ADVENTURES OF ELLERY QUEEN. Scripts, Los Angeles, 1958-1959. 4 boxes.
Television program devised and produced by Albert McCleery. Scripts for 21 episodes. Also two notebooks with production notes.

64 National Broadcasting Company, Inc.
I SPY. Scripts and production materials, Los Angeles, 1966-1968. 14 boxes.

1048 scripts for 28 episodes of television shows produced by David Friedkin and Mort Fine. Also ephemera--correspondence, budgets, production notes.

65 Nelson, Ralph, 1916-   . (director, writer)
    Papers, ca. 1940-   . 71 boxes and 12 oversize packages.
    Collection consists of motion picture and television scripts, pictures, production stills, production notes, budget breakdowns, publicity related ephemera and correspondence. Particularly complete production records, including screenplays for the following: LILIES OF THE FIELD (UA, 1963), SOLDIER IN THE RAIN (AA, 1963), FATE IS THE HUNTER (F, 1964), and FATHER GOOSE (U, 1964). Collection contains both television script and screenplay version for REQUIEM FOR A HEAVYWEIGHT (1956, 1961).
    Unpublished register in library.

66 Nichols, Dudley, 1895-1960. (writer)
    Collection of screenplays by Dudley Nichols. L.A. ca. 1940-1958. 8 boxes.
    Included are a few articles by and about Nichols, as well as a few pieces of ephemera relating to films by him. Also included are the screenplays by Nichols of Eugene O'Neill's LONG VOYAGE HOME (UA, 1940) and MOURNING BECOMES ELECTRA (RKO, 1947), along with production notes and designs. Among the 24 screenplays are: AIR FORCE (WA, 1943), FOR WHOM THE BELL TOLLS (PAR, 1943), PINKY (F, 1949), and RAWHIDE (F, 1951).
    Unpublished register in library.

67 North, Edmund H., 1911-   . (writer)
    Collection of screenplays and related material by Edmund H. North. L.A. 1934-   . 4 boxes.
    Includes scripts for THE DAY THE EARTH STOOD STILL (F, 1951), ONLY THE VALIENT (WA, 1951) and THE PROUD ONES (F, 1956). Also 11 orientation films made by the Signal Corps for the War Department during World War II. Also first draft of PATTON (F, 1970) by Francis Ford Coppola, revisions by North and final screenplay and shooting script.
    Unpublished register in library.

68 Oral History--UCLA Oral History Program.
    Transcripts of interviews, including the following with individuals connected with the motion picture industry:
    a. Bradbury, Ray Douglas, 1920-   (writer).
    b. DePatie, Edmond, 1900-   (executive).
    c. Groves, George, 1901-1976 (sound director).
    d. Hodkinson, William Wallace, 1881-1971 (pioneer motion
        picture distributor).
    e. Hoyningen-Huene, George, 1900-   (photographer).

    f. Johnson, George Perry, 1885-   (collector of Negro motion picture history).
    g. Lavery, Emmet Godfrey, 1902- (writer).
    h. Reilly, Jean Burt (hair stylist).
    i. Sorrell, Herbert Knoll, 1897- (union organizer).
    j. Van der Veer, Willard, 1895-1963 (cameraman).

69 Oral History--An Oral History of the Motion Picture in America.
    A series of taped interviews with producers, directors, actors, etc. relating to the motion picture industry. Interviews were conducted by the UCLA Department of Theater Arts under a grant (1968-1969) from the National Endowment for the Humanities and the American Film Institute. Includes the following transcripts:
    a. Anhalt, Edward, 1914- (writer).
    b. Avery, Tex, 1918- (animation director).
    c. Blanke, Henry, 1901- (production executive).
    d. Carle, C. E. "Teet," 1899- (publicist).
    e. Carre, Ben, 1884- (art director, scenic designer).
    f. Cukor, George, 1899- (director).
    g. DUEL IN THE SUN: Rennahan, Ray, 1898- (cinematographer); Garmes, Lee, 1897- (cinematographer, producer, director); Vidor, King, 1894- (director).
    h. Fleischer, Dave, 1894- (director cartoon production).
    i. Freleng, Friz (animator, producer).
    j. Howe, James Wong, 1899-1976 (cinematographer, director).
    k. Huemer, Richard, 1898- (animator).
    l. Johnson, Nunnally, 1897-1977 (producer, writer).
    m. Klune, Raymond, 1904- (production executive).
    n. Lipton, David, 1904- (executive).
    o. Mahin, John Lee, 1907- (writer).
    p. Mandell, Daniel (film editor).
    q. Mann, Abby, 1927- (writer).
    r. Oliver, Harry, 1888-1973 (art director).
    s. Poe, James, 1921- (writer).
    t. Struss, Karl, ca. 1890- (cinematographer).

70 Oral History--Collection of taped interviews with theater, motion picture, and television professionals. v.p., ca. 1961-1970.
    Ralph Freud (1901-1973), collector. Interviews were conducted by Ralph Freud, Victor Jory, and Professor Freud's students from UCLA's Theater Arts Department. Includes the following:
    a. Ames, Leon, 1903- (actor).
    b. Arzner, Dorothy, 1900- (director).
    c. Bellamy, Ralph, 1905- (actor).
    d. Booth, Shirley, 1907- (actress).
    e. Bradbury, Ray, 1920- (writer).

f. Cabot, Sebastian (actor).
g. Clurman, Harold, 1901-   (stage director).
h. Cukor, George, 1899-   (director).
i. Davis, Bette, 1908-   (actress).
j. Doolittle, James A., 1914-   (theater executive).
k. Duerr, Ed, 1906-   (director, producer in radio and
      TV).
l. Dumbeau, Dug.
m. Erway, Ben.
n. Freud, Ralph, 1901-1973 (theater director, founder of
      UCLA Theater Arts Department).
o. Freund, Karl, 1890-1969 (cinematographer).
p. Hall, Frances.
q. Inness, Jean.
r. Jagger, Dean, 1903-   (actor).
s. Jory, Victor, 1902-   (actor).
t. Kelly, George, 1887-   (writer, director).
u. Lane, Charles, 1899-   (actor).
v. Lawson, John Howard, 1894-1977 (writer).
w. Lemmon, Jack, 1925-   (actor).
x. Loos, Lex.
y. Lunt, Alfred, 1892-1977 (actor) and Lynn Fontanne,
      1887-   (actress).
z. McDowall, Roddy, 1928-   (actor).
aa. McIntire, John, 1907-   (actor).
bb. McNear, Howard, 1909-1969 (actor).
cc. Mishkin, Meyer, 1912-   (Hollywood agent).
dd. Morgan, Dickson.
ee. Pollock, Max.
ff. Seaton, Phyllis (Hollywood talent director & dramatic
      coach).
gg. Tamiroff, Akim, d. 1972 (actor).
hh. Willson, Meredith, 1902-   (composer, writer).
ii. Wynn, Keenan, 1916-   (actor).

71 Ouspenskaya, Maria, 1876-1949. (actress)
      Papers, ca. 1922-1942. 4 boxes and 1 package.
      Papers consist of scripts for dramas and motion pictures
    in which Maria Ouspenskaya appeared, notices, reviews, pub-
    licity material and photographs of various scenes, chiefly the
    motion pictures KINGS ROW (WA, 1941) and DODSWORTH (UA, 1936).
    2 boxes of moving picture scripts from 1933-1942. Included
    among the screenplays are: DANCE GIRL DANCE (RKO, 1940),
    WATERLOO BRIDGE (MGM, 1940), and FRANKENSTEIN MEETS THE WOLF
    MAN (U, 1943).
      Unpublished register in library.

72 Paul, Elliot Harold, 1891-1955. (writer)
      Collection of screenplays and proof sheets of books. ca.
    1942-1945. 1 box (9 items).
      Unpublished register in library.

73 Poe, James, 1921-   . (writer)
       Papers, ca. 1940-   27 boxes.
       The collection includes scripts for radio, television, and
    motion pictures, as well as working notes, research materials,
    movie stills, correspondence, tapes and ephemera. Consider-
    able material relating to AROUND THE WORLD IN 80 DAYS (UA,
    1956), including conference notes, correspondence from Mike
    Todd, depositions for arbitration suit, scripts and clippings,
    photostats and legal documents used in arbitration, pre-trial
    depositions, correspondence and statements from Poe, Todd,
    Farrow, S. J. Perelman. Scripts include: CAT ON A HOT TIN
    ROOF (MGM, 1958), LAST TRAIN FROM GUNHILL (PAR, 1959),
    SANCTUARY (F, 1961), SUMMER AND SMOKE (PAR, 1961), and TOYS IN
    THE ATTIC (UA, 1963).
       Unpublished register in library.

74 Powell, Dick, 1904-1963. (actor)
       Scrapbooks, 1925-1947. 1 box. 18 packages.
       Stills, snapshots, clippings, publicity on Dick Powell,
    Joan Blondell, June Allyson and others.

75 Republic Pictures Corporation.
       Collection of continuity scripts and shooting scripts.
    L.A. ca. 1935-1955. 139 boxes.
       Collection includes large number of films starring Gene
    Autry, Roy Rogers, Monte Hale, John Wayne. Director and cast
    for each film are given on list of continuities.
       Unpublished register in library.

76 Roberts, Charles E., 1894-1951. (writer)
       Collection of screenplays. L.A. v.d. 4 manuscripts.

77 Robson, Mark, 1913-   . (producer, director)
       DADDY'S GONE A-HUNTING. Los Angeles, ca. 1968. 5 boxes
    and 5 oversize packages.
       Collection consists of scripts and related material for
    this movie, produced and directed by Mark Robson.

78 Ross, Sam, 1912-   . (writer)
       Collection of literary manuscripts by Sam Ross. 1941-
    6 boxes.
       Radio scripts 1941-1947; television scripts 1958-1967.
    Included are scripts for several television series: THE
    NAKED CITY, THE FUGITIVE, ADVENTURES IN PARADISE, MANNIX, THE
    ELEVENTH HOUR, THE LEGEND OF JESSE JAMES, BOURBON STREET
    BEAT, THE F.B.I., THE REBEL, HAWAIIAN EYE, RAWHIDE, HONG KONG,
    TALES OF WELLS FARGO.
       Unpublished register in library.

79 Rotha, Paul, 1907-   . (documentary producer, director, historian)
    Material by and about Paul Rotha. [v.p. (England) 1926-1960]. 18 boxes. 6 packages.
    A collection of material by and about Paul Rotha. Included are scripts in various stages, typescripts of published and unpublished articles, scrapbooks and photographs.
    Unpublished register in library.

80 Ruggles, Charles, 1892-1970. (actor)
    Papers, ca. 1905-1960.
    A collection of photographs, keybooks, annotated plays and scripts, clippings, and ephemera relating to the stage and moving picture career of Mr. Ruggles. Includes screenplays of HEAVEN CAN WAIT (F, 1943), IT HAPPENED ON FIFTH AVENUE (AA, 1947), FATHER OF THE BRIDE (MGM, 1950), and THE PLEASURE OF HIS COMPANY (PAR, 1961).
    Unpublished register in library.

81 Saroyan, Aram, 1943-   .
    Papers, ca. 1965- . 12 boxes.
    Includes correspondence from various Hollywood personalities including Walter Matthau and Garson Kanin.

82 Schram, Violet, 1898-   . (actress)
    Collection of materials relating to Violet Schram's acting career, ca. 1914-1963. 3 boxes, 1 oversize package.
    Collection consists largely of still photographs and newspaper clippings.
    Unpublished register in library.

83 Serling, Rod, 1924-1975. (writer)
    Papers, ca. 1945. 17 boxes.
    The collection consists of scripts for movies, television and radio; correspondence; and business records. Included are scripts for TWILIGHT ZONE television program (1958-1964), SEVEN DAYS IN MAY (PAR, 1964), and THE DOOMSDAY FLIGHT (Universal Television, 1966).
    Unpublished register in library.

84 Shapiro, Victor Mansfield, 1893-1967. (publicist)
    Papers, ca. 1915-1942. 6 boxes, 1 package.
    Public relations and promotional materials relating to the motion picture industry. Documented publicity campaigns of Mae West, Charles Chaplin, Harold Lloyd, Rudolph Valentino, Gloria Swanson, and Louis Wohlheim are included, as well as a diary of GONE WITH THE WIND (MGM, 1939). Also scrapbooks, photo albums, a biography of Victor M. Shapiro and manuscripts and notes on Pearl White, Sol Wurtzel, Lois Moran, Norma Talmadge, Elissa Landi, and Sid Grauman. Screenplay for EVERY DAY'S A HOLIDAY (PAR, 1937).
    Unpublished register in library.

85 Silliphant, Stirling, 1918-   . (writer)
       Collection of scripts for motion pictures and television.
    ca. 1957-   . 60 boxes and 2 oversize packages.
       Includes business materials, publicity, correspondence and
    123 episodes for ROUTE 66 television series (1959-1963).
    Among the 18 screenplays are: THE SLENDER THREAD (PAR, 1965),
    THE LIBERATION OF L. B. JONES (COL, 1969), THE NEW CENTURIONS
    (COL, 1971), SHAFT (MGM, 1971), THE POSEIDON ADVENTURE (F,
    1972), and SHAFT IN AFRICA (MGM, 1973).
       Unpublished register in library.

86 Simpson, Russell, 1880-1959. (actor)
       Collection of moving picture stills, clippings, correspon-
    dence. 1917-1942. 1 box.
       The collection contains 158 moving picture stills, also a
    bound album of stills from WAY DOWN EAST (UA, 1920), in all
    of which Russell Simpson, an actor who entered moving pic-
    tures in 1907, appeared. Included also is a scrapbook of
    newspaper clippings.

87 Smith, Paul Gerard, 1895-1968. (writer)
       Collection of screenplays. L.A. v.d. 4 manuscripts.
       Includes screenplay for HURRY, CHARLIE, HURRY (RKO, 1941).

88 Sorrell, Herbert Knoll, 1897-   compiler. (union organizer)
       Scrapbooks, L.A., 1945-1947. 1 box and 4 v. (oversize
    packages).
       Scrapbooks and related material concerning the Hollywood
    Studio Strike, 1946-47, compiled by H. K. Sorrell, labor
    union representative and President of the Conference of
    Studio Unions. Included are clippings, photographs, ephemera,
    material relating to the hearings on the strike conducted in
    L.A. by the Special Subcommittee of the U.S. House of Repre-
    sentatives Committee on Education and Labor, Carroll D. Kearns,
    Chairman, and THE STORY OF THE HOLLYWOOD FILM STRIKE IN CAR-
    TOONS, by Gene Price.

89 Starr, Ben, 1921-   . (writer)
       Collection of scripts for motion pictures, television and
    radio, by Ben Starr and various collaborators. ca. 1948-   .
    6 boxes.
       Includes several drafts, revisions and shooting scripts.
    Among the screenplays are: OUR MAN FLINT (F, 1966), THE BUSY
    BODY (PAR, 1967), and HOW TO COMMIT MARRIAGE (CIO, 1969).
       Unpublished register in library.

90 Stone, Peter, 1930-   . (writer)
       Screenplays, books for musicals, and related materials.
    ca. 1960. 7 boxes.

Collection includes scripts for CHARADE (U, 1963),
ARABESQUE (U, 1966), and THE SECRET WAR OF PRIVATE FRIGG (U,
1967).
Unpublished register in library.

91 Story, Ralph. (television commentator)
RALPH STORY'S LOS ANGELES: television scripts. CBS-TV,
Los Angeles, Jan. 14, 1964- . 216 scripts in 7 boxes.
Television scripts for the documentary RALPH STORY'S LOS
ANGELES, broadcast on CBS-TV, Los Angeles beginning Jan. 14,
1964.
List of scripts in library.

92 Sturges, Preston, 1898-1959. (director, writer)
Papers.
Collection consists of scripts and production materials
for about 16 films Mr. Sturges either wrote, directed or was
involved in some capacity. This material (34 boxes) has been
arranged. Correspondence and personal papers (approx. 60
boxes) have not yet been arranged. Also 34 scrapbooks on
films. The scripts collection includes the various treatments, revisions and versions of different scripts. In some
instances musical scores are included.
Unpublished register for scripts and production material
in library. Set of Sturges screenplays also in UCLA Theater
Arts Library.

93 Tully (Jim) Collection. (writer)
A collection of the manuscripts of books and articles,
published and unpublished, of Jim Tully (1891-1947), noted
American author, comprising manuscript drafts, galley proofs,
movie scripts, radio scripts, and tearsheets from magazines.

94 Turman, Lawrence, 1926- . (producer)
Collection of screenplays and related materials, produced
by Lawrence Turman. L.A., 1960- . 26 boxes and 4 oversize
packages.
Collection includes script of THE GRADUATE (EMB, 1967) as
well as production material, several drafts, business files,
wardrobe stills and exhibitors campaign manual on the film.
Other scripts are: THE YOUNG DOCTORS (UA, 1961), THE BEST MAN
(UA, 1964), THE FLIM FLAM MAN (F, 1966), and PRETTY POISON
(F, 1968).
Unpublished register in library.

95 Vidor, King Wallis, 1894- . (director)
Papers, 1920-1959. 14 boxes.
The collection consists primarily of scripts (20) and
related materials of movies produced and directed by King
Vidor. Included are scripts for THE BIG PARADE (MGM, 1925),
HALLELUJAH (MGM, 1929), OUR DAILY BREAD (UA, 1934), SO RED

THE ROSE (PAR, 1935), STELLA DALLAS (UA, 1937), NORTHWEST PASSAGE (MGM, 1940), and THE FOUNTAINHEAD (WA, 1949). Many scripts annotated. Also production notes, revisions, photographs and correspondence. Key album of photographs for THE JACK KNIFE MAN (FN, 1920).
Unpublished register in library.

96 Wagner, Robert Leicester, 1872-1942. (writer)
Collection of manuscripts, correspondence and ephemera, 1925-1942. 25 boxes.
Much of the correspondence in this collection is from famous movie personalities. There is also a folder of letters from prominent literary figures. The manuscripts, primarily stories intended for film adaptation, are by Rob Wagner and other writers, including one manuscript each by William Saroyan and Peter Bernard Kane.
Unpublished register in library.

97 Webb, James R., ca. 1912-   . (writer)
Papers. v.d. 1 box.
Included are 7 variant scripts of HOW THE WEST WAS WON (MGM, 1962) by James Webb, and related materials.

98 Wellman, Paul Iselin, 1898-1966. (writer)
Papers, ca. 1930-1966. 29 boxes.
This collection consists primarily of literary manuscripts and galleys of Mr. Wellman's published books. Screenplay for THE KISSING BANDIT (MGM, 1949).
Unpublished register in library.

99 Wilson, Richard A., 1915-   . (producer, writer)
Papers, ca. 1945- .
Collection consists of production files for film, radio and stage productions involving Richard Wilson. Included are still photographs, scripts and correspondence. Several files contain material relating to Orson Welles and the Mercury Theater production of MacBeth. Among the screenplays are: THE EGG AND I (U, 1947), a number of MA AND PA KETTLE films (1949-1953), CROSSWINDS (PAR, 1951), THE BIG BOODLE (UA, 1957), and AL CAPONE (AA, 1959).
Unpublished register in library.

100 Wolper Productions, Inc. Los Angeles.
Television scripts and research materials for documentaries produced by Wolper Productions. Los Angeles, ca. 1960-1963. 10 boxes.
Unpublished register in library.

101 Woodfield, William Read.
Papers, 1957-1969. 4 boxes.

Includes television scripts and related production materials for SHAFT and MISSION IMPOSSIBLE. Various drafts of
scripts, photos, clippings, layouts, budgets.
Unpublished register in library.

102 Wynn, Ed, 1886-1966. (actor)
Scrapbooks, 1923-1937.
Clippings on Ed Wynn's career.

103 Zugsmith, Albert, collector, 1910-   . (producer, director,
writer)
Collection of movie scripts, some of which were written
or produced by Albert Zugsmith. v.p., v.d. 9 boxes.

B   MUSIC LIBRARY
Music Librarian: Stephen M. Fry
(213) 825-4882
Hours: M-Sat, 9-5, Sun, 1-9
Material may be viewed only through special arrangement.

1 General Music Corporation Library.
Music manuscripts, ca. 1930-1970. ca. 2,500 folders.
Collection contains film and television scores including
conductor's scores and parts from General Music Corporation
and Sunset Music Corporation libraries. Included are scores
for a number of cartoon series such as PINK PANTHER, ROAD
RUNNER and WOODY WOODPECKER, and for television series GENTLE
BEN, COWBOY IN AFRICA, and JOURNEY TO THE CENTER OF THE EARTH.
Composers include Darrell Calker, Basil Adlam, Frank de Vol,
George Bruns, Malcolm Arnold, Harry Sukman, Earle Hagen,
Herbert Spenser, Walter Greene, Henry Mancini, William Lava
and Lee Zahler.

2 Lubin, Harry. (composer)
Music manuscripts, ca. 1948-mid-1960s. ca. 20 boxes.*
Collection contains music scores for television, film and
records. Television series include LORETTA YOUNG SHOW, ONE
STEP BEYOND, ZANE GREY THEATRE, and OUTER LIMITS. Film
scores are for DISASTER (PAR, 1948), CAGED FURY (PAR, 1948),
MR. RECKLESS (PAR, 1948), WATERFRONT AT MIDNIGHT (PAR, 1948),
and WYOMING MAIL (U, 1950).

3 Mancini, Henry, 1924-   . (composer)
Film scores, 1954-1969. 18 manuscripts.
Collection includes manuscript scores for THE PRIVATE WAR
OF MAJOR BENSON (U, 1955), THE DAYS OF WINE AND ROSES (WA,
1962), EXPERIMENT IN TERROR (COL, 1962), MR. HOBBS TAKES A
VACATION (F, 1962), CHARADE (U, 1963), SOLDIER IN THE RAIN
(AA, 1963), DEAR HEART (WA, 1964), THE PINK PANTHER (UA,

---

*music manuscript boxes: 24"x15"x10"

1964), A SHOT IN THE DARK (UA, 1964), THE GREAT RACE (WA, 1965), ARABESQUE (U, 1966), MOMENT TO MOMENT (U, 1966), WHAT DID YOU DO IN THE WAR, DADDY (UA, 1966), PETER GUNN (1967), TWO FOR THE ROAD (F, 1967), WAIT UNTIL DARK (WA, 1967), GAILY, GAILY (UA, 1969), and ME NATALIE (NG, 1969). Also included are the first drafts of Mancini's book on scoring for films, Sound and Scores (1962).

4 Newman, Alfred, 1901-1970. (musical director)
   Film score recordings, 1936-1962. 41 albums, 47 tapes.
   Studio recordings have all been transferred to tape. The collection includes music for BELOVED ENEMY (UA, 1936), STELLA DALLAS (UA, 1937), WUTHERING HEIGHTS (UA, 1939), HOW GREEN WAS MY VALLEY (F, 1941), SONG OF BERNADETTE (F, 1943), LEAVE HER TO HEAVEN (F, 1945), CENTENNIAL SUMMER (F, 1946), DAVID AND BATHSHEBA (F, 1951), and MARCO POLO (AMI, 1962).

5 North, Alex, 1910-   . (composer)
   Film scores, 1951-1969. 39 manuscripts.
   Collection includes manuscript scores for DEATH OF A SALESMAN (COL, 1951), A STREETCAR NAMED DESIRE (WA, 1951), THE 13TH LETTER (F, 1951), MEMBER OF THE WEDDING (COL, 1952), LES MISERABLES (F, 1952), PONY SOLDIER (F, 1952), VIVA ZAPATA! (F, 1952), DESIREE (F, 1954), GO, MAN, GO (UA, 1954), I'LL CRY TOMORROW (MGM, 1955), MAN WITH THE GUN (UA, 1955), THE RACERS (F, 1955), THE ROSE TATTOO (PAR, 1955), UNCHAINED (WA, 1955), THE BAD SEED (WA, 1956), THE RAINMAKER (PAR, 1956), THE BACHELOR PARTY (UA, 1957), KING AND FOUR QUEENS (UA, 1957), SOUTH SEAS ADVENTURE (SW, 1958), HOT SPELL (PAR, 1958), THE LONG HOT SUMMER (F, 1958), STAGE STRUCK (BV, 1958), THE WONDERFUL COUNTRY (UA, 1959), SPARTACUS (parts 1 & 2, U, 1960), THE MISFITS (UA, 1961), SANCTUARY (F, 1961), ALL FALL DOWN (MGM, 1962), THE CHILDREN'S HOUR (UA, 1962), CLEOPATRA (F, 1963), CHEYENNE AUTUMN (WA, 1964), THE OUTRAGE (MGM, 1964), THE AGONY AND THE ECSTASY (F, 1965), WHO'S AFRAID OF VIRGINIA WOOLF? (WA, 1966), THE DEVIL'S BRIGADE (UA, 1968), THE SHOES OF THE FISHERMAN (MGM, 1968), 2001: A SPACE ODYSSEY (1968-- not used for the released film), A DREAM OF KINGS (NGP, 1969), and HARD CONTRACT (F, 1969).

6 Toch, Ernst, 1887-1964. (composer)
   Collection (in process of being catalogued. size and in- clusive dates not yet determined).
   Includes film scores for LADIES IN RETIREMENT (COL, 1941), ADDRESS UNKNOWN (COL, 1944), and NONE SHALL ESCAPE (COL, 1944). Also music for European radio plays and correspondence.

7 Ward, Edward, 1896-1971. (composer)
   Collection of film music by Edward Ward, 1935-1940. 19 v.
   Included are reduced scores, piano-vocal scores, and selec- tions for a large number of MGM films such as WIFE VS.

SECRETARY (1930), GRAND HOTEL (1932), NIGHT AT THE OPERA
(1935), CAMILLE (1936), AFTER THE THIN MAN (1936), SAN
FRANCISCO (1936), DOUBLE WEDDING (1937), VACATION FROM LOVE
(1938), and THE WOMEN (1939).

C   THEATER ARTS LIBRARY, University Research Library
    Librarian: Audree Malkin
    (213) 825-4880
    Hours: M-F, 9-6; Sat, 12-4
    Open to all who have occasion to consult its holdings.

1   Alcoa Collection, 1959-1961.   9 boxes.
        Collection of scripts for the television series ONE STEP
    BEYOND, ALCOA PREMIERE, and FRED ASTAIRE PRESENTS. 136 epi-
    sodes in all. Most episodes include treatments, outline,
    credits-sequences listing, and cast list.

2   Art Direction.
        Story boards, continuity sketches, set designs, blueprints,
    1945-1976.
        Story boards for 19 Stanley Kramer productions (1945-1960):
    HOME OF THE BRAVE (UA, 1945), CHAMPION (UA, 1949), CYRANO
    DE BERGERAC (UA, 1950), THE MEN (UA, 1950), DEATH OF A SALES-
    MAN (COL, 1951), EIGHT IRON MEN (COL, 1952), THE FOUR POSTER
    (COL, 1952), THE HAPPY TIME (COL, 1952), HIGH NOON (COL,
    1952), THE MEMBER OF THE WEDDING (COL, 1952), MY SIX CONVICTS
    (COL, 1952), THE SNIPER (COL, 1952), THE 5000 FINGERS OF
    DR. T. (COL, 1953), THE JUGGLER (COL, 1953), NOT AS A STRANGER
    (UA, 1955), THE PRIDE AND THE PASSION (UA, 1957), THE DEFIANT
    ONES (UA, 1958), ON THE BEACH (UA, 1959), INHERIT THE WIND
    (UA, 1960).
        Story boards for several television commercials. Partial
    story boards by Gregg Toland for SONG OF THE SOUTH (RKO,
    1946). Unproduced Disney motion picture story boards. Con-
    tinuity sketches for DESIRE UNDER THE ELMS (PAR, 1958) and
    DEVIL'S DISCIPLE (UA, 1959).
        Blueprints and set designs for BUT NOT FOR ME (PAR, 1959)
    and KISSES FOR MY PRESIDENT (WA, 1964). Blueprints for ALL
    THE PRESIDENT'S MEN (WA, 1976).

3   Barrett, Tony, 1917-1974. (writer)
        Collection, 1946-1973. 130 boxes.
        Radio and television production materials and scripts.
    Television material for a variety of programs, particularly
    MOD SQUAD (126 episodes, 1967-1972), including various drafts,
    final scripts, budgets, outlines, cast lists, call sheets,
    shooting schedules, daily production reports, correspondence
    and miscellaneous notes. 40 screenplays by miscellaneous
    authors, including WILD HORSE MESA (RKO, 1947) and UNDER THE
    TONTO RIM (RKO, 1947). Radio scripts include DANGEROUS
    ASSIGNMENT (1951-1953), TALES OF THE TEXAS RANGERS (1951-1952),

DEFENSE ATTORNEY (1951–1952), HOLLYWOOD STAR PLAYHOUSE (1951–1952), and SUSPENSE (1951–1956).
Unpublished register in library.

4 CAPTAIN FROM CASTILE (F, 1947).
5 research notebooks for the film.

5 CHARLEY VARRICK (U, 1973).
Collection of memos, scripts and treatments related to the production of the film, 1972–1973. 18 items in 2 boxes.
Unpublished register in library.

6 Disney (Walt) Productions.
23 cartoon continuities and shooting scripts, 1937–1939.

7 Duff, Warren, 1904–1973. (writer)
Script Collection, ca. 1950s–early 1970s. 108 items in 7 boxes.
Original television scripts, screenplays and stories written by Mr. Duff and others. Includes outlines, drafts, pilot scripts and revisions. Television shows for which there are scripts include AMOS BURKE, SECRET AGENT; THE F.B.I., IRONSIDE and MANNIX. Screenplays include HONDO (WA, 1953) and APPOINTMENT WITH DANGER (PAR, 1951).
Unpublished register in library.

8 Film Festival Programs, 1960-   .
Collection of over 500 programs from major United States and foreign film festivals. Kept up-to-date.

9 HOLLYWOOD TELEVISION THEATRE, 1970–1976.
Scripts for 37 productions, including ANDERSONVILLE TRIAL, DOUBLE SOLITAIRE, INCIDENT AT VICHY, MAN OF DESTINY, SCARECROW, SHADOW OF A GUNMAN, STEAMBATH, THE CHINESE PRIME MINISTER, THE LADIES OF THE CORRIDOR, and THE LAST OF MRS. LINCOLN.

10 Lobby Cards, ca. 1919-   . ca. 500.
Includes many early and rare items such as material from Christie Comedies. Also included are title cards used for silent films.

11 Metro-Goldwyn-Mayer Ideas for Motion Pictures.
52 synopses, ideas for motion pictures by a number of writers, including A. E. Hotchner, Edward G. Robinson, Jr., Jack Kerouac, Jean Anouilh, Terence Rattigan, Theodore White, Frank Gilroy.
Unpublished register in library.

12 Motion Picture Thematic Cue Sheets, 1920–1930. ca. 950 items.
Music cue sheets for silent films of the twenties.

13 Oral History--Jason E. Squire Thesis Supplement.
      Interviews, 1970-1971. 1 box.
      Transcripts of recorded interviews with members of the
   motion picture industry. Included are the following:
      a. Detmers, Fred H. (executive) and Dr. Frank P. Brackett
            (research).
      b. Donahue, Tim (head of budgeting).
      c. Durwood, Stanley H. (president, American Multi.
            Cinema).
      d. Fellman, Nat O. (president, National General Theatres).
      e. Forbes, Gordon B. (management).
      f. Green, Marshall (production manager).
      g. Kopaloff, Don (agent).
      h. Kramer, Stanley, 1913-   (producer, director).
      i. Lederer, Richard, 1916-   (Warner Bros. executive).
      j. Levison, Art (assistant director).
      k. Lipton, David A. (Universal executive).
      l. McCarthy, M. J. (salesman).
      m. Mayer, Roger L. (MGM executive).
      n. Meyer, Russ, 1922-   (producer, director).
      o. Pollack, Sydney, 1934-   (director).
      p. Rittenberg, Saul (MGM legal department).
      q. Rosenberg, Lee (literary agent).
      r. Rotcop, J. Kenneth (story editor).
      s. Said, Fouad (president, Cinemobile Systems).
      t. Silliphant, Stirling, 1918-   (writer, producer).
      u. Stulberg, Gordon, 1923-   (executive).
      v. Weitz, Barry J. (talent agent).
      w. Weitzman, Lew (literary agent).
      x. Yorkin, Bud, 1926-   and Norman Lear, 1922-
            (producers).
      Unpublished register in library.

14 Photograph Collection, 1905-   .
      Collection contains over 190,000 production stills, por-
   traits, publicity stills, and other miscellaneous photographs
   dating from 1905 to present. A continuing program of acquiring stills from current productions keeps the collection up
   to date. Production stills are for American and some foreign
   films. A general portrait file includes photographs of film
   personalities from the 1930s to the present.
      Special collections include:
      a. J. C. Jessen Photograph Collection, 1905-1929.
            Over 2,000 photographs of early studios and 900
         portraits of performers. In addition to photographs
         of such pioneer studios as Biograph, Vitagraph,
         Triangle, The New York Motion Picture Company, Key-
         stone, Selig and Universal, there are many of notable
         individuals such as Thomas Edison, D. W. Griffith,
         Thomas Ince, Mack Sennett, Jesse Lasky, C. B. DeMille,
         the Talmadge Sisters and Mary Pickford.

b. Richard J. Biermann Stills Collection, 1923-1929.
   Over 200 motion picture production stills.
c. Francis Faragoh Photograph Collection, 1920s-1950s.
      ca. 500 motion picture production stills and por-
   traits of performers.
d. Richard Dix Stills Collection, 1920-1939.
      Over 5,000 motion picture stills from productions
   featuring Richard Dix. Large number of miscellaneous,
   unidentified stills as well as nearly 2,000 identified
   stills from 36 productions.
e. George B. Seitz Stills Collection, 1919-1942.
      Over 2,000 motion picture stills from George B.
   Seitz's productions, including serials, one with Pearl
   White (THE BLACK SECRET, 1919) and feature films,
   primarily of the 1930s and early 1940s. A large number
   of stills are from the various ANDY HARDY films.
f. Columbia Pictures Stills Collection, 1950-1960.
      Over 60,000 motion picture production stills and
   188 keybooks.
g. Twentieth Century-Fox Stills Collection, 1950-1971.
      ca. 100,000 motion picture production stills from
   288 American and European films released by Fox primarily during the 1950s and 1960s. Also included are
   stills from a few films of the early 1970s. In addition there are stills of motion picture personalities,
   as well as stills for publicity news release. Also
   keysets, proof sheets and color transparencies.
Unpublished inventories for most of collections in library.

15 Poster Collection, 1915-___. ca. 800
   This large collection includes posters, many early and rare
for American as well as Polish and Czechoslovakian motion
picture productions.

16 Programs, 1915-___. ca. 900
   Collection of programs for major motion picture productions
contains many early and rare items.

17 Radio Broadcasts, 1934-1960.
   Collection from The Library of American Radio, 1934-1960.
14 v.
   Index to radio broadcasts in library.

18 Radio Scripts, 1943-1954.
   Collection of more than 1,200 scripts which includes the
complete AMOS 'N' ANDY series (354 episodes, 1943-1953), and
OUR MISS BROOKS (222 scripts, 1948-1954). Scripts also for
THE BOB HOPE SHOW (1949-1950) and PHILCO RADIO TIME starring
Bing Crosby (1946-1947).
   Unpublished register in library.

110

19 Roddenberry, Gene, 1921-   . (producer, writer)
    STAR TREK Archive, 1966-1969.
    Roddenberry's complete files for three years of production
of the STAR TREK television series. Included are scripts for
82 episodes, production material, business records and correspondence. Also scripts for shows not produced and story
ideas.
    Unpublished register in library.

20 ROOM 222 Archive, 1968-1973.
    Scripts, outlines, notes, treatments, drafts, miscellaneous
revision pages and floor plans for over 50 episodes of the
television series.
    Unpublished register in library.

21 Screenplay Collection, 1922-   .
    Collection of more than 5,000 unpublished scripts for
American, British and some foreign language films. Between
1,500-2,000 scripts are from Fox Film Corp. and Twentieth
Century Fox; the period 1929-1949 is particularly well represented. Another large segment of the collection is devoted
to scripts from Metro-Goldwyn-Mayer, dating back to 1925 with
DANCE MADNESS. Included from MGM are the ANDY HARDY,
DR. KILDARE, and MAISIE film series which are virtually complete, and a number of short features, such as ROBERT BENCHLEY
COMEDIES, PETE SMITH SPECIALTIES, and OUR GANG series. There
is also a small Industrial Films Collection (1953-1962) which
contains 7 screenplays on scientific, social and industrial
topics.

22 Smothers, Tom, 1937-   and Dick, 1939-   . (actors)
    Television script collection, 1967-1975.
    Scripts are from THE SMOTHERS BROTHERS COMEDY HOUR (1967-
1968), THE SUMMER BROTHERS SMOTHERS SHOW (1968), THE SMOTHERS
BROTHERS SUMMER SHOW (1970), and THE SMOTHERS BROTHERS SHOW
(NBC-TV, 1975).
    Music scores from the Smothers Brothers shows are in UCLA
Music Library.
    Films and tapes of the Smothers Brothers shows are in the
National Academy of Television Arts and Sciences Library at
UCLA.
    Unpublished register in library.

23 Stone, Andrew L., 1902-   . (producer, director, writer)
    Collection, 1947-1972. 3 boxes.
    Screenplays, treatments, step outlines for 14 films, in-
cluding FUN ON A WEEKEND (UA, 1947), THE STEEL TRAP (F, 1952),
A BLUEPRINT FOR MURDER (F, 1953), THE DECKS RAN RED (MGM,
1958), CRY TERROR (MGM, 1958), and THE SECRET OF MY SUCCESS
(MGM, 1965).

24 Sturges, Preston, 1898-1959. (director, writer)
       Collection, 1930s-1940s.
       Collection contains screenplays, unpublished scripts,
    revisions and notes, miscellaneous correspondence and unpub-
    lished autobiography by Sturges. Also a sizable collection
    (over 60) of unproduced screenplays by various authors, as
    well as story outlines, synopses and suggestions for films.
       The Sturges screenplays are duplicates of those held by
    the UCLA Department of Special Collections. The Theater
    Arts Library has the following: IF I WERE KING (PAR, 1938),
    THE GREAT MCGINTY (PAR, 1939), THE LADY EVE (PAR, 1940),
    CHRISTMAS IN JULY (PAR, 1940), PALM BEACH STORY (PAR, 1941),
    SULLIVAN'S TRAVELS (PAR, 1941), THE MIRACLE OF MORGAN'S
    CREEK (PAR, 1942), GREAT MOMENT (PAR, 1942), HAIL THE CON-
    QUERING HERO (PAR, 1943), MAD WEDNESDAY (RKO, 1945),
    BEAUTIFUL BLONDE FROM BASHFUL BEND (F, 1948), and UNFAITH-
    FULLY YOURS (F, 1948).

25 Subject File, 1920-   .
       An extensive collection of articles, pamphlets, clippings,
    program notes, reviews and other ephemera about personalities,
    films, and subjects relating to all aspects of motion pic-
    tures, radio and television from 1920 to the present. Con-
    siderable amount of material relates to foreign as well as
    American motion pictures. Clippings are from a variety of
    sources including newspapers and film magazines.

26 Television Scripts, 1958-   .
       Collection contains over 2,800 scripts for a vast number
    of television programs, including such series as MISSION
    IMPOSSIBLE (all episodes, 1966-1970), THE REAL McCOYS (78
    episodes, 1959-1961), KRAFT TELEVISION THEATER (1953-1956),
    MAYBERRY R.F.D. (1968-1970), ANDY GRIFFITH SHOW (1964-1968),
    and THE ROOKIES (1972).

27 THE TEN COMMANDMENTS (PAR, 1956).
       Screenplay and production stills. 4 boxes.

28 Twentieth Century-Fox Press Clippings, 1960, 1963. 3
    scrapbooks.
       Scrapbooks on Marilyn Monroe in LET'S MAKE LOVE (1960),
    Alan Ladd in ONE FOOT IN HELL (1960), and Elizabeth Taylor in
    CLEOPATRA (1963).

29 Wexler, Haskell, 1926-   . (cinematographer, director)
       Collection, 1960s-1976. 24+ boxes.
       Screenplays, both produced and unproduced, television
    scripts, treatments, stories and other material submitted to
    Mr. Wexler. Included among the nearly 300 screenplays are
    the following: WHO'S AFRAID OF VIRGINIA WOOLF? (WA, 1966),
    THE THOMAS CROWN AFFAIR (UA, 1968), THE LEARNING TREE (WA,

1969), THEY SHOOT HORSES, DON'T THEY? (CIN, 1969), MEDIUM
COOL (PAR, 1969), HARRY AND TONTO (F, 1974), HAROLD AND MAUDE
(F, 1974), THE CONVERSATION (PAR, 1974), ONE FLEW OVER THE
CUCKOO'S NEST (UA, 1975), and BOUND FOR GLORY (UA, 1976).
Unpublished register in library.

UNIVERSITY OF CALIFORNIA, SAN DIEGO (UCSD)
The University Library
La Jolla, California   92037

MANDEVILLE DEPARTMENT OF SPECIAL COLLECTIONS
Head: Ronald Silveira de Braganza
(714) 452-2533
Hours: M-F, 10-5
Material may be viewed only through special arrangement.

1   Roy Harvey Pearce Collection.
      Screenplays. 1 box.
      Small collection of screenplays includes BALL OF FIRE
   (RKO, 1941), HOLD BACK THE DAWN (PAR, 1941), L'ASSASIN HABITE
   AU 21 released as THE MURDERER LIVES AT NUMBER 21 (MAG, 1947),
   THE BRIDGE OF SIGHS (1947), and PORTRAIT OF JENNIE (SRO,
   1948).

2   Rogers, Will, 1879-1935. (actor, writer)
      Folio scrapbook containing newspaper clippings on life and
   death of Will Rogers. 130 pg.

UNIVERSITY OF CALIFORNIA,
SANTA BARBARA (UCSB)
University Library
Santa Barbara, California   xxxxx

DEPARTMENT OF SPECIAL COLLECTIONS
Head: Christian Brun
(805) 961-3420
Hours during school year: M-Th, 8am-11pm; F, 8-5; Sat, 9-6; Sun,
   12-4. Otherwise: M-F, 8-5
Material open to the public.

1   Anderson, Dame Judith, 1898-   . (actress)
      Papers, 1930s- . 29 boxes.
      Collection includes stage plays, screenplays, television
   scripts, radio scripts, prompting books, programs, contracts,
   financial records, clippings, personal correspondence, and

photographs. Screenplays include: GIANT (WA, 1956), THE TEN
COMMANDMENTS (PAR, 1956), and A MAN CALLED HORSE (NGP, 1970).
Television scripts include a number for HALLMARK HALL OF
FAME (1967, 1969, 1973), ROBERT TAYLOR'S DETECTIVES (1959),
and TALES OF THE PLAINSMAN (1959).

UNIVERSITY OF CALIFORNIA, SANTA CRUZ (UCSC)
University Library
Santa Cruz, California 95060

DEPARTMENT OF SPECIAL COLLECTIONS
Head: Rita Bottoms
(408) 429-2547
Hours for regular session: M-F, 10-12, 1-4. For recess schedules
    an appointment is required.
All material open to the public.
Photograph services available but not on premises.

1 Motion Picture Photograph Collection, 1911-1975. ca. 12-15 ft.
      Collection of material primarily from Preston Sawyer,
   Santa Cruz Sentinel feature writer who also worked in film
   distribution. Includes production stills, publicity portraits,
   lobby cards, snapshots. Much of material relates to filmmaking in the Santa Cruz area. Among film personalities for
   whom there is considerable material are: Charles Ray, Madge
   Bellamy, William S. Hart, Zasu Pitts, Wallace Reid, Mary Miles
   Minter, Mary Pickford, George O'Brien, Noah Beery, Viola Dana,
   Wallace Beery, and Victor Schertzinger. Many snapshots of
   character actors and technical crews of the 1920s. Photographs of local motion picture theaters date from teens to
   1940s. Photographs of southern California and Santa Cruz area
   motion picture studios in 1920s. Snapshots of location filming for FOOLISH WIVES (U, 1922) and EVANGELINE (UA, 1929).
   Set construction photographs for HUNCHBACK OF NOTRE DAME (U,
   1923). Over 300 lobby cards for silent films, some hand
   tinted. Most of cards are for Paramount-Artcraft, but considerable number also for Fox, Universal, First National,
   Mutual and Century Comedy. 1 full color poster THE SEA WOLF,
   1913. 6 cartoon cells from PINOCCHIO (RKO, 1940).

UNIVERSITY OF COLORADO (UCo)
Norlin Library
Boulder, Colorado 80309

SPECIAL COLLECTIONS DEPARTMENT
Head: Dr. Ellsworth Mason
(303) 492-6144
Hours: M-F, 9-12, 1-5
Material open to the public for reference use.

1 Maclaren-Ross, Julian.
    Collection, ca. 1958-1964.
    Holograph collection of plays, radio and television dramas,
notes for short stories, serial plays for broadcasting, reviews and articles.

2 Screenplay Collection, 1915-1973.
    Collection includes approximately 25 screenplays, among
which are BIRTH OF A NATION (UA, 1915), VIVA, VILLA! (MGM,
1934), THE BEST YEARS OF OUR LIVES (RKO, 1946), DRAGONWYCK
(F, 1946), ARCH OF TRIUMPH (UA, 1948), JULIUS CAESAR (MGM,
1953), THE LONG, HOT SUMMER (F, 1958), and MINNIE AND
MOSKOWITZ (U, 1971).

UNIVERSITY OF IDAHO (UI)
University Library
Moscow, Idaho 83843

DEPARTMENT OF SPECIAL COLLECTIONS AND ARCHIVES
Head: Charles A. Webbert
(208) 885-7951
Hours: M-F, 8-12, 1-5
Material open to the public.

1 Screenplays and Television Scripts.
    Small collection includes screenplay for ROMEO AND JULIET
(MGM, 1936) and television scripts for 77 SUNSET STRIP.

UNIVERSITY OF OREGON (UO)
Library
Eugene, Oregon 97403

DEPARTMENT OF SPECIAL COLLECTIONS
Curator: Martin Schmitt
(503) 686-3069

Hours: M-F, 8-12, 1-5
Material open to the public.

1 Adams, Frank Ramsay, 1883-1963. (writer)
      Papers, 1908-1955. 15 ft.
      Consists of manuscripts of published and unpublished short
   stories, of musical comedies, plays, motion picture scripts,
   treatments, continuities and scenarios, a collection of pub-
   lished stories and books, published sheet music, scrapbooks
   and correspondence. Among the screenplays are: PEG 'O' MY
   HEART (MGM, 1933), TARZAN AND HIS MATE (MGM, 1933), WAGONS
   WESTWARD (REP, 1940). Correspondents include: Chambrun and
   Margulies (agents), Marian deForest (agent), First National
   Pictures, Fox Film Corp., Miriam Meredith (agent), Paramount
   Famous Lasky Corp., Paul R. Reynolds (agent), RKO Studios,
   Universal Pictures Corp.
      Inventory with collection.

2 Baker, Samm Sinclair, 1909-   . (writer)
      Manuscripts, 1938-1952. 3 ft.
      Author a radio script writer, advertising executive, and
   author of "how-to-do-it" books. Manuscripts include drafts,
   final copies, and galleys of 4 books. 7 of the radio scripts
   are for the FAMOUS JURY TRIALS series, Mutual Broadcasting
   System (1938-1939).
      Inventory with collection.

3 Ball, William David, 1885-   . (writer)
      Miscellaneous papers, 1920-1965. 1 box.
      Author wrote short stories and photoplays, and was editor
   of Writers Markets and Methods and president of the Palmer
   Institute of Authorship. The papers include manuscripts of
   short stories, a series of letters written in 1925 when Ball
   was in New York working on story line of motion picture
   FLAMING YOUTH.

4 Ballard, Willis Todhunter, 1903-   . (mystery, western
   writer)
      Papers, 1927-1966. 6 ft.
      Author has written under a variety of pseudonyms, includ-
   ing Todhunter Ballard, P. D. Ballard, Neil McNeil, John Hunter,
   Parker Bonner, Sam Bowie, Hunter D'Allard, Harrison Hunt, John
   Shephard, Brian Agar, Willard Kilgore, Dave Ballard, John
   Grange, and Robert Wallace.
      Papers consist of correspondence, book manuscripts, tele-
   vision scripts, screenplays, published magazine pieces and
   books, a complete publication record and record of earnings,
   and scrapbooks of notices and reviews. Also a file of organ-
   izational correspondence with Western Writers of America,
   1960-1966.
      Inventory with collection.

5 Beau, Henry J., 1911-   . (composer)
   The Henry Beau Collection of American popular music: stock
arrangements, popular song arrangements by Henry Beau, and
miscellaneous sheet music, 1925-1971. 876 pieces.
   Includes musical arrangements for radio and television
programs such as THE JIM NABORS HOUR (1969-1971) and THE
JONATHAN WINTERS SHOW (1967-1968). Also 6 television scripts,
1966-1970.
   Inventory with collection.

6 Behn, Harry, 1898-1973. (writer)
   Papers, 1914-1968. 1 1/2 ft.
   Papers include 28 screen treatments, screenplays, con-
tinuities, written 1926-1939, among them PROUD FLESH (MGM,
1925), LA BOHEME (MGM, 1926), HELL'S ANGELS (UA, 1930), and
TEXAS RANGERS (PAR, 1936). Dialogue continuity for William
Faulkner's HONOR. Also manuscript plays, correspondence,
scrapbook of clippings, photos, playbills and programs.
   Inventory with collection.

7 Bendick, Robert, 1917-   . (author, producer, director)
   Television scripts, 1952-1964. 1 box.
   Various production materials and scripts for variety of
television programs, among them: WIDE WIDE WORLD (1955-1956),
17th Annual EMMY AWARDS SHOW, and TONIGHT show (1960). Material dealing with programming during pioneer days of commercial television, 1946-1948. Also production materials for
THIS IS CINERAMA (CIN, 1952).
   Inventory with collection.

8 Blocklinger, Peggy O'More, 1895-1970. (writer)
   Papers, 1927-1965. 6 ft.
   Her books published under a variety of pseudonyms, most
often Peggy O'More and Jeanne Bowman.
   Papers include manuscripts of 37 books, together with
synopses and alternate versions, short story, essay, and
poetry manuscripts, television scripts, and professional correspondence. Also a collection of books and articles, clippings, photographs, and scrapbooks.
   Inventory with collection.

9 Booth, Edwin, 1906-   . (writer)
   Papers, 1946-1966. 13 ft., incl. 166 manuscripts.
   Author also writes as Don Blunt and Jack Hazard.
   Papers include manuscripts of books, novelettes, short
stories, and television scripts. Manuscripts usually present
in several states, from outlines to final drafts, with source
notes, maps and casts of characters.
   Inventory with collection.

10 Branch, Houston, 1905-1968. (writer)
      Papers, 1919-1958. 11 ft.
      Includes manuscripts of novels, plays, screen stories,
    screen treatments, shooting scripts, production materials,
    and television scripts.
      Inventory with collection.

11 Brentano, Lowell, 1895-1950. (writer, editorial director and
    executive of Brentano's, Inc.)
      Papers, 1917-1952. 6 ft., incl. about 4,300 letters.
      Includes correspondence with writers, agents, publishers,
    and motion picture companies; manuscripts of novels, plays,
    movie treatments and synopses, short stories and magazine
    articles. Major correspondents include: Fox Film Corp. (1930-
    1934), William Morris Agency (1932-1936), Warner Bros. (1933-
    1942), RKO Pictures (1932), Dorothy Armbruster, George Bernard
    Shaw, and Jerry Wald.
      Inventory with collection.

12 Bright, Verne, 1893-   . (poet)
      Papers, 1917-1962. 3 ft., incl. about 450 letters.
      Includes correspondence and manuscripts of poems, prose
    pieces, radio scripts, and W.P.A. writings.
      Inventory with collection.

13 Clements, Calvin J., 1915-   . (writer)
      Papers, 1958-1966. 3 ft.
      Collection includes large number of television scripts for
    such programs as THE DETECTIVES (1959-1961), GUNSMOKE (1965-
    1969), LAREDO (1965-1966), THE RIFLEMAN (1959-1962), and WAGON
    TRAIN (1964). Also scripts in various stages and production
    material for FIRECREEK (WA, 1968).
      Inventory with collection.

14 Collins, Richard J., 1914-   . (screenwriter, television
    producer)
      Papers, 1932-1967. 9 ft.
      Papers include motion picture scripts, in various stages,
    outlines, treatments, production notes, among which are
    scripts for: RULERS OF THE SEA (PAR, 1939), LADY SCARFACE
    (RKO, 1941), MISS SUSIE SLAGLE'S (PAR, 1945), and RIOT IN
    CELL BLOCK 11 (AA, 1954). Television scripts and related
    material for variety of programs, including BREAKING POINT
    (1963-1964) and CHRYSLER THEATRE (1964-1965). Personal and
    professional correspondence. Major correspondents are
    Marjorie Cantor, Frank Dorsey, Arnaud d'Usseau, Ned Russell.
    Also a contract file, 1936-1962.
      Inventory with collection.

15 Columbia Broadcasting System, Inc. CBS Television.
      GUNSMOKE Script Collection, 1966-1970. 106 episodes.

Inventory listing by season, production number, states whether includes outline, first, second, final draft, revised final, second revised final, shooting schedule and credits. All literary rights held by CBS Television.

16 Cox, William Robert, 1901-   . (adventure, western writer)
     Papers, 1921-1968. 7 ft.
     Includes manuscripts of novels, short stories, screenplays and television scripts. Correspondence with other writers, agents, and publishers.
     Inventory with collection.

17 Curry, Thomas Albert, Jr., 1900-   . (western, detective writer)
     Papers, 1922-1967. 12 ft., incl. about 350 letters.
     Papers include manuscripts of novels, novelettes, comic strip treatments, radio scripts, and motion picture treatments. Correspondence is with publishers and editors.
     Inventory with collection.

18 Daugherty, James Henry, 1889-1974. (artist, writer)
     Manuscripts and illustrations, 1930-1964. 6 ft.
     Originally a muralist, Daugherty decorated motion picture theaters, then became a book illustrator and author. Collection includes mural sketches, drawings, and cartoons as well as book manuscripts and illustrations.
     Inventory with collection.

19 DeYoung and Roald, architects, Portland, Ore.
     Architectural plans and photographs, ca. 1927. 1 box, 1 roll plans.
     Collection consists of original plans and photographs of the construction of the New Heathman Hotel, Portland in 1927; photographs of the interior of the Paramount theater, Portland; photographs of designs and finished buildings in Portland and elsewhere in Oregon.

20 Disque, Brice Pursell, Jr., 1904-1960. (writer, magazine editor)
     Papers, 1923-1958. 12 ft.
     Collection includes over 300 radio scripts--drafts and final copies of production scripts, and proposals with pilot scripts. Among them are GANG BUSTERS (116 scripts, 1938-1942), MARCH OF TIME (35 scripts, 1936), and THIS WAS NEWS (21 scripts, 1938-1939). Also correspondence and material relating to his magazine and radio work.
     Inventory with collection.

21 Fessier, Michael, 1905-   . (writer)
     Papers, 1927-1967. 5 ft.

Consists of manuscripts of short stories, plays, television scripts, screenplays, novels, radio scripts, collection of published pieces, correspondence, reviews and publicity material. Screenplays include: HE STAYED FOR BREAKFAST (COL, 1940), FRONTIER GAL (U, 1946), TRIPOLI (PAR, 1950), and RED GARTERS (PAR, 1954).

Inventory with collection.

22 First National Theaters, Inc., Portland, Ore.
Financial records, 1921-1954. 3 ft.
Includes records of predecessor firm, the Yakima Amusement Co. Both firms leased and owned motion picture theaters in the Pacific Northwest.

23 Flynn, John Thomas, 1882-1964. (writer, newspaper editor, radio commentator)
Papers, 1928-1961. 45 ft.
Collection consists of correspondence, manuscripts of books, articles, speeches, lectures, and radio scripts. Radio scripts are included for the National Broadcasting Co., 1949, for the program BEHIND THE HEADLINES, 1949-1960, and for programs over Liberty Broadcasting System, 1951-1952.

An Inventory of the Papers of John T. Flynn was published by the University of Oregon Library in 1966 as Occasional Paper no. 3.

24 Glidden, Frederick Dilley, 1908-1975. (western writer)
Papers, 1933-1966. 10 ft., incl. about 3,000 letters.
Author wrote under pseudonym Luke Short.
Papers consist of correspondence, manuscripts of novels, novelettes, short stories, articles, television scripts and screenplays, and published magazine pieces and books. Includes screenplay for BLOOD ON THE MOON (RKO, 1948). Correspondence primarily with Glidden's agent, Marguerite Harper.
Inventory with collection.

25 Goldstone, Nathan C., 1904-1966. (agent)
Screenplays, screen treatments, and other literary properties. n.d. 1 box.
Goldstone was senior member of the Goldstone-Tobias Agency, Inc., Beverly Hills, Calif., founded in 1932. The properties include: screenplays, "The Winner," by Houston Branch and "The Phantom Strikes," by Paul Gaer; screen adaptation, "The Delightful Defector," by Alden Nash; screen treatment, "Puccini," by Mary Loos Sale. Agency rights to these properties are held by Mrs. Nathan C. Goldstone.

26 Green, Paul Eliot, 1894-   . (playwright, teacher)
Screenplays and scripts, 1925-1942. 11 pieces.
Collection includes screenplays, screen treatments, continuities and screen stories. Among the screenplays are:

KENTUCKY PRIDE (F, 1925), VOLTAIRE (WA, 1933), CAROLINA (F, 1934), and HERE COMES MR. JORDAN (COL, 1941).
Inventory with collection.

27 Hawkins, John, 1910-____. (writer)
 Papers of John and Ward Hawkins, 1937-1972. 15 ft.
 Includes correspondence, fiction manuscripts, screenplays, screen treatments and television scripts. Television scripts, shooting schedules, cast lists, notes are for a variety of programs, particularly SHANNON, MANHUNT, RAWHIDE, and BONANZA.
 Inventory with collection.

28 Hawkins, Ward, 1912-____. (writer)
 Screenplays and television plays, 1967-1969. 1 box.
 Collection includes four versions of unproduced screenplay "Cascade."

29 Hoyt, Vance Joseph, 1889-1967. (writer, physician, naturalist)
 Papers, 1913-1965. 4 ft.
 Collection includes scrapbook of reviews, notices, photographs, and mementos relating to SEQUOIA (MGM, 1934), film for which Hoyt was author and technical director. Also manuscript of book, screenplays (including THE COURAGE OF LASSIE, (MGM, 1946), radio scripts, scrapbooks of old-time motion picture actors, Mexican revolution scenes and various loose photographs.
 Inventory with collection.

30 Josephy, Alvin M., Jr., 1915-____. (writer, editor of American Heritage books)
 Papers, 1946-1968. 6 ft.
 Papers include manuscripts of books, short stories, articles, screenplays, screen treatments, television program formats, and scripts for Time magazine color projects in the 1950s. Also material relating to author's work in American Indian rights movement.
 Inventory with collection.

31 Kober, Arthur, 1900-1975. (writer, columnist)
 Papers, 1930-1961. 1 ft., incl. 278 letters.
 Manuscripts of short stories, sketches, plays and television scripts. Also correspondence concerning contracts and motion picture jobs, and clippings.
 Inventory with collection.

32 Lait, Jacquin L., 1893-1954. (writer, theater critic)
 Papers, 1917-1938. 3 ft.
 Papers include manuscripts of novels, short stories, plays and scripts or scenarios for films. There are scrapbooks of newspaper pieces and a folder of minor correspondence.
 Inventory with collection.

33 Lynch, Margaret Frances. (writer, actress)
    Radio and television scripts, phono-records of radio pro-
grams, and kinescopes of television programs, 1944-1966.
69 ft.
    Margaret Lynch was the writer of, and appeared in the radio
and television program ETHEL AND ALBERT. The collection has
the following scripts for that series: 1,340 fifteen minute
and 32 half-hour radio scripts, 1944-1950; 113 half-hour television scripts, 1950-1966. There are also four kinescopes of
the show from the early fifties. The collection includes 48
ten-minute scripts for THE KATE SMITH HOUR, 1950-1952 and 759
fifteen minute scripts for CBS radio's COUPLE NEXT DOOR, 1957-
1960. Miscellaneous material consists of 233 NBC radio
MONITOR scripts, 1963-1965; Swedish and Dutch translations of
ETHEL AND ALBERT scripts; phono-records of ABC radio broadcasts of ETHEL AND ALBERT shows, 1949; and promotional
material.
    Inventory with collection.

34 McGivern, Maureen Daly, 1922-   . (writer)
    Papers, 1938-1973. 6 ft.
    Collection includes personal and professional correspon-
dence, manuscripts of novels, short stories, articles and
television scripts. Among the television scripts are a number
for SIMON LOCKE, POLICE SURGEON.
    Inventory with collection.

35 McGraw, Eloise Jarvis, 1915-   . (children's story writer)
    Papers, 1949-1966. 3 ft., incl. about 1,000 letters.
    Collection includes manuscripts of novels, plays, short
stories, biographies, and radio scripts.
    Inventory with collection.

36 Nathan, Paul S.
    Production reports, 1937-1948. 3 ft., incl. about 1,350
reports.
    Paul S. Nathan, writer of the "Rights and Permissions"
column in Publishers Weekly, was employed by Paramount Pictures, 1937-1948, to view and report on all new plays in New
York and vicinity, concerning story material, actors, designers, and other details of possible motion picture value.
Each report includes a critical review, summary of plot, comments on actors and production, notes on features of special
interest to Paramount Pictures.
    A chronological list and title index is with the reports.

37 Newton, Dwight Bennett, 1916-   . (western writer)
    Papers, 1944-1966. 1 1/2 ft.
    Papers include book manuscripts, correspondence and tele-
vision scripts. Among the television scripts are a number

for TALES OF WELLS FARGO, 1957-1959. Also a file of correspondence concerning Western Writers of America.
Inventory with collection.

38 Ottenheimer, Albert M. (actor, writer, director)
Papers, 1929-1964. 4 1/2 ft., incl. about 2,000 letters.
Papers include play manuscripts, original radio scripts
for CHRONICLES OF KATZ (1929) and THIS IS YOUR WORLD (1943-
1944), television and motion picture scripts, fiction and
nonfiction manuscripts.
Inventory with collection.

39 Pogany, Willy, 1882-1955. (artist, illustrator, costume
designer)
Illustrations and other art work, 1913-1954. 244 pieces.
Collection includes original drawings, sketches, etchings,
watercolors, and oils. Among them are illustrations for
motion picture set designs for WONDER BAR (FN, 1934), DANTE'S
INFERNO (F, 1935), and MODERN TIMES (UA, 1936). Also costume
sketch for Douglas Fairbanks' THE THIEF OF BAGDAD (UA, 1924).
Inventory with collection.

40 Portland, Ore. Radio Station KOIN.
Corporate records, 1926-1952. 2 v.
Includes articles of incorporation and minutes of meetings.

41 Rapp, William Jourdan, 1895-1942. (writer, magazine editor)
Papers, 1916-1942. 6 ft.
Papers consist of manuscripts of plays, novels, serials,
short stories and radio scripts, including a number of radio
serials such as WHIZZER and BILLY AND BETTY.
Inventory with collection.

42 Robinson, Charles William, 1889-1955. (attorney)
Scripts for radio program, THE MIGHTY MEEK, 1942-1948.
218 scripts.
The program was broadcast over radio station KOIN, Portland, Oregon.

43 Sconce, Haywood Pressley, 1905-1959. (Baptist minister)
Papers, 1945-1959. 5 ft., incl. 93 reels tape recordings.
Collection includes program notes and tapes for CHRISTIAN
CELEBRITY TYME, a religious radio program founded and directed
by Sconce.

44 Smith, Wallace, 1888-1937. (newspaperman, novelist, artist)
Papers, 1916-1935. 3 ft.
Papers include manuscripts of short stories, articles,
motion picture scripts, correspondence, book jackets and
magazine covers, about 400 sketches and drawings, photograph
album and clippings of Smith's stories. Included is musical

play, "May Wine" (1935) based on a story by Smith and Erich von Stroheim. With manuscript is testimony in arbitration between the two.
Inventory with collection.

45 Steiner, Fred. (composer, arranger, conductor)
    Music manuscripts, 1944-1969.
    Consists of sketches and orchestra scores of music for various radio and television programs, including THIS IS YOUR FBI (radio, 1949-1952), THE RADIO READER'S DIGEST (1945), and THE GUNS OF WILL SONNETT (television, 1967-1969).
    Inventory with collection.

46 Steiner, George, 1900-1967. (composer, arranger, conductor)
    Music manuscripts, 1914-1964. 6 ft.
    Steiner was associated with Paramount Studios in New York as a composer of background and mood music. The manuscripts include original compositions, arrangements, arrangements for radio, motion picture music, and school notebooks. There is music for Paramount newsreels, cartoons, short subjects, for the television program BULLWINKLE and for commercials. There is also a collection of published pieces.
    Inventory with collection.

47 Stevenson, Janet, 1913-   . (writer)
    Papers, 1929-1966. 4 ft.
    Papers include manuscripts of short stories, articles, biographies, plays, television scripts, screenplays, radio scripts, and poems.
    Inventory with collection.

48 Stordahl, Axel, 1913-1963. (composer, arranger)
    Music scores and arrangements, 1936-1960. 145 ft., incl. about 1,500 pieces.
    Stordahl was with the Tommy Dorsey band as player, composer, and arranger. He was associated with the radio show, HIT PARADE, as composer and arranger. He did arrangements for Frank Sinatra, Eddie Fisher, Gisele MacKenzie, Nanette Fabray, Dinah Shore, Dean Martin, and Bing Crosby, and was musical director for the television series, MCHALE'S NAVY.
    The collection consists of scores and arrangements for orchestra and voice, often for specific artists or groups. It is arranged in a numerical order devised by Mr. Stordahl.
    Inventory with collection.

49 Stuart, Charles E.
    Transcriptions of radio broadcasts from Republic of China radio stations XGOY (Chungking) and XGOUS (Nanking), Nov. 1943-Jan. 1949. 8 ft., incl. 105 phonorecords.

In 1939 Stuart, an amateur radio operator, commenced monitoring broadcasts for the Board of Information, Republic of China, emanating from Chungking, and later from Nanking.

The transcriptions are typed, and include news broadcasts, speeches, messages, announcements, and some cultural programs. Except for some personal messages, the material represents official Republic of China releases or reports from accredited foreign correspondents. The phonorecords consist of 81 12-inch and 24 16-inch records of miscellaneous broadcasts. There is also a file of logs, correspondence concerning the broadcasts and transcriptions, and a file of correspondence with the Federal Communications Commission about licenses and renewals.

50 Taylor, Matthew Ambrose, 1897-1966. (writer)
     Papers, 1931-1961. 1 1/2 ft.
     Many of his stories were adapted for radio and television, and some were made into motion pictures. The papers consist of published and unpublished short stories, plays, radio and television scripts, and a collection of published magazine pieces. Also correspondence with film companies.
     Inventory with collection.

51 Thompson, Thomas, 1913-   . (western writer)
     Papers, 1938-1966. 13 ft., incl. about 5,000 letters.
     Collection includes manuscripts of novels in various stages, 116 television scripts, most of them in original form, revised, and as shooting scripts, particularly for BONANZA and WAGON TRAIN. With the television scripts are filed correspondence and memoranda concerning story lines, scene or dialogue changes, casting, and credit lines. Screenplay for FORBIDDEN VALLEY (U, 1938). Correspondence, particularly that of three literary agencies, reflects the publishing history of the Western novel and its related form, the Western television script, from 1946 to 1962. In addition, there are extensive and important files from major Western authors. Also files of letters from the Western Writers Association and the Writers Guild of America, West.
     Inventory with collection.

52 Warren, Charles Marquis, 1912-   . (writer)
     Papers, 1942-1972. 5 ft.
     Includes professional correspondence, screenplays, television scripts, book and article manuscripts. In addition to screenplays by Warren, the collection includes scripts by Sy Bartlett, Jonathan Latimer and Ranald MacDougall. Screenplays include: THE STREETS OF LAREDO (PAR, 1949), ONLY THE VALIANT (WA, 1951), THE NAKED JUNGLE (PAR, 1954), and CHARRO (NGP, 1969).
     Inventory with collection

53 Woodman, Ruth Cornwall, 1895-1970. (writer)
    Radio and television scripts for DEATH VALLEY DAYS and
miscellaneous papers, 1913-1917, 1930-1969. 12 ft.
    Collection includes scripts and associated material for
204 DEATH VALLEY DAYS radio (1930-1944) and television (1952-
1957) programs, written by Woodman. There is also an index
to the scripts, notebooks from summer research trips, and
correspondence with Death Valley acquaintances. Screenplay
for LAST OF THE PONY EXPRESS (COL, 1953). Correspondence includes a 1913-1917 diary and copies of 46 letters written
from Vassar College (1914-1916) and correspondence with
agents and publishers.
    Inventory with collection.

54 Wright, Robert Vincent. (television writer)
    Television scripts, 1961-1968. 1 box, incl. 32 items.
    Synopses, outlines, and production copies of scripts for
major television series, including BONANZA, DR. KILDARE,
MAVERICK, MISSION IMPOSSIBLE, SURFSIDE, and THE VIRGINIAN.
    Inventory with collection.

UNIVERSITY OF REDLANDS (UR)
Armacost Library
1200 East Colton Avenue
Redlands, California 92373

DEPARTMENT OF SPECIAL COLLECTIONS
Supervisor: Alice Crabtree
(714) 793-2121, Ext. 472
Hours: M-Th, 8am-11pm; F, 8-5; Sat, 10-5; Sun, 1pm-11pm
Material open to the public.

1 Wallace, Charles A., 1930-   . (writer, director, producer)
    Collection, 1956-1974. 8 file drawers, 2 cartons.
    Collection includes television scripts, screenplays, pro-
duction papers, contracts, correspondence, research material,
outlines, notes, clippings, original stories and commercials.
Included among the approximately 240 television scripts are
STEVE ALLEN SHOW (1959-1960), WIDE WIDE WORLD (1956-1958),
BLACK SADDLE (1958-1959), TRACKDOWN (1958-1959), TWENTY-SIX
MEN (ca. 1958), and ZANE GREY THEATRE (ca. 1957-1958).
Screenplays are both by Wallace and other writers and include
WEST SIDE STORY (UA, 1961), THEY SHOOT HORSES, DON'T THEY?
(CIN, 1969), and TIGER BY THE TAIL (AIP, 1970) which is listed
under working title "Dead Heat."
    Script inventory in library.

UNIVERSITY OF SANTA CLARA (UStC)
Orradre Library
Santa Clara, California 95053

RESEARCH COLLECTION
University Librarian: Dr. Victor Novak
(408) 984-4415
Hours: M-F, 8am-12 midnight; Sat, 9-5; Sun, 1pm-12 midnight
Material may be viewed only through special arrangement.

1 DANIEL BOONE.
    Television scripts, 1965-1970. 160 episodes.

2 Newman, Lionel. (composer, conductor)
    Motion picture music scores, 1947-1967. 130 v.
    Conductor's scores for 130 Twentieth Century-Fox films,
including BILL AND COO (1947), NIGHTMARE ALLEY (1948), HALLS
OF MONTEZUMA (1951), HOW TO MARRY A MILLIONAIRE (1953),
GENTLEMEN PREFER BLONDES (1953), SEVEN CITIES OF GOLD (1955),
ON THE THRESHOLD OF SPACE (1956), 23 PACES TO BAKER STREET
(1956), AN AFFAIR TO REMEMBER (1957), THE SUN ALSO RISES
(1957), THE LONG HOT SUMMER (1958), and DOCTOR DOLITTLE (1967).

UNIVERSITY OF SOUTHERN CALIFORNIA (USC)
Doheny Library
University Park
Los Angeles, California 90007

DEPARTMENT OF SPECIAL COLLECTIONS
Department Head: Dr. Robert L. Knutson
(213) 741-6058
Hours: M-F, 8-5; Sat, 9-5 when classes are in session.
Material open to the public.
Photograph duplication services available on campus.

1 Allen, Steve, 1921-   . (actor, writer)
    Collection, ca. 1952-1960. 20 ft.
    Promotional material, business correspondence, television
scripts for THE STEVE ALLEN PLYMOUTH SHOW (1956-1960) and THE
TONIGHT SHOW. Also included are screenplays for THE BENNY
GOODMAN STORY (U, 1955) and COLLEGE CONFIDENTIAL (U, 1960).

2 Anhalt, Edward, 1914-   . (writer)
    Collection, 1949-1969. 9 ft.
    Scripts, production notes, drafts, treatments, synopses,
outlines, publicity clippings, research photos, and correspondence for film and television; miscellaneous materials

relating to the 1960 Writers Guild of America strike; and
biographical memoir written in 1965. Screenplays include
THE YOUNG SAVAGES (UA, 1961), BECKET (PAR, 1964), THE BOSTON
STRANGLER (F, 1968), and THE MADWOMAN OF CHAILLOT (WA, 1969).
   Index to collection.

3 Anthony, John J., 1898-1970. (radio commentator)
      Collection, 1937-1952. 15 ft.
      Radio transcriptions, tapes, scripts and files from several
   programs involving Anthony.

4 Art Direction.
      Mattes, proofs, blueprints, set and costume design sketches,
   1936-1963. 18 ft.
      Most of the approximately 50 films represented are MGM
   productions, including MUTINY ON THE BOUNTY (1936), THE
   WIZARD OF OZ (1939), WOMAN OF THE YEAR (1942), THE YEARLING
   (1946), and THE BAND WAGON (1953). Considerable amount of
   material for CLEOPATRA (F, 1963). Approximately 50 costume
   design sketches for various Warner Brothers productions, including those for Eleanor Parker in THE WOMAN IN WHITE (1948)
   and Lauren Bacall in DARK PASSAGE (1947).

5 Astaire, Fred, 1899-   . (actor)
      Papers, 1960. 1 1/2 ft.
      Collection contains the manuscript and galley proofs of
   his autobiography, Steps in Time, published in 1960.

6 Backus, Jim, 1913-   and Henny. (actor and actress)
      Collection, early 1940s-1967. 7 ft.
      Consists mainly of screenplays for films in which Mr. or
   Mrs. Backus appeared; radio scripts for THE JIM BACKUS SHOW
   ("Hot Off the Line"); and recordings of the early 1940s War
   Department JUBILEE radio programs as well as approximately
   25 miscellaneous radio programs in which Jim or Henny Backus
   participated. Also a scrapbook and pictorial illustrations
   relating to Mr. Backus' book What Are You Doing After the Orgy?
   and a script of the 1967 television version of DAMN YANKEES.
   Included among the 19 screenplays are ANDROCLES AND THE LION
   (RKO, 1952), REBEL WITHOUT A CAUSE (WA, 1955), and HURRY SUN-
   DOWN (PAR, 1967).
      Index to collection.

7 Bainter, Fay, 1891-1968. (actress)
      Collection, 1906-1967. 4 ft.
      Collection contains stills and photographs from approxi-
   mately 15 films and 20 stage plays; scripts of 15 stage plays
   and 6 television shows; miscellaneous photographs, personal
   documents, and magazine articles; clippings, programs and
   correspondence relating to Fay Bainter's stage appearances.
      Index to collection.

8 Bakaleinikoff, Mischa, 1890-1960. (composer)
       Collection, no dates available. ca. 80 ft.
       Music scores and manuscripts.

9 Bickford, Charles, 1889-1967. (actor)
       Collection, 1925-1967. 2 ft.
       Scrapbooks, stills, radio transcriptions, clippings, pub-
   licity, photographs, and correspondence, including letters
   from Carl Laemmle and John Frankenheimer. Also, theater programs and awards. Included are radio transcriptions for THE
   SCREEN GUILD PLAYERS program (1944-1949) and THE FREE COMPANY.

10 Brahm, John, 1893-   . (director)
       Collection, 1920-1966. 4 ft.
       Collection includes the director's annotated shooting
   scripts for THE LODGER (F, 1944) and THE MIRACLE OF OUR LADY
   OF FATIMA (WA, 1952); 2 television scripts; still books for
   BROKEN BLOSSOMS (IML, 1937), THE THIEF OF VENICE (F, 1952),
   and SPECIAL DELIVERY (COL, 1955); a number of stills from
   SINGAPORE (U, 1947); photographs of early stage productions
   in Berlin and Vienna (1920-1930); miscellaneous items including
   clippings, publicity and theater programs; approximately 40
   musical transcription discs from Brahm films and an oral
   history/interview of Brahm on cassettes.

11 Brecher, Irving, 1914-   . (writer)
       THE LIFE OF RILEY. Radio tapes, 1944-1951. 10 ft.
       Approximately 325 radio transcriptions transferred to
   tape. Broadcast dates included.
       Index to collection.

12 Burke, Billie, 1885-1970. (actress)
       Collection, 1907-1950. 4 ft.
       Approximately 240 production stills from Burke films in-
   cluding PEGGY (TRI, 1916), ARMS AND THE GIRL (PAR, 1920),
   DINNER AT EIGHT (MGM, 1933), and THE WIZARD OF OZ (MGM, 1939);
   miscellaneous publicity and promotional photographs; 50 radio
   scripts including THE PEPSODENT SHOW, THE CHASE AND SANBORN
   PROGRAM, THE EDDIE CANTOR SHOW, and THE MARTIN AND LEWIS SHOW;
   books, sheet music, lobby cards, pressbooks, telegrams, and
   3 scrapbooks of clippings and programs; 10 volumes of The
   Theatre magazine (1909-1926); personal photographs including
   4 oversize portraits of Dorothy Arzner; screenplay for PEGGY
   (TRI, 1916).

13 Burns, George, 1896-   and Gracie Allen, 1906-1964. (actor
    and actress)
       Collection, 1931-1959. 74 ft.
       Collection contains 82 volumes of radio scripts (1932-
   1950) and 57 volumes of television scripts (1950-1958) for
   THE BURNS AND ALLEN SHOW, plus miscellaneous scripts from

stage, radio and television shows featuring Burns and Allen. Approximately 12 scrapbooks and 11 boxes containing clippings, publicity, photographs, magazine articles, and cartoons of "Gracie Allen: I Always Say" which appeared in the New York Evening Journal (1936-1937). Also, approximately 600 disc recordings and approximately 220 16mm films and kinescopes of THE BURNS AND ALLEN SHOW.

14 Burton, Jay. (writer)
     Scripts and sketches, 1948-1959. 8 ft.
     Items are grouped according to the particular television program for which they were written. Approximately 150 sketches and scripts for THE TEXACO STAR THEATRE (1948-1953); 36 sketches and scripts for THE BUICK-BERLE SHOW (1954-1955); 76 scripts for THE PERRY COMO SHOW (1955-1959); 4 scripts for THE JULIUS LAROSA SHOW (1957). Also included are 11 volumes of monologues written mostly for Milton Berle.
     Index to collection.

15 Carlock, Marvin and Mary.
     Television scripts and films, 1949-1954. 16 ft.
     29 volumes of scripts and 174 reels of 16mm film from the television series FIRESIDE THEATRE. Also included are miscellaneous television scripts from programs produced by Frank Wisbar.

16 Carroll, Pat, 1927-   . (actress)
     Collection, 1967-1975. 2 ft.
     Files contain story boards, correspondence, scripts and production materials pertaining to Pat Carroll's work in commercials. Also included are television scripts for THE CAROL BURNETT SHOW and GETTING TOGETHER and for pilots and specials. Screenplay for WITH SIX YOU GET EGG ROLL (NGP, 1968).

17 Chaplin, Saul, 1912-   . (songwriter, music director, producer)
     Scripts and production items, 1953-1960. 1 ft.
     Pre-production planning cross plot and scripts in various stages for CAN-CAN (F, 1960). Also included are 5 screenplays: THE LAST TIME I SAW PARIS (MGM, 1954), JUPITER'S DARLING (MGM, 1955), INTERRUPTED MELODY (MGM, 1955), HIGH SOCIETY (MGM, 1956), and THE TEAHOUSE OF THE AUGUST MOON (MGM, 1956).

18 Clippings Files - Motion Picture and Television. 190 ft.
     Information gathered from various sources, including magazines and newspapers.
     Name File. Information on individuals, institutions, and organizations.
     Production File. Includes reviews and other production information on motion pictures and television.

Subject File. Information on a wide variety of topics
dealing with the entertainment industry.

19 Colt, Samuel. (son of Ethel Barrymore)
    Collection, ca. 1911-1959. 1/2 ft.
    Books, miscellaneous theatre programs, letters, piano
score, and unpublished manuscript written by Lionel Barrymore.

20 Conley, Leland and Renie.
    Collection, late 1950s and 1960s. 258 items.
    Collection dealing with costume designs of Renie Conley
includes 160 costume and production stills, 4 portfolios of
costume sketches for various films and television episodes
totalling 93 items. Principal films included are THE BIG
FISHERMAN (BV, 1959), SNOW WHITE AND THE THREE STOOGES (F,
1961), CLEOPATRA (F, 1963), and CIRCUS WORLD (PAR, 1964).
Included are fabric charts for men's and women's costumes for
THE BIG FISHERMAN. Also 1 notebook: "Costume Breakdown for
CLEOPATRA--Handmaidens."

21 Connors, Chuck, 1921-   . (actor)
    Collection, 1958-1975. 35 ft.
    Collection contains television scripts for THE RIFLEMAN
(1961-1963), BRANDED (1964-1966), COWBOY IN AFRICA (1967-
1968), ARREST AND TRIAL (1963-1964), THE KRAFT MUSIC HALL
(1962), THE DINAH SHORE CHEVY SHOW (1960), THE 12TH ANNUAL
EMMY AWARDS (1960), and THE DON KNOTTS SHOW (1970); screenplays for RIDE BEYOND VENGEANCE (COL, 1966) and THE SEA WOLF
(IL LUPO DEI MARI, 1970); scripts of stage plays Mary, Mary
(1971) and The Button (1974); scrapbooks of clippings and
publicity materials; stills from television productions; personal photographs; correspondence and political files pertaining to Ronald Reagan and Richard Nixon; 4-16mm prints for
episodes of BRANDED; awards and plaques; music manuscript,
including instrumental score, for THE RIFLEMAN.

22 Cooper, Dame Gladys, 1888-1971. (actress)
    Collection, 1888-1965. 22 ft.
    Contains scripts, contracts, programs, correspondence,
scrapbooks, and clippings relating to approximately 25 motion
pictures (1916-1960), 5 radio programs (1935-1954) and 90
plays (1905-1968) which Ms. Cooper optioned or appeared in.
Also scripts, call sheets, shooting schedules, correspondence
and clippings pertaining to approximately 30 television shows
(mainly THE ROGUES, 1964-1965); papers relating to the manage-
ment of the Playhouse Theatre (London, 1922-1934); programs
from 45 benefit performances given between 1908 and 1956 for
such organizations as The Church of England Waifs and Strays
Society; materials pertaining to the acting careers of Philip
Merivale (1923-1946), Sally Cooper (1936-1946) and Joan Buck-
master (1924-1950); miscellaneous clippings and playbills

from 29 plays dating back to 1888; approximately 50 magazines
(1934-1964), 50 music scores (1924-1950) and 90 photos and
stills. Included among the screenplays are THE CHALK GARDEN
(U, 1964) and SEPARATE TABLES (UA, 1958).
Index to collection.

23 Cotten, Joseph, 1905-   . (actor)
       Collection, 1931-1962. 3 ft.
       Collection contains 6 scrapbooks, including ones on CITIZEN
KANE (RKO, 1941) and THE MAGNIFICENT AMBERSONS (RKO, 1942);
publicity, reviews and clippings relating to other films in
which Cotten appeared; screenplays for SINCE YOU WENT AWAY
(UA, 1944), I'LL BE SEEING YOU (UA, 1944), and DUEL IN THE
SUN (SRO, 1946); typescript of HORSE EATS HAT with Orson
Welles' notes; miscellaneous stills and photographs.
       Index to collection.

24 Cukor, George, 1899-   . (director)
       Collection, 1932-1963. 1/2 ft.
       Consists of correspondence, telegrams, photographs, stills
and a television script for THIS IS YOUR LIFE honoring Bessie
Love (1965). Majority of correspondence is from Laurette
Taylor (1933-1935) and between Cukor and Moss Hart (1945-
1959).

25 David, Mack, 1912-   . (composer, lyricist)
       Collection, 1924-1968. 23 ft.
       Collection consists mainly of sheet music (approximately
550 items) dating from 1924, screenplays and miscellaneous
material such as correspondence, budgets, contracts and advertising brochures relating to several films. Among the screenplays are INVITATION TO A GUNFIGHTER (UA, 1964), GUESS WHO'S
COMING TO DINNER (COL, 1967), and KRAKATOA--EAST OF JAVA
(CIN, 1969). Also included are 14 reels of audio tape containing a variety of music and 2 audio tapes of David's autobiography in his own words.

26 Davis, Luther, 1921-   . (writer, producer)
       ARSENIC AND OLD LACE. Scripts and related material, 1969.
3 ft.
       Includes drafts of the television script, a model of
the set for the television production, reviews of the television program and a printed copy of the script for the stage
play version.

27 DeFore, Don, 1917-   . (actor)
       Collection, ca. 1947-1967. 5 ft.
       Collection contains approximately 31 screenplays, 9 reels
of film (mostly television) including 1955 and 1956 films of
the Emmy Awards Show, and 16 radio transcriptions of late
1940s programs including LUX RADIO THEATRE and THE FAMILY

THEATRE. Movie magazines, publicity materials, playbills, pressbooks, clippings, photos, business papers and personal items are included. Among the screenplays are THE HUMAN COMEDY (MGM, 1943), GOING MY WAY (PAR, 1944), THE AFFAIRS OF SUSAN (PAR, 1945), DRAGNET (SCG, 1947), and MY FRIEND IRMA (PAR, 1949).
Index to collection.

28 DeMille, Cecil B., 1881-1959. (producer, director)
      Collection, 1920-1952. 4 ft.
      Contains 17 stereopticon slides from FOOL'S PARADISE (PAR, 1921); 1 bound volume entitled "Mr. Cecil B. DeMille Appraisal of Personal Property in his Study at Famous Players-Lasky Studio" (1920); 3 scrapbooks of foreign publicity for THE CRUSADES (PAR, 1935) and THE GREATEST SHOW ON EARTH (PAR, 1952); 1 scrapbook containing still photographs of DeMille's country estate; 1 scrapbook from the World Premiere of UNION PACIFIC (PAR, 1939); 1 scrapbook of theater clippings, posters and programs relating to Henry C. DeMille and David Belasco.

29 DeMille, William C., 1878-1955. (director, writer, producer)
      Collection, 1896-1953. 8 ft.
      Consists primarily of scripts and essays written by Mr. DeMille and his wife, Clara Beranger, and includes materials pertaining to the theatrical careers of William, Cecil and Henry DeMille. Includes approximately 60 screenplays; 17 play scripts (1903-1940); drama and cinema articles written by DeMille between 1909-1940; clippings, playbills, correspondence, and miscellaneous production materials; approximately 34 albums containing photographs from silent films produced or directed by DeMille. Among the screenplays are THE EXPLORER (EDK, 1915), COMMON GROUND (PAR, 1916), CRAIG'S WIFE (PAT, 1928), MAD LOVE (MGM, 1935), SMILIN' THROUGH (MGM, 1941), UNCONQUERED (PAR, 1947), and THE GREATEST SHOW ON EARTH (PAR, 1952).
      Index to collection.

30 Devine, Andy, 1905-1977. (actor)
      Collection, 1951-1957. 10 ft.
      Collection contains radio and television scripts for WILD BILL HICKOK. The radio scripts cover the years 1951 to 1954 and the television scripts 1952 to 1957. Also included are a number of phonograph records.

31 De Wolfe, Billy, 1907-1974. (actor)
      Collection, 1925-1974. 6 ft.
      Clippings, scrapbooks, vaudeville photo album, musical arrangements, posters, awards, stills from stage, motion picture and television productions; autographed photographs from show business personalities; publicity materials and studio biography; costume props and theater programs. Miscellaneous

scripts from his stage appearances include HOW TO SUCCEED IN
BUSINESS WITHOUT REALLY TRYING. Also, the screenplay for
DIXIE (PAR, 1943) and television scripts for THE DORIS DAY
SHOW and LOVE AMERICAN STYLE.
Index to collection.

32 Dieterle, William, 1893-1972. (director)
        Collection, ca. 1935-1950. 5 ft.
        Advertising and publicity stills, research materials, out-
lines, memos, correspondence, clippings, photographs and mis-
cellaneous production items. There is material for the
following films: THE STORY OF LOUIS PASTEUR (WA, 1935), THE
WHITE ANGEL (FN, 1936), THE LIFE OF EMILE ZOLA (WA, 1937),
BLOCKADE (UA, 1938), JUAREZ (WA, 1939), THE HUNCHBACK OF NOTRE
DAME (RKO, 1939), DR. EHRLICH'S MAGIC BULLET (WA, 1940),
DISPATCH FROM REUTERS (WA, 1940), ALL THAT MONEY CAN BUY (RKO,
1941), TENNESSEE JOHNSON (MGM, 1942), KISMET (MGM, 1944), and
SEPTEMBER AFFAIR (PAR, 1950). Some screenplays included.
        Index to collection.

33 Doniger, Walter, 1917-____. (writer, producer, director)
        PEYTON PLACE. Television scripts and set drawings, 1963-
        1968. 27 ft.
        Collection includes scripts for 473 episodes plus hair-
dressers' and property and set designers' scripts.

34 Dorr Historical Collection, 1932-1948. 2 1/2 ft.
        Choral recordings and tapes made by St. Luke's Choristers,
founded in 1930 by William Ripley Dorr; stills from films in
which Choristers appeared; sheet music.
        Index to recordings in collection.

35 Duning, George, 1908-____. (composer)
        Collection, 1945-1973. 9 ft.
        Collection contains 103 folders of motion picture scores
including SALOME (COL, 1953), MISS SADIE THOMPSON (COL, 1953),
FROM HERE TO ETERNITY (COL, 1953), PICNIC (COL, 1955), 3:10
TO YUMA (COL, 1957), PAL JOEY (COL, 1957), THE WORLD OF SUZIE
WONG (PAR, 1960), and TOYS IN THE ATTIC (UA, 1963); 34 folders
of scores from television programs including THE BIG VALLEY,
STAR TREK, MANNIX, and THEN CAME BRONSON; scrapbooks and tapes
from Mr. Duning's career.

36 Dunne, Philip, 1908-____. (writer, director, producer)
        Collection, 1950-1964. 12 ft.
        Files contain notes for all of the productions on which
Dunne worked. Each file deals with individual films and
covers pre-production memos from actual story conferences to
post-production editing. For each film which Dunne scripted
and directed there is a bound copy of the final shooting
script with photographs of the production. Screenplays

include HOW GREEN WAS MY VALLEY (F, 1941), PINKY (F, 1949),
THE ROBE (F, 1953), and TEN NORTH FREDERICK (F, 1958). Also,
5 reels of taped self-interviews by Mr. Dunne, working copies
of 15 novels adapted by Dunne for the screen, and publicity
materials, clippings, and miscellaneous magazines.
Index to collection.

37 Durante, Jimmy, 1893-   . (comedian, actor)
Approximately 200 scripts and transcriptions of Durante's
radio programs, 1943-1947. 6 ft.

38 Duryea, Dan, 1907-1968. (actor)
Collection, 1924-1968. 13 ft.
Collection contains approximately 70 screenplays (1941-
1966); television scripts for approximately 50 episodes of
THE AFFAIRS OF CHINA SMITH (1952-1956); approximately 75 miscellaneous television scripts for programs in which Mr. Duryea
acted; television scripts and call sheets for approximately
60 episodes of PEYTON PLACE (1967-1968); and scripts of 6
stage plays (1952-1956). Also included are 8 scrapbooks
(1924-1967), correspondence, publicity booklets, articles,
story treatments, and programs. Among the screenplays are
BALL OF FIRE (RKO, 1941), THE LITTLE FOXES (RKO, 1941), THE
PRIDE OF THE YANKEES (RKO, 1942), and WINCHESTER '73 (U,
1950).
Index to collection.

39 Eddy, Nelson, 1901-1967. (actor, singer)
Collection, 1928-1967. 24 ft.
Contains over 2,200 publicity and personal stills including
stills from approximately 25 motion pictures; scripts of 16
films and 29 television programs; phonograph records of the
NELSON EDDY RADIO SHOW (1944-1949) and the KRAFT MUSIC HALL
(1947-1949); approximately 15 scrapbooks (1933-1967) dealing
with Mr. Eddy's career; booklets of concert programs (1928-
1950); and approximately 100 personal photographs. Screenplays include DANCING LADY (MGM, 1933), NAUGHTY MARIETTA
(MGM, 1935), and MAYTIME (MGM, 1937).
Index to collection.
Restricted at the request of the donor. Special permission must be obtained from the Head of the Department of
Special Collections.

40 Edens, Roger, 1905-1970. (composer, musical supervisor,
producer)
Collection, ca. 1935-1968. 38 ft.
Correspondence, memos, personal files relating to
Mr. Edens' career at MGM and other studios. Included are
original arrangements for such stars as Judy Garland and Ethel
Merman, sheet music from other composers, books, records, and
transcriptions. Scripts in various stages for many MGM

musicals including GOOD NEWS (1947), EASTER PARADE (1948),
ON THE TOWN (1949), SHOW BOAT (1951), AN AMERICAN IN PARIS
(1951), and FUNNY FACE (PAR, 1957).

41 Eilers, Sally, 1908-   . (actress)
      Collection, 1927-1939. 4 ft.
      Includes 8 oversize scrapbooks of clippings and stills for
QUICK MILLIONS (F, 1931), DANCE TEAM (F, 1932), ALIAS MARY
DOW (U, 1935), STRIKE ME PINK (UA, 1936), LADY BEHAVE (REP,
1937), and EVERYBODY'S DOING IT (RKO, 1938), among others.

42 Farnum, William, 1876-1953. (actor)
      Collection, 1897-1953. 10 ft.
      Play scripts, personal photographs, theater programs,
handbills, correspondence, clippings, and publicity relating
to the theater and motion picture careers of William and
Dustin Farnum. Also, scrapbooks containing photographs from
stage appearances and motion picture stills, including a
number from TALE OF TWO CITIES (F, 1917) and THE CONQUEROR
(F, 1917).

43 Fine, Mort. (writer, producer)
      I SPY. Scripts and production material, 1964-1968. 3 ft.
      Included are approximately 40 scripts, rough drafts,
correspondence, production reports, shooting schedules, cast
lists, and call sheets.
      Index to collection.

44 Fleischer, Richard, 1916-   . (director)
      Collection, 1946-1970. 46 ft.
      Collection includes approximately 33 screenplays; miscel-
laneous items (mostly clippings and sketches) relating to 21
films; research materials, photographs, correspondence,
drafts, budgets, story board sketches, shooting schedules,
call sheets, general publicity items and contracts. Among
the films for which there is material are: FANTASTIC VOYAGE
(F, 1966), DR. DOLITTLE (F, 1967), THE BOSTON STRANGLER (F,
1968), THE SEVEN MINUTES (F, 1969), and TORA, TORA, TORA (F,
1970).
      Index to collection.

45 Flicker, Theodore J., 1930-   . (director, writer)
      Collection, 1958-1964. 10 ft.
      Deals mainly with Flicker's career as a theatrical direc-
tor. Includes play scripts, playbills, tapes of stage performances and improvisations, correspondence, and 3 scrapbooks
of clippings and photographs.

46 Fordin, Hugh, 1935-   . (writer)
      Collection, 1952-1974. 5 ft.

149 cassette tapes of interviews with 90 professional associates and friends of Arthur Freed conducted by Hugh Fordin for his book, The World of Entertainment; the manuscript and galley proof of The World of Entertainment; 29 tapes of music recorded from soundtracks of Arthur Freed productions; miscellaneous files dealing with, among others, Rouben Mamoulian and Vincente Minnelli; production and set stills from SINGIN' IN THE RAIN (MGM, 1952) and THAT'S ENTERTAINMENT (UA, 1974).

47   Freed, Arthur, 1894-1973. (producer)
        Collection, ca. 1930-1970. 78 ft.
        Includes scripts, drafts, treatments, memos, correspondence, call sheets, books, budgets, financial papers, sheet music, magazines, plaques, awards, stills, phonograph records, costume and set sketches pertaining to Mr. Freed's career primarily in making MGM musicals. Among the screenplays (including several unproduced) are GOOD NEWS (MGM, 1947), EASTER PARADE (MGM, 1948), THE BARKLEYS OF BROADWAY (MGM, 1949), ON THE TOWN (MGM, 1949), SINGIN' IN THE RAIN (MGM, 1952), THE BAND WAGON (MGM, 1953), IT'S ALWAYS FAIR WEATHER (MGM, 1955), SILK STOCKINGS (MGM, 1957), and BELLS ARE RINGING (MGM, 1960).

48   Freeman, Y. Frank, 1890-1969. (studio executive)
        Collection, 1953-1969. 2 ft.
        Contains plaques, awards, clippings, photographs, and books.

49   Freiberger, Fred. (writer, producer)
        Television scripts and production material, 1956-1968.
        10 ft.
        Scripts, shooting schedules, production reports, correspondence, cast lists, memos, call sheets, and miscellaneous production items pertaining to approximately 25 episodes of STAR TREK; 58 television scripts for BEN CASEY (1961-1963); and 7 screenplays (some unproduced) written by Freiberger.
        Index to collection.

50   Friedman, Phil M., ca. 1891-1974. (casting director)
        Collection, ca. 1930-1950. 1 1/2 ft.
        Phil M. Friedman worked at Universal (for Carl Laemmle), Fox, Pickford-Lasky Productions, and Warner Brothers.
        Collection includes books, casting directories, photographs (many autographed by stars such as Tom Mix, Joan Bennett, and Akim Tamiroff), studio publicity shots, correspondence, pamphlets, clippings, and miscellaneous articles.

51   Gable, Clark, 1901-1960. (actor)
        Collection, 1931-1960. 7 ft.
        Stills, personal photographs, snapshots, publicity photographs, scrapbook of clippings on GONE WITH THE WIND (MGM, 1939), scrapbook of photographs and clippings on Carole

Lombard, stillbook from POLLY OF THE CIRCUS (MGM, 1932) and
numerous photographs of Marion Davies. Among the screenplays
are Carole Lombard's shooting script for MADE FOR EACH OTHER
(UA, 1939), RUN SILENT, RUN DEEP (UA, 1958), NEVER SO FEW
(MGM, 1959), and IT STARTED IN NAPLES (PAR, 1960). Also a
number of unproduced scripts and Gable's Oscar for his per-
formance in IT HAPPENED ONE NIGHT (COL, 1934).

52 Garnett, Tay, 1898-   . (director, writer, producer)
      Collection, 1928-1963. 5 ft.
      Collection contains approximately 39 screenplays, most
annotated by Garnett, including ONE-WAY PASSAGE (WA, 1932),
CHINA SEAS (MGM, 1935), BATAAN (MGM, 1943), THE POSTMAN ALWAYS
RINGS TWICE (MGM, 1946), and CATTLE KING (MGM, 1963); scripts
for approximately 20 episodes of THREE SHEETS TO THE WIND
(1942), a half-hour radio program produced and directed by
Garnett and starring John Wayne; and 2 scrapbooks containing
reviews, clippings, programs and posters relating to Tay
Garnett's career from 1928 to 1937.
      Index to collection.

53 Gershman, Ben. (writer)
      Radio and television scripts, 1947-1955. 1 ft.
      Consists of radio scripts for HOLLYWOOD STAR THEATRE (1948)
and radio and television scripts for THE ADVENTURES OF OZZIE
AND HARRIET (1947-1955).

54 Glucksman, Ernest D. (producer, director, writer)
      Collection, ca. 1950s-1976. 18 ft.
      Presentations, proposals, treatments and scripts for a
wide variety of television shows; business files, production
papers, screenplays and play scripts. Collection includes
correspondence, memos, contracts and legal materials pertaining to Glucksman's activities as personal manager,
especially on behalf of Jerry Lewis (1960s) as well as production papers for a number of Jerry Lewis films produced by
Glucksman (1959-1964). Television shows for which there is
material (files, proposals, budgets, correspondence) include
THE CHEVY SHOW (ca. 1955), COLGATE COMEDY HOUR with Dean
Martin and Jerry Lewis (ca. 1955-1956), THE JERRY LEWIS SHOW
(ca. 1963), LOVE FROM A TO Z, and the Kirk Douglas version of
DR. JEKYLL AND MR. HYDE. Also included in the collection are
television casting files, Winters/Rosen Productions files
(1970s) and miscellaneous comedy files.
      Index to collection.

55 Goodman, Hal and Larry Klein. (writers)
      Radio and television scripts, 1946-1967. 4 ft.
      Collection includes radio scripts for THE BOB HOPE SHOW
(1948-1950), THE DEAN MARTIN AND JERRY LEWIS SHOW (1951-1952),
THE EDGAR BERGEN HOUR (1955-1956), and THE PEPSODENT SHOW

STARRING BOB HOPE (1946-1948); and approximately 140 television scripts (1955-1967) written for Steve Allen, Milton Berle, Edgar Bergen, and for the MARGIE series.

56 Gosden, Freeman, 1899-   and Charles Correll, 1890-1972.
    (actors)
        Collection, 1926-1955. 10 ft.
        (Creators of the AMOS 'N' ANDY characters)
        Collection includes 50 volumes of scripts for half-hour AMOS 'N' ANDY radio program (1943-1955); 3 volumes of scripts for SAM 'N' HENRY radio program (1926-1927); and approximately 15 scrapbooks containing clippings, photos, publicity and cartoons relating to the AMOS 'N' ANDY radio show. Also, synopses of scripts, lists of story titles, correspondence and miscellaneous scripts for other radio shows on which Gosden and Correll appeared, including BOB HOPE'S PEPSODENT SHOW (1947) and THE JACK BENNY PROGRAM (1949). In addition, there are plaques, awards, and reviews of AMOS 'N' ANDY television show (1951).

57 Grauman, Walter. (director)
        Collection, ca. late 1950s-1960s. 68 ft.
        Television scripts, including THE UNTOUCHABLES, treatments, photographs, correspondence, memos, notes, 16mm prints and kinescopes of television programs. Included is a kinescope of NBC MATINEE THEATRE production of WUTHERING HEIGHTS with Tom Tryon.

58 Greg Garrison Productions. (TV production company)
        THE DEAN MARTIN SHOW. Scripts, budgets, and papers, 1966-1969. 6 ft.

59 Gunzburg, Milton L. (producer, inventor)
        Collection, ca. 1950s. 4 ft.
        Material dealing with Natural Vision and the 3-D film processes, including film ends, trims, tests, titles, filters, glasses, and BWANA DEVIL (UA, 1952) trailer and miscellaneous papers.

60 Hamner, Robert. (writer)
        Collection, 1960-1968. 6 ft.
        Television scripts, many annotated by Hamner, for such series as LOST IN SPACE (1967), MISSION IMPOSSIBLE (1968), A MAN CALLED SHENANDOAH (1966), RUN FOR YOUR LIFE (1967), THE FUGITIVE (1965), HAWAIIAN EYE (1962), MY FRIEND TONY (1968), 77 SUNSET STRIP (1963), STAR TREK (1966), and THE NAME OF THE GAME (1968).

61 Harte, Betty, 1883-1965. (actress)
        Collection, 1909-1965. 2 ft.

Original short stories written by Harte; photographs and stills; posters; 2 small scrapbooks containing clippings relating to Betty Harte's career as an actress with Selig Polyscope Co. (1909-1916).

62 Head, Edith, 1907-   . (costume designer)
    BUTCH CASSIDY AND THE SUNDANCE KID (F, 1969). Sketches, costume plot and screenplay. 1 notebook.

63 Hiers, Walter (1893-1933) and Gloria Williams. (actor and actress)
    Collection, 1917-1945. 1 ft.
    Stills and photographs, 22 oversize photographs, 2 glass magic lantern slides (1917), concert programs, lobby cards for SHORT CHANGE (EDU, 1924), and 2 packages of negatives.

64 Higham, Charles, 1931-   . (writer)
    Collection, 1922-1973. 1 1/2 ft.
    Scrapbook on Anastasia Reilly (Ziegfeld Follies star), 1922-1928, and Leila Hyams (screen actress), 1926-1932; Paramount press sheets and publicity materials (1930-1931); miscellaneous music cue sheets from Paramount releases (1928); and stills and photographs from a variety of motion pictures. Also included are manuscripts, galleys, and stills from Higham's books: Kate: The Life of Katherine Hepburn, Cecil B. DeMille and Warner Brothers.

65 Humphrey, Hal, 1912-1968. (television columnist and critic)
    Collection, 1950-1968. 28 ft.
    Television materials, including columns and publicity; books; papers; files; and location photographs.

66 Imhoff, Roger, 1875-1958. (actor)
    Collection, ca. 1920-1937. 1 ft.
    Contains a scrapbook of unidentified photographs and stills and a scrapbook of telegrams (1923) and clippings from Imhoff's stage appearances; miscellaneous theater programs and copies of the New York Star, a national theatrical weekly; and play scripts written by Imhoff.

67 Jacobs, Arthur P., 1922-1973. (producer)
    THE CHAIRMAN (F, 1969). Production material. 6 ft.
    Collection includes budgets, script drafts, stills, correspondence and publicity material.

68 Jarre, Maurice, 1924-   . (composer)
    Collection, ca. 1965-1969. 2 1/2 ft.
    Original music scores composed by Jarre for films including THE COLLECTOR (COL, 1965), DR. ZHIVAGO (MGM, 1965), IS PARIS BURNING? (PAR, 1966), NIGHT OF THE GENERALS (COL, 1967), and THE FIXER (MGM, 1968). Also, musical scores of songs composed by Jarre.

69 Kaufman, Millard. (writer)
      Collection, 1951-1958. 3 ft.
      Scripts in various stages, step outlines, and notes.
    Screenplays include TAKE THE HIGH GROUND (MGM, 1953), BAD
    DAY AT BLACK ROCK (MGM, 1954), RAINTREE COUNTY (MGM, 1957),
    IMITATION GENERAL (MGM, 1958), NEVER SO FEW (MGM, 1959), and
    THE WAR LORD (U, 1965). Also, radio script for SUSPENSE
    (1951).

70 Knight, Arthur, 1916-   . (film critic and historian)
      Papers and tapes, 1957-1966. 4 ft.
      Papers consist of the manuscript and illustration layouts
    of his book, The Liveliest Art (1957). Also included are 70
    tapes primarily from WNYC radio program "Knight at the
    Movies," 1958-1960. Interviews/discussions with such film-
    makers as Jacques Tati, John Sturges, George Stevens, Leo
    McCarey, Stanley Donen, William Wyler, and Rene Clair. Music
    track from AND NOW MIGUEL (U, 1966) and miscellaneous tapes.
      Individual tapes indexed in Tape Catalogue available at
    the Special Collections desk.

71 Kovacs, Ernie, 1919-1962. (actor, writer)
      Collection, 1951-1957. 5 ft.
      Consists mainly of materials pertaining to Kovacs' tele-
    vision career. Included are scripts, treatments, notes, cue
    sheets and production materials relating to 3 television
    shows: KOVACS UNLIMITED (1952-1953), THE ERNIE KOVACS SHOW
    (1953-1957), and THE TONIGHT SHOW (1955-1957). Scripts for
    miscellaneous television shows and screenplay and publicity
    items for OPERATION MADBALL (COL, 1957).
      Index to collection.

72 Laszlo, Ernest, 1905-   . (cinematographer)
      Collection, 1943-1968. 3 ft.
      Collection includes approximately 50 shooting scripts
    (some unproduced); 2 television scripts and 2 short subject
    scripts of films made while Laszlo was in the Army; stills,
    clippings, and periodicals relating to Mr. Laszlo's career.
    Among the screenplays are TWO YEARS BEFORE THE MAST (PAR,
    1946), THE BIG WHEEL (UA, 1949), THE MOON IS BLUE (UA, 1953),
    KISS ME DEADLY (UA, 1955), and FOUR FOR TEXAS (WA, 1963).
      Index to collection.

73 Lehman, Ernest, 1920-   . (writer, producer, director)
      Collection, 1920-1968. 20 ft.
      Collection contains approximately 130 screenplays and
    approximately 120 synopses of potential properties; produc-
    tion materials, script drafts, outlines, publicity, memos,
    correspondence, budgets, and contracts. There is material
    for the following films: THE PRIZE (MGM, 1963), THE SOUND OF
    MUSIC (F, 1965), WHO'S AFRAID OF VIRGINIA WOOLF? (WA, 1966),

and HELLO DOLLY! (F, 1969). Among the miscellaneous screenplays are a number for 20th Century-Fox musical comedies.
   Index to collection.

74 Lesser, Sol, 1890-____. (producer, motion picture industry
pioneer)
      Collection, 1903-1967. 11 ft.
      Includes 48 screenplays (1933-1951); scenarios of 14 stage
plays (1905-1920); correspondence, contracts, scrapbooks,
production books, publicity, and photographs; approximately
230 stills from more than 30 films; pamphlets, booklets, magazines and glass transparencies relating to the history of
motion pictures; approximately 100 books and 36 volumes of
miscellaneous periodicals and yearbooks (1903-1967); a 16mm
film on the Hollywood Museum as designed by Sol Lesser and
James Fletcher. Among the screenplays are THE TERROR OF TINY
TOWN (COL, 1933), PECK'S BAD BOY (F, 1934), WHISPERING SMITH
SPEAKS (F, 1935), RAINBOW ON THE RIVER (RKO, 1936), O'MALLEY
OF THE MOUNTED (F, 1936), IT HAPPENED OUT WEST (F, 1937), and
a considerable number from the TARZAN series.
      Index to collection.

75 Sol Lesser/Mervyn LeRoy Collection of Early Motion Picture
Devices.
      Included are motion picture cameras, projectors, still
cameras, stereo cameras, viewers, magic lanterns, zoetropes,
tripods, lenses, miscellaneous glass plates, and chromatrope
slides.

76 Leven, Boris, ca. 1900-____. (art director, production
designer)
      Collection, 1933-1975. 7 ft.
      Approximately 150 art director's sketches from Mr. Leven's
films and other productions; theater music and dance programs; production design sketches from numerous motion pictures including TILLIE AND GUS (PAR, 1933), THE SHANGHAI
GESTURE (UA, 1941), TALES OF MANHATTAN (F, 1942), WEST SIDE
STORY (UA, 1961), and STAR! (F, 1968). Additional set and
location stills, sketches, scripts and notes from other Leven
films including CRISS-CROSS (U, 1949), SUDDEN FEAR (RKO, 1952),
and JONATHAN LIVINGSTON SEAGULL (PAR, 1973). Preliminary
notes for MANDINGO (PAR, 1975) and BLACK SUNDAY (PAR, 1977;
preliminary sketches for NEW YORK, NEW YORK. Also cassettes
of interviews with Leven.
      Index to collection.

77 Lewin, Albert, 1894-1968. (writer, producer, director)
      Collection, 1909-1968. 25 ft.
      Stills, scrapbooks, manuscripts written by Lewin; business
and personal correspondence including letters from Jean
Renoir, George Cukor, Man Ray, John Wayne, and between Lewin
and his wife, Millie; correspondence relating to The Unaltered

Cat, a book by Lewin; publicity, personal photographs, clippings and sheet music; bound musical scores for THE CUBAN LOVE SONG (MGM, 1931) and MUTINY ON THE BOUNTY (MGM, 1935). Screenplays include THE PICTURE OF DORIAN GRAY (MGM, 1945), THE PRIVATE AFFAIRS OF BEL AMI (UA, 1947), and PANDORA AND THE FLYING DUTCHMAN (MGM, 1951).

78 Lewis, Jerry, 1926-   . (actor, writer, producer, director)
     Collection, ca. 1960-1969. 75 ft.
     Includes screenplays; production records; call sheets, shooting schedules, production reports, sketches, inter-office communications, payroll, budgets, cash receipts; stills, proof sheets, personal photographs, and music scores. Films for which there are scripts and production papers include THE BELLBOY (PAR, 1960), CINDERFELLA (PAR, 1960), THE LADIES MAN (PAR, 1960), THE ERRAND BOY (PAR, 1962), IT'S ONLY MONEY (PAR, 1962), THE DISORDERLY ORDERLY (PAR, 1963), THE NUTTY PROFESSOR (PAR, 1963), WHO'S MINDING THE STORE (PAR, 1963), THE PATSY (PAR, 1964), THE FAMILY JEWELS (PAR, 1965), THREE ON A COUCH (COL, 1966), and HOOK, LINE AND SINKER (COL, 1969).

79 Littlefield, Constance. (writer)
     Collection, 1943-1951. 1 1/2 ft.
     Approximately 90 fan magazines containing articles written under the pseudonym Constance Palmer. Titles include Movieland, Screen Guide and Silver Screen. Also, 6 notebooks of holographic notes for her articles.

80 Lord, Jack, 1922-   . (actor)
     Collection, ca. 1957-1975. ca. 100 ft.
     Includes vast number of scripts and production materials (call sheets, cast lists, light tests) for television program HAWAII FIVE-O. Also clippings, play scripts and screenplays including THE AMERICANIZATION OF EMILY (MGM, 1964), A FINE MADNESS (WA, 1966), and AVANTI (UA, 1972).

81 McCormick, Constance.
     Clippings, 1934 to date. 47 ft.
     Newspaper and magazine clippings about motion picture personalities compiled by Constance McCormick.

82 McHugh, Jimmy, 1894-1969. (songwriter)
     Collection, ca. 1929-1955.
     Collection includes original music manuscripts and orchestrations; original lead sheets; scores for McHugh songs such as "I'm in the Mood for Love" and "I Can't Give You Anything But Love, Baby"; biographical information on McHugh and miscellaneous clippings.
     Collection not yet fully catalogued.

83   Mann, Abby, 1927-   . (writer)
        Collection, 1950s and 1960s. 35 ft.
        Includes play scripts, television scripts, screenplays,
     outlines, drafts, and research materials. Among the screen-
     plays are JUDGMENT AT NUREMBURG (UA, 1961), A CHILD IS WAIT-
     ING (UA, 1963), and SHIP OF FOOLS (COL, 1965). Television
     materials for ANDERSONVILLE and AFTER THE FALL.

84   Marion, Frances, 1890-1973. (writer)
        Collection, ca. 1914-1973. 3 ft.
        Contains books; scrapbooks of clippings and correspondence
     pertaining to her book, Off With Their Heads (1972); treat-
     ments and short stories written by Marion; photographs, stills,
     clippings and programs relating to the acting careers of
     Frances Marion and Fred Thomson; newspaper and magazine
     articles; plaques and awards.

85   Mayo, Virginia, 1920-   . (actress)
        Collection, 1930s-1976. 12 ft.
        Personal and business correspondence, telegrams, fan
     letters, theater and motion picture programs, scrapbooks and
     clippings, stills, photographs, fan magazines, publicity,
     pressbooks, awards and trophies. Included are television
     scripts for BURKE'S LAW (1964) and NIGHT GALLERY (1971);
     screenplay for YOUNG FURY (PAR, 1965); and radio transcrip-
     tions of THE BOB HOPE SHOW (1946), THE SCREEN GUILD PLAYERS,
     and THE CHESTERFIELD PLAYERS. Also, a special scrapbook of
     letters from prominent political and motion picture person-
     alities including Richard Nixon, Dwight Eisenhower, Samuel
     Goldwyn, and Adolph Zukor.
        Index to collection.

86   Menjou, Adolphe, 1890-1963. (actor)
        Collection, 1915, 1947-1961. 1 ft.
        Collection consists of 2 scrapbooks of clippings detailing
     the "Red Menace" in Hollywood and America (1947-1955) with
     emphasis on the "Hollywood Ten" and Mr. Menjou's involvement
     in the anti-communist movement; reports and bulletins on
     Hollywood hiring and assignment practices (1951-1952); maga-
     zines and pamphlets dealing with the anti-communist movement
     (1948-1961); miscellaneous stills from HEARTS IN EXILE (1915);
     and a book and reports by Vincent W. Hartnett.

87   Metro-Goldwyn-Mayer Screenplay Collection.
        Approximately 20,000 items in all covering the years 1918
     to 1958. Collection includes both features and shorts (ca.
     2,500 titles). Each title often includes a synopsis, treat-
     ment, and shooting schedule as well as several drafts.

88   Newman, Alfred, 1901-1970. (composer, conductor)
        Collection, 1933-1969. 20 cartons.

Scores of original motion picture music and published operatic and instrumental scores; bound vocal scores and bound conductor books of film scores for KEYS OF THE KINGDOM (F, 1944), ALL ABOUT EVE (F, 1950), LOVE IS A MANY SPLENDORED THING (F, 1955), and HOW THE WEST WAS WON (MGM, 1962), among others; music notes; books on music; song books and sheet music; tapes of film scores by Newman and contempories. Screenplays include ALEXANDER'S RAGTIME BAND (F, 1938), HOW GREEN WAS MY VALLEY (F, 1941), A TREE GROWS IN BROOKLYN (F, 1945), GENTLEMAN'S AGREEMENT (F, 1947), PINKY (F, 1949), and CAMELOT (WA, 1967).

Index to collection.

89 Novros, Lester. (producer)
Stills and photographs, 1930s and 1940s. 1 envelope.
Small collection of black and white stills and photographs of motion picture personalities.

90 Oakie, Jack, 1903-____. (actor)
Collection, ca. 1936-1966. 4 ft.
Contains scripts, books, theater programs, photographs and stills, 1 scrapbook of clippings, and 98 transcriptions of JACK OAKIE COLLEGE radio program (1936-1939). Television scripts for STUDIO ONE (1958), THE REAL MCCOYS (1962), and MISTER ED (1964). Screenplays include THE LIFE OF RILEY (U, 1949), AROUND THE WORLD IN 80 DAYS (UA, 1956), THE RAT RACE (PAR, 1960), LOVER COME BACK (U, 1961), and POCKETFUL OF MIRACLES (UA, 1961).

91 Pacific Pioneer Broadcasters.
Collection, 1937-1958. 16 ft.
Consists primarily of scripts for radio and television shows and for television commercials (approximately 90 volumes) including DEALER IN DREAMS (radio, 1940-1941), MURDER IS MY HOBBY (radio, 1945), and QUEEN FOR A DAY (television, 1952-1953). Also, promotional materials for films distributed by Four Star Distribution Corp. and for THE DICK POWELL THEATRE and QUEEN FOR A DAY television shows. Approximately 23 disc recordings; commercials and radio spots.
Individual tapes indexed in Tape Catalogue available at the Special Collections desk.

92 Paramount Research Department.
Research materials, 1937-1957. 12 ft.
Stills, photographs, sketches and documents used in set and costume design, location scouting and for reference pur-poses. Among the Paramount releases represented are THE HITLER GANG (1944), THE LOST WEEKEND (1945), STALAG 17 (1953), REAR WINDOW (1954), and THE TEN COMMANDMENTS (1956).

93 Parker Advertising.
        Collection, ca. 1968. 6 ft.
        Hundreds of short 16mm and 35mm commercials made for tele-
    vision, most of which are for Datsun automobiles. Also, radio
    commercials on audio tape and some slide materials.

94 Parsons, Louella, 1880-1972. (columnist)
        Tapes, 1935-1958. 4 ft.
        21 reels of tape dubbed from transcriptions of HOLLYWOOD
    HOTEL, THE LOUELLA PARSONS PROGRAM and miscellaneous radio
    programs featuring Louella Parsons.

95 Pasternak, Joe, 1901-   . (producer)
        Collection, 1931-1966. 20 ft.
        Includes correspondence, stills and other photographs,
    treatments and approximately 67 screenplays including 100 MEN
    AND A GIRL (U, 1937), DESTRY RIDES AGAIN (U, 1939), SONG OF
    RUSSIA (MGM, 1943), ANCHORS AWEIGH (MGM, 1945), THE GREAT
    CARUSO (MGM, 1951), THE MERRY WIDOW (MGM, 1952), PLEASE DON'T
    EAT THE DAISIES (MGM, 1960), and JUMBO (MGM, 1962).
        Index to collection.

96 Patent Material, ca. 1916-1950. ca. 90 ft.
        Patent materials relating to motion pictures, phonograph
    equipment and wireless telegraphy.

97 Photograph Collection. ca. 130 ft.
        Included are production, publicity and set stills, research
    photos and candid shots. Most of material is for motion pic-
    tures, some for television.

98 Posters and Lobby Cards, ca. 1920s-   .

99 Powers, Sally. (casting director)
        Television scripts, 1970-1973. 5 ft.
        Included in the collection are scripts for THE PARTRIDGE
    FAMILY, THE PAUL LYNDE SHOW, HONEYMOON SUITE, TEMPERATURE'S
    RISING, THE GIRL WITH SOMETHING EXTRA. Also, the final shoot-
    ing script for QB VII (1974) written by Edward Anhalt.

100 Pressbook Collection.
        Extensive collection covering all the major studios from
    the early sound period to date.

101 Radio Script Collection, ca. 1934-1951. 12 ft.
        Collection includes 19 volumes of scripts for THE ADVEN-
    TURES OF SAM SPADE (1946-1951); 21 volumes of THE FAT MAN
    (1946-1951); and scripts for THE CHASE AND SANBORN HOUR (1937-
    1939), CAVALCADE OF AMERICA (1941-1947), and MEN WITH WINGS
    (1938).

102 Randall, Tony, 1920-   . (actor)
     THE ODD COUPLE. Television scripts, 1970-1974. 2 ft.
     Also included are miscellaneous items such as appointment
     calendars, correspondence, and clippings.

103 Reagan, Ronald, 1911-   . (actor, politician)
     Collection, 1930-1944, 1966. 29 ft.
     Includes 56 volumes of DEATH VALLEY DAYS radio scripts
     (1930-1944); films and videotapes of Governor Reagan's Cali-
     fornia gubernatorial campaign and other speeches.

104 Reynolds, Adeline deWalt, 1862-1961. (actress)
     Collection, ca. 1940s-1961. 5 ft.
     Stills, location photographs, clippings, correspondence,
     framed photographs, and materials pertaining to Ms. Reynolds
     and her daughter, Mary Reynolds Adams, who performed on the
     radio program ONE MAN'S FAMILY (1956-1959). Also included is
     still book from THE TUTTLES OF TAHITI (RKO, 1942).
     Included is a list of Adeline deWalt Reynolds Collection
     at the Lincoln Center Library for the Performing Arts, New
     York, N. Y.

105 Roach (Hal) Studios Collection.
     Collection, ca. 1914-1954. 88 ft.
     Consists mainly of financial papers and ledgers, payroll
     notebooks, paid vouchers, invoices, and business files. Also
     included are television materials from the 1950s, television
     scripts for RACKET SQUAD and PUBLIC DEFENDER, and radio
     scripts for THIS IS YOUR F.B.I. (1949).

106 Rodman, Howard. (writer)
     Collection, 1940s-1969. 3 ft.
     Contains radio scripts, treatments, and outlines for THE
     COUPLE NEXT DOOR (1940s) and JOE POWERS OF OAKVILLE (1946);
     television scripts for STUDIO ONE (1955), GENERAL MOTORS
     THEATRE (1954), ALCOA-GOODYEAR THEATRE (1959), ONE STEP
     BEYOND (1960s), and NAKED CITY (1960), among others; miscel-
     laneous short stories written by Rodman. Screenplays include
     AN AMERICAN DREAM (WA, 1966), MADIGAN (U, 1968), COOGAN'S
     BLUFF (U, 1968), and WINNING (U, 1969).
     Index to collection.

107 Romero, Cesar, 1907-   . (actor)
     Collection, 1927-1961. 4 ft.
     Includes 31 scrapbooks of clippings documenting Mr. Romero's
     career; 21 envelopes of stills, clippings, correspondence,
     periodicals and programs; and a number of 8x10 stills from
     films in which Romero appeared.

108 Rubin, Benny, 1899-   . (actor)
     Collection, 1921-1971. 2 ft.

Collection contains photographs (including ones of Jerry Lewis, Louis Armstrong and Jack Dempsey), television scripts for ADAM-12 and THE PARTNERS, books, plaques, papers, and clippings.

109 Ruby, Harry, 1895-1974. (composer, writer)
  Sheet music and correspondence, 1928-1968. 1 ft.
  Sheet music for 5 songs composed by Ruby including "I Want to Be Loved by You" (1928) and "Money Doesn't Grow on Trees" (1967). Also, approximately 85 pieces of correspondence (1929-1968).
  Index to collection.

110 Schaefer, William and Margaret.
  Collection, 1909-1942. 2 ft.
  Collection contains material relating to William Schaefer's career as assistant to Jack Warner. Includes miscellaneous advertising materials and film programs; copies of Vitagraph Bulletin of Life Portrayals (1911-1915), the Vitagraph house organ; 4 copies of The Edison Kinetogram (Nov. 1, 1909-Dec. 15, 1909); and a notebook of Vitaphone releases listing name of act or artist, scene, songs or music played, classification, trailers, and features with cast and synopses (1927-1930). In addition, there is a research scrapbook for YANKEE DOODLE DANDY (WA, 1942) containing photographs of George M. Cohan and family, photostats of clippings from the period, play-bills, publicity, and photographs of the New York theatrical district and theatres, ca. 1927.

111 Scheurer, Stanley K. (script supervisor)
  Collection, 1912-1965. 2 ft.
  Consists of scripts, notebooks, and pressbook pertaining to CLEOPATRA (F, 1963); 5 annotated shooting scripts includ-ing THE COUNTRY GIRL (PAR, 1954), I WANT TO LIVE! (UA, 1958), and VON RYAN'S EXPRESS (F, 1965); approximately 60 movie magazines (1912-1932); publicity booklets for United Artists and Fox Film Corp. (1930-1931); 1 scrapbook of publicity clippings for many silent films; and miscellaneous film clippings.
  Index to collection.

112 Schildkraut, Joseph, 1896-1964. (actor)
  Stills, n.d.
  Approximately 100 still photographs of Mr. Schildkraut from various screen performances.

113 Screenplay Collection, ca. 1920s-   . 96 ft.
  All the major studios are represented.

114 Seltzer, Walter, 1914-   . (producer, executive)
  Scripts and publicity material, 1956-1972. 5 ft.

15 shooting scripts including ONE-EYED JACKS (PAR, 1961), PARIS BLUES (UA, 1961), THE WAR LORD (U, 1965), WILL PENNY (PAR, 1968), and SOYLENT GREEN (MGM, 1973), and related publicity material. Also, 5 scrapbooks of publicity campaigns for Seltzer films.
Index to collection.

115 Shagan, Steve, ca. 1923-   . (writer, producer)
        Collection, 1973-1975. 1 ft.
     Consists of final shooting script for SAVE THE TIGER (PAR, 1972); manuscript and galleys of Save the Tiger novelization; shooting script for A CITY OF ANGELS (1973) released as HUSTLE (PAR, 1975); and original manuscript and galley proofs of A City of Angels novelization.

116 Sheldon, Sidney, 1917-   . (writer, director)
        Collection, ca. 1947-1972. 35 ft.
     Television scripts and research files from various Sheldon projects including NANCY, THE PATTY DUKE SHOW, and I DREAM OF JEANNIE. Screenplays include THREE GUYS NAMED MIKE (MGM, 1951), YOU'RE NEVER TOO YOUNG (PAR, 1955), THE BUSTER KEATON STORY (PAR, 1957), and ROMAN CANDLE (UA, 1961), plus drafts of screenplay projects. Also, 7-16mm episodes of I DREAM OF JEANNIE (1965-1968) and 1-35mm print of HELL'S ANGELS ON WHEELS (US, 1967).

117 Shepard, Richmond. (actor)
        Collection, ca. 1963-1970. 1 ft.
     Contains the manuscript of Mime--The Technique of Silence, a book written by Shepard; articles by Shepard; program notes, clippings, stills and photographs pertaining to the Richmond Shepard Mime Theatre; and miscellaneous programs, publicity, and magazines with articles about Shepard.

118 Sisk, Robert, 1903-1964. (producer)
        Collection, 1920-1963. 6 ft.
     Collection contains 60 screenplays, 17 screen treatments, scripts or synopses of 5 stage plays, miscellaneous production materials relating to and scripts of approximately 225 episodes of THE LIFE AND LEGEND OF WYATT EARP television series (1955-1963), approximately 60 television scripts for THE CALIFORNIANS (1957-1959), personal scrapbooks, catalogues of unproduced properties; approximately 250 publicity photographs from motion pictures, television and stage productions; 55 group photos of Sisk with various show business personalities; miscellaneous correspondence and film production materials; assorted papers relating to the Screen Producers Guild; plaques, books, and magazines.
     Index to collection.

119   Slide, Anthony, 1944-   . (film historian, writer)
         Collection, 1911-1975. 3 ft.
         Files contain interviews and correspondence with various
      silent film personalities including Lillian Gish, Anita Loos,
      Hal Roach, and Blanche Sweet. Taped interviews with Lillian
      Gish/Anita Loos, Ralph Graves, Blanche Sweet, George Walsh,
      and Ruth Waterbury, among others. Also included are stills,
      the manuscript of The Griffith Actresses by Anthony Slide,
      early film magazines, and material relating to Vitagraph.
         Index to collection.

120   Small, Edward, 1891-1977. (producer)
         Collection, n.d. available. 25 ft.
         Includes various script drafts, letters, preview cards,
      budgets, pressbooks, posters, reviews, production and publicity
      stills (approximately 9,750), research materials, and con-
      tracts relating to Mr. Small's motion picture productions.

121   Solomon, Aubrey. (producer, writer)
         Collection, 1914-1973. 1/2 ft.
         Contains 1 taped interview with Delmer Daves, 1 printed
      interview with Nunnally Johnson (1973), 1-35mm print of HUB
      CAPERS by Solomon, and a list of Fox releases (1914-1925).

122   Sothern, Ann, 1909-   . (actress)
         Approximately 100 films of the television program PRIVATE
      SECRETARY (syndication title: SUSIE), 1952-1954.

123   Stahl, John, 1886-1950. (director)
         Collection, 1922-1955. 5 ft.
         Contains approximately 20 screenplays; correspondence,
      telegrams, and memos; publicity clippings and reviews of many
      of Stahl's films; books (mostly novels); synopses and treat-
      ments; and approximately 50 photographs and stills. Also,
      sketchbooks from IMMORTAL SERGEANT (F, 1943) and THE KEYS OF
      THE KINGDOM (F, 1944), research book for PARNELL (MGM, 1937),
      and still book from LEAVE HER TO HEAVEN (F, 1945). Among the
      screenplays are THE LADY SURRENDERS (U, 1930), STRICTLY DIS-
      HONORABLE (U, 1931), BACK STREET (U, 1932), IMITATION OF LIFE
      (U, 1934), MAGNIFICENT OBSESSION (U, 1935), PARNELL (MGM,
      1937), THE FOXES OF HARROW (F, 1947), and FATHER WAS A FULL-
      BACK (F, 1949).
         Partial index to collection.

124   Stern, Stewart, 1922-   . (writer)
         Collection, 1951-1973. 5 ft.
         Writing and research materials: scripts, reviews, publicity,
      pressbooks, stills, outlines, treatments, research notes, cor-
      respondence, and shooting schedules relating to Stern projects
      (some unproduced). Screenplays include REBEL WITHOUT A CAUSE
      (WA, 1955), THE JAMES DEAN STORY (WA, 1957), THE UGLY AMERICAN

(U, 1963), RACHEL, RACHEL (WA, 1968), and SUMMER WISHES,
WINTER DREAMS (COL, 1972). Also, television scripts for
PHILCO PLAYHOUSE, GULF PLAYHOUSE, and PLAYHOUSE 90.
Index to collection.

125 Stone, Andrew L., 1902-   . (producer, director, writer)
    Collection, 1926-1972. 7 1/2 ft.
    Production materials, treatments and scripts, pressbooks,
    stills, correspondence, reviews, books, and periodicals re-
    lating to 36 of Andrew L. Stone's films. Screenplays include
    ADORATION (FN, 1928), STOLEN HEAVEN (PAR, 1938), STORMY
    WEATHER (F, 1943), CONFIDENCE GIRL (UA, 1952), CRY TERROR
    (MGM, 1958), THE LAST VOYAGE (MGM, 1960), SONG OF NORWAY
    (CIN, 1970), and THE GREAT WALTZ (MGM, 1972).

126 Taped Interviews, ca. 1959-   . ca. 500.
    Oral History.
        The American Society of Cinematographers conducted oral
    history interviews, primarily with cinematographers. The
    following tapes on file at USC were dubbed from the Soci-
    ety's collection: John Arnold, Jacob A. Badaracco, Fred J.
    Balshofer, Spencer Bennet, Charles G. Clarke, William
    Daniels, Arthur Edeson, George Folsey, James Wong Howe,
    Reggie Lyons, Arthur C. Miller, Virgil Miller, Victor
    Milner, George Mitchell, Hal Mohr, Ray Overbaugh, Lewis
    Physioc, Gregory Peck, Ray Rennahan, Charles Rosher, Harold
    Rosson, Joseph Ruttenberg, John Seitz, Henry Sharp, Karl
    Struss, Phillip Tannura, James Van Trees, Paul C. Vogel,
    Joseph Walker, and Gilbert Warrenton.

    Class Session Tapes and other Interviews.
        Sources for these several hundred interviews consist of
    Arthur Knight's classes, Sol Lesser's classes, and indi-
    vidual donations. Most are recordings of class sessions
    with various guests from the industry, including producers,
    directors, writers, performers, and executives.

    University of Southern California Film Conference.
        Recordings of the Film Conference sessions held annually
    since 1971.

    Tape Catalogue containing index to individual tapes avail-
    able at Special Collections desk.

127 Television Script Collection, 1950s-   . 12 ft.
        Includes titles for ADAM-12, BOOTS AND SADDLES, COMBAT,
    DICK POWELL'S ZANE GREY THEATRE, HAVE GUN--WILL TRAVEL, I LOVE
    LUCY, THE RED SKELTON HOUR, STAR TREK, UNION PACIFIC, and a
    few scripts for made-for-TV movies such as THE MARCUS-NELSON
    MURDERS.

128 Tiomkin, Dimitri, 1899-___. (composer)
       Collection, ca. 1927-1964. 125 ft.
       Included are personal papers, screenplays, photographs,
    correspondence, phonograph records, click tracks, and scores
    for most of the major films done by Tiomkin including LOST
    HORIZON (COL, 1937), MOON AND SIXPENCE (UA, 1942), IT'S A
    WONDERFUL LIFE (RKO, 1946), HIGH NOON (UA, 1952), HIGH AND
    THE MIGHTY (WA, 1954), FRIENDLY PERSUASION (AA, 1956), and 55
    DAYS AT PEKING (AA, 1963). Among the screenplays are RED
    RIVER (UA, 1948), HIGH NOON (UA, 1952), I CONFESS (WA, 1953),
    STRANGE LADY IN TOWN (WA, 1955), RIO BRAVO (WA, 1959), TOWN
    WITHOUT PITY (UA, 1961), and THE GUNS OF NAVARONNE (COL, 1961).
    Scrapbooks dating from the late 1920s cover Tiomkin's career
    as concert pianist and film composer. Also, musical scores
    from Frank Capra's WHY WE FIGHT series.

129 Tokar, Norman, 1920-___. (director, producer, actor)
       Collection, 1936-1972. 6 ft.
       Contains material on radio, television and motion pictures.
    Includes approximately 430 scripts for THE ALDRICH FAMILY
    radio program (1939-1952); scripts, photographs, cast lists,
    and production materials for the television show LIFE WITH
    LUIGI (1952); casting books for miscellaneous television pro-
    grams such as LEAVE IT TO BEAVER (1957) and THE ROBERT
    CUMMINGS SHOW; approximately 15 television scripts for CHARLIE
    CHAN (1958); production stills from various television shows
    and from many Walt Disney features including RASCAL (BV, 1969)
    and THE UGLY DACHSHUND (BV, 1966); story board sketches for
    Disney projects; general radio literature and brochures; radio
    transcription discs.
       Index to collection.

130 Tuttle, William, 1911-___. (make-up artist)
       Approximately 140 costume and life masks of various per-
    sonalities associated with Metro-Goldwyn-Mayer Studios. Among
    them are Debbie Reynolds, Natalie Wood, Paul Newman, Fred
    Astaire, Gene Kelly, and Hurd Hatfield.

131 Twentieth Century-Fox Set Stills, 1932-1953. 22 ft.
       Set stills for approximately 220 motion pictures.

132 Twentieth Century-Fox Screenplay Collection, 1916-1971.
       Collection includes approximately 2,300 titles for films
    produced by both Fox Film Corp. and 20th Century-Fox. With
    most final scripts there are also drafts and conference notes.

133 Universal Studios Collection. 1,081 ft.
       Large collection of business records, papers and scripts
    from Universal Studios. Collection not yet catalogued. No
    dates available.

134 Vidor, King, 1894-   . (director)
         Collection, 1909-1959. 8 ft.
         Collection includes 13 screenplays; general production
correspondence including items from David O. Selznick, Samuel
Goldwyn and Pare Lorentz; miscellaneous newspaper and magazine clippings and reviews; production materials such as
drafts, notes, story outlines, research materials, and publicity; and Vidor's memoirs for an autobiography. Among the
films for which there is material are OUR DAILY BREAD (UA,
1934), SO RED THE ROSE (PAR, 1935), THE TEXAS RANGERS (PAR,
1936), STELLA DALLAS (UA, 1937), THE CITADEL (MGM, 1938),
NORTHWEST PASSAGE (MGM, 1940), H.M. PULHAM, ESQ. (MGM, 1941),
AN AMERICAN ROMANCE (MGM, 1944), and DUEL IN THE SUN (SEZ,
1946).
         Index to collection.

135 Wallace, Irving. (writer)
         Collection, 1934-1967. 10 1/2 ft.
         Play scripts, television scripts, screenplays, treatments,
published and unpublished stories and articles, poems, and
copies of books written by Wallace. Among the screenplays
are SPLIT SECOND (RKO, 1953), SINCERELY YOURS (WA, 1955),
and PARIS DOES STRANGE THINGS (WA, 1957).
         Index to collection.

136 Weingarten, Lawrence, 1893-1975. (producer)
         Collection, 1929-1964. 6 ft.
         Collection contains 13 scrapbooks of clippings, stills,
letters and advertisements relating to films produced by
Mr. Weingarten, including DON'T GO NEAR THE WATER (MGM, 1957)
and THE UNSINKABLE MOLLY BROWN (MGM, 1964); approximately 40
accolades, awards or prizes; daily production reports from 4
films produced in 1930; and detailed budget estimates from 11
films including A DAY AT THE RACES (MGM, 1937).
         Index to collection.

137 Weisbart, David, 1915-1967. (producer)
         Collection, 1950-1967. 7 ft.
         Collection consists of screenplays, correspondence, stills,
budgets, and general production materials relating to approximately 13 films produced by Weisbart; miscellaneous scripts
and treatments pertaining to 56 unproduced films and television
shows; synopses of approximately 30 properties (1950-1960);
and extensive memos and correspondence from the story department at Twentieth Century-Fox (1950-1959). Screenplays include LOVE ME TENDER (F, 1956), APRIL LOVE (F, 1957), THE
PLEASURE SEEKERS (F, 1964), and VALLEY OF THE DOLLS (F, 1967).
         Index to collection.

138 Windsor, Claire, 1898-1972. (actress)
         Collection, 1921-1972. 12 ft.

Collection includes approximately 29 scrapbooks of clip-
pings (1921-1965); photographs and portraits of Claire
Windsor; correspondence and a file of telegrams from Bert
Lytell (1923-1927); movie magazines; still books from WHAT'S
WORTH WHILE (PAR, 1921), SON OF THE SAHARA (FN, 1924), DANCE
MADNESS (MGM, 1926), and several Lois Weber productions;
pressbook and tape of an interview with Claire Windsor in
1968.

139 Wise, Robert, 1914-   . (editor, producer, director)
       Collection, 1943-1971. 48 ft.
       Screenplays, most annotated, of 28 films directed by Wise,
from THE CURSE OF THE CAT PEOPLE (RKO, 1944) to THE
ANDROMEDA STRAIN (U, 1971); and production materials such as
drafts, stills, correspondence; research materials, publicity
and budgets. There is material for the following films: WEST
SIDE STORY (UA, 1961), TWO FOR THE SEESAW (UA, 1962), THE
HAUNTING (MGM, 1963), THE SOUND OF MUSIC (F, 1965), THE SAND
PEBBLES (F, 1966), STAR! (F, 1968), and THE ANDROMEDA STRAIN
(U, 1971). Also, miscellaneous materials (mostly sketch
books) relating to EXECUTIVE SUITE (MGM, 1954), SOMEBODY UP
THERE LIKES ME (MGM, 1956), and I WANT TO LIVE! (UA, 1958),
among others.

140 Wolper Productions.
       Videotape cassettes from film originals, ca. 1962-1970s.
ca. 400.
       Collection consists primarily of documentaries, including
series on "Hollywood and the Stars" and biographies. Also a
few feature length entertainment films.

141 Wray, Fay, 1907-   . (actress)
       Collection, ca. 1924-1950s. 13 ft.
       Collection contains scrapbooks dealing with the careers of
Ms. Wray and her two husbands, John Monk Saunders (writer,
1895-1940) and Robert Riskin (writer, 1897-1955); stills,
including publicity photos from films in which Ms. Wray
appeared and a photo album from THE WEDDING MARCH (PAR, 1928);
19 screenplays written by Riskin including MR. DEEDS GOES TO
TOWN (COL, 1936) and YOU CAN'T TAKE IT WITH YOU (COL, 1938);
12 short 16mm films produced by Riskin during World War II
and a 16mm print of the Capra-Riskin feature MEET JOHN DOE
(WA, 1941); miscellaneous items such as contracts, magazines
and personal photographs.

142 Wynn, Ed, 1886-1966. (comedian, actor)
       290 theatre posters from the late 19th and early 20th
century.

UNIVERSITY OF WASHINGTON LIBRARIES (UW)
Seattle, Washington 98195

SPECIAL COLLECTIONS
Head: Robert D. Monroe
(206) 543-0742
Hours: M-F, 8-5
All material open to the public.

1 Motion picture photographs.
        Small collection of motion picture stills, 1917-1930.

UTAH STATE HISTORICAL SOCIETY (USHS)
603 East South Temple
Salt Lake City, Utah 84102

LIBRARY
Coordinator of Collections and Preservation: Jay Haymond
(801) 533-5755
Hours: M-F, 8-5
Material open to the public.

1 Filmmaking in Utah.
        Stills, clippings, promotional material and films.
    1 1/2 ft.
        Small collection focused on films made about Utah; films
    made in Utah, and films made by Utahns or with Utahns as
    actors, directors, etc.

General Index

broadcasts see radio broadcasts, television broadcasts

Bronco Billy Girl, HCAA:32

Brook, Clive, 1887-1974 (actor), AFI:3a

Brook, Peter, 1925- (director), NWFSC:4c

Brown, Bruce (director, writer, producer), NWFSC:4d

Brown, Jeanne DeVivier (talent coordinator), PPB:13g

Brown, Joe E., 1892-1973 (actor), AMPAS:22

Browne, Frank L., 1880- (actor, theater manager), AMPAS:23

Bruns, George (composer), UCLA(B):1

Buck, Jules, 1917- (producer), SU:1

BUCK ROGERS (radio), PPB:15

Bucquet, Harold S., 1892-1946 (director), AMPAS:24

budget personnel see Index by Occupation

Burke, Billie, 1885-1970 (actress), HuL:1; SU:3; USC:12

Burns, George, 1896- (actor), USC:13

THE BURNS AND ALLEN SHOW (radio), USC:13

THE BURNS AND ALLEN SHOW (television), USC:13

Burr, Raymond, 1917- (actor), MSL:1

Burton, Jay (writer), USC:14

BUTCH CASSIDY AND THE SUNDANCE KID (F, 1969), USC:62

Bute, Mary Ellen (director, writer, producer), NWFSC:4e

Butler, Frank (actor), PPB:13h

Bylek, Rudolph, 1885- (technical director, art director), HCAA:5

Cabot, Bruce, 1906- (actor), AHS:4c

Cabot, Sebastian, 1918- (actor), UCLA(A):70f

Caddo Co. Productions, AMPAS:88

Cagney, James, 1904- (actor), SU:3

California Theatre, Los Angeles, AMPAS:32

Calker, Darrell, d. 1964 (composer), UCLA(B):1

THE CAMEL PROGRAM (radio), PPB:15

cameramen see Index by Occupation under Cinematographers

cameras, AMPAS:63, 84; ASC:1, 2; CMSI:1; HCAA:10; LAMNH(A):2, 3, 8, 14, 15, 17

Canova, Judy, 1916- (actress), OC:2

Cantor, Eddie, 1892-1964 (actor, comedian), UCLA(A):20

Canutt, Yakima, 1895- (stuntman, director), AHS:4d

Capra, Frank, 1897- (director), OC:2

CAPTAIN FROM CASTILE (F, 1947), UCLA(C):4

Cargo, David F. (Governor, New Mexico), NMSR:1

Carle, C. E. "Teet", 1899- (publicist), UCLA(A):69d

Carlock, Marvin, USC:15

Carlock, Mary, USC:15

Caron, Leslie, 1931- (actress), AFI:2a

Carré, Ben, 1884- (art director, scenic designer), UCLA(A):69e

Carroll, Carroll, 1902- (writer), PPB:13i

Carroll, Frank J., 1879-1944 (producer), AMPAS:25

Carroll, Pat, 1927- (actress), USC:16

Carroll, William A., 1876-1928 (actor), AMPAS:26

cartoon continuities, UCLA(C):6

casting directors see Index by Occupation

Century Comedy, UCSC:1

THE CHAIRMAN (F, 1969), USC:67

Chambrun and Margulies (agency), UO:1

Chandler, George, 1902- (actor), AFI:6

Chandler, Raymond, 1888-1959 (writer), UCLA(A):21

Dawley, J. Searle, 1877–1949
(director), AMPAS:31

Dawn, Norman O., 1886– (cinematographer, special effects
photographer), AFI:1d

THE DEAN MARTIN SHOW (television), USC:58

DEATH VALLEY DAYS (radio), UO:53;
USC:103

DEATH VALLEY DAYS (television),
UO:53

DeFore, Don, 1917– (actor),
USC:27

De Forest, Lee, 1873–1961 (radio
inventor, pioneer), FC(A):1

De Forest, Marian (agent), UO:1

DeMille, Cecil B., 1881–1959
(producer, director), OC:2;
UCLA(C):14a; USC:28, 29

DeMille, Henry C., 1850–1893
(stage actor, playwright),
USC:28, 29

DeMille, William C., 1878–1955
(director, writer, producer),
USC:29

DePatie, Edmond, 1900– (executive), UCLA(A):68b

Deren, Maya, 1917–1961 (director,
writer, experimental filmmaker), SFMMA:1

Desmond, William, 1878–1949
(actor), HCAA:9

detective shows see mystery and
detective shows

Detmers, Fred H. (executive),
UCLA(C):13a

Deutsch, Adolph, 1897– (composer), CSULB:1

devices, motion picture see
cinema devices (antique);
equipment, motion picture

Devine, Andy, 1905–1977 (actor),
USC:30

De Vol, Frank (composer),
UCLA(B):1

De Wolfe, Billy, 1907–1974
(actor), USC:31

DeYoung and Roald (architects),
UO:19

Dick, Oliver Lawson, 1920–
(writer), UCLA(A):26

Dickson, W. Kennedy Laurie, 1860–
1937 (camera inventor),
LAMNH(A):8

Dieterle, William, 1893–1972
(director), USC:32

director cartoon production see
Index by Occupation under
Animators/Animation Directors

directors
see Index by Occupation
film credits, AMPAS:5

Disney, Roy O., 1893–1971 (executive), DP:6

Disney, Walt, 1901–1966 (animator,
producer, executive), DP:3, 7,
12k, 12n; LAMNH(A):3;
UCLA(A):9

Disneyland, AnPL:1; DP:8, 12a

Disney (Walt) Productions, AnPL:1;
ASC:3; DP:1, 3, 4, 5, 6, 7, 9,
10, 11, 12; UCLA(C):6; USC:129

Disney World see Walt Disney
World

Disque, Brice Pursell, Jr., 1904–
1960 (writer, magazine editor),
UO:20

distribution companies
Four Star Distribution Corp.,
USC:91
General Film Company, AMPAS:75
Janus Films, NWFSC:4ff
New Line Cinema, NWFSC:4z

distributors, AMPAS:8
see Index by Occupation

Dix, Richard, 1894–1949 (actor),
UCLA(C):14d

DR. KILDARE motion picture series,
AMPAS:24; UCLA(C):21

documentaries
motion picture, STC:1;
UCLA(A):79
television, LAPL(C):3;
UCLA(A):91, 100; USC:140

documentary filmmakers
Flaherty, Robert J., STC:1;
UCLA(A):26
Ivens, Joris, AMPAS:56
Lorentz, Pare, USC:134
Maysles, Al, NWFSC:4r
Maysles, David, NWFSC:4r

KOATV, Denver, Colorado, SHSC:4

KOIN, Portland, Oregon radio station, UO:40, 42

KPFK, Los Angeles, MSM:1

Kahlenberg, Richard (executive), NWFSC:4dd

Kalem Co., AMPAS:91; GPL:1

Kaper, Bronislaw, 1902- (composer), AFI:1j

Karloff, Boris, 1887-1969 (actor), BYU:6, 7

Karlson, Phil, 1908- (director), UCLA(A):47

Kaufman, Millard (writer), USC:69

Keaton, Buster, 1895-1966 (comedian), AFI:14; AMPAS:110

Kelly, Gene, 1912- (actor), AFI:2a

Kelly, George, 1887- (writer, director), UCLA(A):70t

Kent, Ted (film editor), AFI:2b

Keystone, AMPAS:95; UCLA(C):14a

Kiesling, Barret C., 1894- (publicist), OC:3

Kilgore, Willard see Ballard, Willis Todhunter

Kirkham, Arthur P., OHS(A):2

Klein, Larry (writer), USC:55

Klune, Raymond, 1904- (production executive), SU:1; UCLA(A):69m

Knight, Arthur, 1916- (film critic, historian), USC:70, 126

KNIGHT AT THE MOVIES (radio), USC:70

Knox, Donald E. (writer), AFI:2a

Kober, Arthur, 1900-1975 (writer, columnist), UO:31

Koch, Howard, 1902- (writer), AFI:1k

Kohlmar, Fred, 1905-1969 (producer), SU:1

Kohn, Max, SHSC:2

Koko the Klown, DP:9

Kolar, Boris, 1933- (animator), NWFSC:4q

Kopaloff, Don (agent), UCLA(C):13g

Korty, John, 1936- (director, producer, animator, writer), NWFSC:4m

Koszarski, Richard (writer), AFI:2b

Kovacs, Ernie, 1919-1962 (writer, actor, comedian), UCLA(A):48; USC:71

Kramer, Stanley, 1913- (producer, director), UCLA(A):49; UCLA(C):2, 13h

Krugman, Lou (actor), PPB:13p

Laemmle, Carl, 1867-1939 (producer, executive), HCAA:17; USC:9

Laemmle Film Service, HCAA:17

Lait, Jacquin, L., 1893-1954 (writer, theater critic), UO:32

Lake, Stuart N., 1890- (writer), HuL:3

Lambs Club, HCAA:11

La Mesa, California, motion picture production in, SDHS:1, 3

Lane, Charles, 1899- (actor), UCLA(A):70u

Langdon, Harry, 1884-1944 (actor), AMPAS:110

Lantz, Walter, 1900- (animator), LAMNH(A):3

Lasky, Jesse L., 1880-1958 (producer, executive), AMPAS:59; HCAA:18; HPM(B):1; HuL:4; UCLA(C):14a

LASSIE (television), AFI:6

Laszlo, Ernest, 1905- (cinematographer), USC:72

Laughton, Charles, 1899-1962 (actor), UCLA(A):50

Laurel, Stan, 1890-1965 (actor), CSUF(B):1

Laurel and Hardy, CSUF(B):1

Lauria, Lew (actor), PPB:13q

Lava, William, d. 1970 (composer), UCLA(B):1

Lavery, Emmet Godfrey, 1902- (writer), UCLA(A):68g

Lawrence, Florence, 1888-1938 (actress), LAMNH(A):10

Roach (Hal) Productions <u>see</u>
Roach (Hal) Studios
Roach (Hal) Studios, CSUF(B):1;
HCAA:29; HL:1; USC:105, 119
Roberson, Chuck (stuntman),
AHS:4p
ROBERT BENCHLEY COMEDIES motion
picture series, UCLA(C):21
Roberts, Charles E., 1894-1951
(writer), UCLA(A):76
Robinson, Charles William, 1889-
1955 (attorney), UO:42
Robinson, Edward G., 1893-1972
(actor), UCLA(A):9
Robson, Mark, 1913-   (producer,
director), UCLA(A):77
Roddenberry, Gene, 1921-   (pro-
ducer, writer), UCLA(C):19
Rodman, Howard (writer), USC:106
Rogers, Will, 1879-1935 (actor,
writer), UCSD:2
Romero, Cesar, 1907-   (actor),
USC:107
Rooks, Conrad (producer, direc-
tor, writer), NWFSC:4x
ROOM 222 (television), UCLA(C):20
Rosenberg, E. J. (producer),
PPB:18
Rosenberg, Lee (literary agent),
UCLA(C):13q
Rosher, Charles, 1885-   (cinema-
tographer), USC:126
Ross, Frank, 1904-   (producer),
SU:1
Ross, Sam, 1912-   (writer),
UCLA(A):78
Rossellini, Roberto, 1906-1977
(director), NWFSC:4y
Rosson, Harold, 1895-   (cinema-
tographer), AFI:1r; USC:126
Rotcop, J. Kenneth (story editor),
UCLA(C):13r
Rotha, Paul, 1907-   (Eng. docu-
mentary producer, director,
writer, film historian),
UCLA(A):79
ROUTE 66 (television), UCLA(A):85
Rozsa, Miklos, 1907-   (com-
poser), CSULB:1
Rubin, Benny, 1899-   (actor),
USC:108

Ruby, Harry, 1895-1974 (com-
poser), USC:109
Ruggles, Charles, 1892-1970
(actor), UCLA(A):80
Rush, Edna Miller (actress),
AFI:1aa
Rush, Jim (actor), AFI:1aa
Rutledge, Evelyn (sound editor),
AFI:1o
Ruttenberg, Joseph, 1889-
(cinematographer), AFI:1s;
USC:126

Sage, George Byron, ca. 1900-
1974 (story analyst), AFI:24
Said, Fouad (pres., Cinemobile
Systems), UCLA(C):13s
St. Luke's Choristers, USC:34
Sais, Marin, ca. 1895-
(actress), AMPAS:91
salesman <u>see</u> Index by Occupation
San Diego, California, motion
picture production in, SDHS:1,
2, 3, 4; SDPL:1, 2
Santa Barbara Motion Picture
Company, AMPAS:16
Santa Cruz, California, motion
picture production in, UCSC:1
Santschi, Tom, 1879-1931 (actor),
HCAA:30
Saroyan, Aram, 1943-   UCLA(A):81
Saunders, John Monk, 1895-1940
(writer), USC:141
SAVROLA (television), UCLA(A):23
Sawyer, Preston (journalist, film
distributor), UCSC:1
scenic artists,<u>see</u> Index by
Occupation under Artists
Schaefer, Margaret, USC:110
Schaefer, William (administrative
assistant), USC:110
Schallert, Edwin, 1890-1968
(columnist), AMPAS:92
Schary, Dore, 1905-   (producer,
director, writer, executive),
AFI:2a
Schertzinger, Victor, 1880-1941
(director, composer), UCSC:1
Scheurer, Stanley K. (script
supervisor), USC:111

Todd, Mike, 1907–1958 (producer), UCLA(A):73
Tokar, Norman, 1920– (director, producer, actor), USC:129
Toland, Gregg, 1904–1948 (cinematographer), UCLA(C):2
TORA, TORA, TORA! (F, 1970), AMPAS:101
Torchia, Emily (publicist), AFI:2a
Tourneur (Maurice) Productions, AMPAS:16
Tracy, Robert (music editor), AFI:1o
trade union organizer see Index by Occupation
trade unions, Hollywood, UCLA(A):42, 88
Tremayne, Les, 1913– (actor), PPB:13, 13aa
Triangle Film Corp., AMPAS:16, 95; UCLA(C):14a
Tryon, Glenn, 1894– (actor), CSUF(B):1
Tully, Jim (writer), UCLA(A):93
Tunberg, Karl, 1907– (writer, producer), AMPAS:102
Turman, Lawrence, 1926– (producer), UCLA(A):94
Turner, Florence, 1885–1946 (actress), LAMNH(A):23
Turrell, Saul J. (executive, Janus Films), NWFSC:4ff
Tuttle, William, 1911– (make-up artist), USC:130
Twentieth Century Fox Film Corp., AFI:2c, 24, 25, 29; AMPAS:42; HuL:3; SU:1; TCF:1, 2; UCLA(C):14g, 21, 28; UCSC:1; UO:1, 11; USC:73, 111, 131, 132, 137; UStC:2

USO Camp Shows, AMPAS:104
unions see trade unions
United Artists, AFI:16; FFSL:1; UCLA(A):49, 58; UCLA(C):2; USC:111
United Detroit Theatres Corp., AMPAS:98
United States Government and motion pictures, AMPAS:78;

HCAA:21; UCLA(A):67; USC:86, 141
Universal/Universal-International, AMPAS:16, 37, 42, 88, 103; FFSL:1; HCAA:17, 34; HuL:3; UCLA(A):13, 43; UCLA(C):13k, 14a; UCSC:1; UO:1; US:1, 2, 3; USC:133
University of Southern California Film Conference, USC:126
Utah, motion picture production in, USHS:1

Vague, Vera (Barbara Jo Allen), ca. 1904– (actress), AMPAS:110
Valentino, Rudolph, 1895–1926 (actor), SU:3
Van der Veer, Willard, 1895–1963 (cameraman), UCLA(A):68j
Van Guysling, George, 1865–1946 (general manager for Biograph), LAMNH(A):24
Van Riper, Kay, 1908–1948 (writer, actress), AMPAS:105
Van Trees, James, d. 1973 (cinematographer), USC:126
Vidor, King, 1894– (director), UCLA(A):69g, 95; USC:134
Vista Vision, UCLA(A):13
Vitagraph, ASC:2; FFSL:1; LAMNH(A):5; UCLA(C):14a; USC:110, 119
Vitaphone, USC:110
Vogel, Amos (film critic), NWFSC:4gg
Vogel, Paul C., 1899– (cinematographer), USC:126
Voiss, Dr. Daniel (psychiatrist), NWFSC:4hh
von Stroheim, Erich, 1885–1957 (director, actor), AFI:2b, 30; UCB:3; UO:44
Von Zell, Harry, 1906– (announcer, actor), PPB:13bb

WNYC, New York, USC:70
Wagner, Jack (actor), SU:6
Wagner, Max (writer), SU:6
Wagner, Robert Leicester, 1872–1942 (writer), UCLA(A):96

Index by Occupation